How to Do
Everything

Palm® Pre™

About the Authors

Rick Broida has devoted 20 years to writing about computers and technology. His credits include more than a dozen books, including *How to Do Everything with Your Zune* and *How to Do Everything with Your Palm Handheld* (the latter with Dave Johnson). He writes or has written for a wide range of magazines, including *PC World*, *Popular Science*, and *Wired*. His work appears daily on CNET's Cheapskate Blog, BNET's Business Hacks, and PC World's Hassle-Free PC. When not writing, he can be found on the basketball court, in front of the TV, or with his nose in an e-book.

Dave Johnson writes about technology from Seattle, Washington. There, he blogs daily for BNET's Business Hacks and writes a weekly digital photography newsletter for *PC World*. He's the author of more than three dozen books that include *How to Do Everything with Your Digital Camera*, *Robot Invasion: 7 Cool and Easy Robot Projects*, *How to Do Everything with MP3 and Digital Music*, and *How to Do Everything with Your Palm Handheld* (the latter two with Rick Broida). His short story for early readers, *The Wild Cookie*, lives on as an interactive storybook on CD-ROM. Dave is a wildlife photographer and plays drums in The Batch 10, a band best known for its punctuality.

About the Technical Editor

Bonnie Cha is a senior editor for CNET.com, covering smartphones. When she's not testing the latest gadgets, you can find her chasing after her crazy lab or surfing in the chilly waters of Northern California.

How to Do
Everything

Palm® Pre™

Rick Broida
Dave Johnson

New York Chicago San Francisco Lisbon
London Madrid Mexico City Milan New Delhi
San Juan Seoul Singapore Sydney Toronto

The McGraw-Hill Companies

Cataloging-in-Publication Data is on file with the Library of Congress

McGraw-Hill books are available at special quantity discounts to use as premiums and sales promotions, or for use in corporate training programs. To contact a representative, please e-mail us at bulksales@mcgraw-hill.com.

How to Do Everything: Palm® Pre™

1234567890   DOC DOC   109876543210

ISBN   978-0-07-163952-1
MHID   0-07-163952-7

Sponsoring Editor Megg Morin	**Technical Editor** Bonnie Cha	**Composition** Glyph International
Editorial Supervisor Janet Walden	**Copy Editor** Lisa Theobald	**Illustration** Glyph International
Project Manager Vipra Fauzdar, Glyph International	**Proofreader** Claire Splan	**Art Director, Cover** Jeff Weeks
Acquisitions Coordinator Meghan Riley	**Indexer** Claire Splan **Production Supervisor** George Anderson	**Cover Designer** Jeff Weeks

Cover images used with permission of Palm, Inc.; Google, Inc.; and Waterbar.

Google Maps is a trademark of Google, Inc. Maps Data © 2009 TeleAtlas.

Palm, Pre and WebOS are trademarks of Palm, Inc.

Images used with permission from Aliph; Arkon Resources, Inc.; Body Glove International, LLC; Ecosol, Inc.; GN Netcom, Inc.; Griffin Technology, Inc.; Palm, Inc.; Seidio, Inc.; and Smartphone Experts.

For Sarah and Ethan. Too many hours in the basement, not enough with you.

—Rick

For Marin (Secret doves!)

—Dave

Contents at a Glance

Contents

Acknowledgments

Thanks, as always, to all the great folks at McGraw-Hill who are always wonderful to work with—especially Megg Morin and Meghan Riley, who put up with missed deadlines and helped us obtain photo rights without inflicting excessive guilt (which we were already feeling). Thanks, too, to supah-genius tech editor Bonnie Cha, the person single-handedly responsible for making this book factually accurate (and not mostly made-up, which is how we originally wrote it). We'd also like to thank the media-relations folks supporting Palm, such as Zeenat Subedar, who made it possible for us to get our hands on a pair of Pres to write this book, and Sarah Williams, who helped us with product images for the book's cover.

Dave adds: Thanks to my family—Kris, Evan, Marin, and Hobbes—for helping me get through yet another book. I'd be remiss not to thank Kristin Hersh, Bob Mould, Jack White, and The Decemberists, because their music was the soundtrack that helped me get my half of the book done. And, technically, this isn't an acknowledgment in the traditional sense, per se, but I apologize for Rick, to everyone who thinks they deserve an apology. You know who you are.

Rick adds: I apologize for myself as well. After all, I was the one who brought Dave on board this project. So I *boing-fwip* that apology out to all you readers. Anyway, I couldn't have done this without the support of my family, who endured my seemingly endless evening and weekend disappearances. And because we're apparently thanking musicians for some reason, my big shout-out goes to Brendan Benson, whose entire catalog—when played in the background—makes work a pleasant experience.

Dave further adds: Brendan, beware. Rick has an unhealthy crush on you.

Rick even further adds: Oh, please. You have five cats and a wall-size poster of Downtown Julie Brown. You think anyone's going to take you seriously?

Introduction

Cell phones have been around for decades. And though mobile phones were not especially common until about 10 or 15 years ago, today it's not unusual to run into people who have completely done away with their home phone, making a mobile phone their sole means of communication.

That's awesome, and the Palm Pre has come along at just the right time. As you'll see in Chapter 1, we like to think of the Palm Pre as the first phone of the 21st century. Sure, other phones are pretty amazing as well, but the Pre is fundamentally different. It's modern in a way that most other phones haven't even started to think about yet.

That's why we wrote this book: The Pre is an incredible device that, while very user-friendly and easy to explore on your own, is so chock-full of potential that we knew we had to tell its story. This book is designed to help you get the most you possibly can out of your new phone purchase.

As an aside, let us point out that the title of the book is *How to Do Everything: Palm Pre*, but that's a little misleading. And not for the obvious reason—that we don't show you how to boil eggs or go hang gliding with your Pre. No, what we mean is that the Pre is just the first of what will no doubt be a number of phones sold by Palm that run the WebOS operating system. And while the phones will look a little different—some will have sliding keyboards, others won't, for example—this book can help you understand and explore any of them.

This book starts at the beginning, which we have discovered to be a much better starting point than, say, midway through. Chapter 1 is a hands-on tour of your Pre, where we poke, prod, and explain every aspect of the phone. Be sure to check out the section on gestures, for example, so you can master all the waves and wiggles you can make with your fingertips to control the phone. The next chapter gets you up and running with your Pre—if you haven't already done it, we'll show you how to bring your online world to the phone.

Chapters 3 through 5 focus on accomplishing the most important kinds of tasks you need to do every day. We start out in Chapter 3 with the most important part of the Pre: its phone-dialing app. By the end of the chapter, you won't just know how to dial the phone; you'll understand all the subtle time-saving tricks we dug up for you as well.

We also talk about text messaging and instant messaging. Chapters 4 and 5 also cover how to customize your Pre and thoroughly describe the core applications—including Email, search, Calendar, and Contacts.

In the last half of the book, you'll learn how to use your Pre on the go as a music player, video machine, USB flash drive, Web browser, and more. We'll tell you how to install new apps and—here's something totally cool—how to configure your Pre to install "homebrewed" apps that aren't in the official Pre App Catalog. And while people rarely have trouble with their Pres, problems do happen occasionally. We have those covered as well in Chapter 12.

We wrote this book so you could sit down and read it through like a novel (spoiler: the App Catalog did it). But if you're looking for specific information, we made it easy to find.

You can find special elements to help you get the most out of the book:

- **Notes**   These provide extra information that is handy for trivia contests but isn't essential to understanding the current topic.
- **Tips**   These tell you how to do something better, faster, or smarter.
- **"How to" and "Did You Know?" Sidebars**   These talk about related topics that are pretty darned interesting, if you ask us, but you can skip them if you prefer.
- **Words in special formatting**   Within the text, you'll also find new terms in italics, while specific phrases that you will see on the screen or that you need to type yourself appear in bold.

Want to email us? You can send questions and comments to us here:

Dave: questions@davejoh.com
Rick: rick.broida@gmail.com

We welcome you to visit Business Hacks (http://blogs.bnet.com/businesstips), where we post tech tips and tricks for business users every day.

Rick also invites you to read his Cheapskate Blog (www.news.com/cheapskate), where you'll find an awesome tech deal every day of the week.

If you can't get enough of Dave, you might also want to visit his Web site at davejoh.com. You can check out his other books and photography. Speaking of which, Dave also writes a free, weekly email newsletter for *PC World* magazine called Digital Focus. You can subscribe to Digital Focus by visiting pcworld.com and clicking the Newsletters link.

Thanks, and enjoy reading the book!

1

Get to Know Your Palm Pre

HOW TO...

- Choose a Sprint service plan
- Learn your way around your Pre
- Shut down and restart your Pre
- Identify the parts of the Pre
- Use gestures to control the Pre
- Work with apps
- Open and use the keyboard
- Use special keys such as the ORANGE, SHIFT, and SYMBOL keys
- Select, copy, and paste text

Congratulations! You've purchased one of the most amazing smartphones ever devised. We like to think of the Palm Pre as the first phone of the 21st century. Sure, other phones are pretty amazing as well, but the Pre is fundamentally different. Even Apple's iPhone is tethered to a desktop computer and, therefore, to the 20th century. The Pre, on the other hand, doesn't rely on a "sync" cable to get its data. It doesn't come with a docking station. It doesn't require any desktop software such as iTunes, Palm Desktop, or ActiveSync. Instead, the Pre finds your contacts, calendar, and other personal data where you, a citizen of the 21st century, store it: *online*. In the pages and chapters to come, we'll tell you how to get the most out of your new purchase by rounding up all sorts of handy tips, tricks, and shortcuts that will make your Pre an indispensable part of your life.

A Brief History

Before we get into the nuts and bolts of using your Pre, you might be interested in knowing how we got here. After all, the Pre didn't come from a company you might expect to create such a revolutionary phone, such as Apple or Microsoft. Don't really

1

care about this stuff? No problem; Dave's kids don't care about the history of rock and roll, even though he rambles on about the cultural impact of the Beatles and the Pretty Things *ad nauseum*. If you like, you can skip this section so you can get straight to the good stuff: Using your Pre. But you can come back here any time. We'll be here, waiting.

So who or what is Palm, anyway?

It turns out that Palm was at the forefront of smartphones before the term even existed. It all started in 1994 with, oddly enough, a block of wood. Jeff Hawkins, founder of a little-known company called Palm Computing, envisioned a pocket-sized computer that would organize calendars and contacts, and maybe let travelers retrieve their email from the road. This idea of a "personal digital assistant," or PDA, was by no means new, but previous attempts—such as Apple's highly publicized Newton MessagePad—had failed to catch on with consumers.

Hawkins envisioned his PDA to be tiny in comparison to other portables—roughly the size of a deck of cards—so he sawed himself a block of wood and carried it around in his pocket to see if it would be comfortable to carry and use. Eventually, Hawkins was able to sell the idea to a company called U.S. Robotics (known at the time for its modems) and that led to the Pilot 1000 in 1996.

The Pilot—which would eventually be renamed PalmPilot and then just Palm— went on to become the fastest-growing computer platform in history, reaching the million-sold mark faster than the IBM PC or Apple Macintosh. In its heyday in the late '90s, the Palm line included a wide variety of pocket-sized gadgets all running the simple Palm OS.

The Palm OS was not limited to PDAs, though. A number of early smartphones— including the Kyocera 7135, the Samsung 1300, and the Treo—would combine the Palm OS with phone functionality. At the time, they were dazzling. But the Palm OS couldn't keep up. Other phones came along with similar features, and eventually gadgets such as Microsoft's Windows Mobile devices and the Apple iPhone all but sent the once venerable Palm to its grave. The once-huge PDA market dried up, and people started using phones to do all the things that PDAs once did.

(As an aside, we had front-row seats to all this early smartphone and PDA excitement. Rick started a magazine about Palm OS devices called *Tap*, which later became known as *Handheld Computing* on newsstands everywhere. Eventually, Rick was the editor of *Handheld Computing* while Dave was editor of its sister publication, *Mobility Magazine*. And Rick and Dave together wrote a number of books about various Palm gadgets. But we digress.)

By 2008, pundits, analysts, and bloggers all agreed that Palm had to do something pretty amazing soon, or else the company would be just another footnote in the history of handheld technology. When Palm announced the Pre at the 2009 Consumer Electronics Show in Las Vegas, it proved to be just the ticket and became an instant hit and an object of anticipation for six months. Why? Because it's elegant. Because it's different. And because the demonstrations made it look like a brilliant metamorphosis of all the things people expect to be able to do with a phone or portable media device.

Choose a Service Plan

Like any mobile phone, you'll need to get a service plan before you can use your Palm Pre. Keep in mind, though, that the Pre works best with a combination voice and data plan. If you get a voice-only plan, you won't be able to do any of the cool Web-connected Internet stuff, such as email, installing additional apps, or Web surfing. You might as well just buy two cans and a string.

If you haven't made your choice yet, then we have some suggestions for you. Of course, pricing and feature details tend to change over time, so you'll want to visit a Sprint store or check out the Sprint Web site for current details. Sprint offers a number of plans for individuals and families.

Note Things can change, especially when it comes to mobile phone plans, packages, and prices, but right now—as we write this book—Sprint requires Pre customers to sign up for one of their Simply Everything/Everything Data Plans or a Business Essentials plan with messaging and data.

If you're looking for a phone just for yourself, for example, Sprint offers a number of voice and data plans (remember that these numbers are current now and may change). All the plans offer unlimited data and messaging and are differentiated by how many minutes of voice you get each month:

450 minutes + unlimited data	$69.99/month
900 minutes + unlimited data	$89.99/month
Unlimited	$99.99/month

If you're buying a plan for the whole family, you can share minutes on two lines, and additional lines are an additional $19.99/month each:

1500 minutes + unlimited data	$129.99/month
3000 minutes + unlimited data	$169.99/month
Unlimited	$189.99/month

Keep in mind that Sprint's Everything data plans really do include, well, just about everything—especially compared to other mobile phone carriers. You get turn-by-turn GPS navigation, Sprint TV, unlimited text messaging, and virtually as much stuff as you can download. So, as we indicated, you probably won't have a choice. But if you do, we highly encourage you to pick one of the voice and data plans; to be honest, we believe that there's absolutely no reason to own a Pre if you don't have Internet access along with your voice service.

Note Actually, even with the Everything plan, Sprint does impose a download limit of 5GB per month, so it's not really *unlimited* in the truest sense. On the other hand, 5GB is a *lot* of data. We don't think most people would ever run into this limit, and certainly we never did while writing this book.

Take a Guided Tour

While it would do your self esteem a world of good if you read this whole book in its entirety before cracking open the box that your Pre came in, we understand that you've probably already become familiar with the phone—at least the basics—before you even got to this first chapter. That's cool. Turn on the Pre and you'll see all sorts of buttons, icons, and such. What is it all? What does it do? How can you avoid cutting your thumb on the sharp edge of the keyboard? Don't worry—we're here to guide you. Let's take a stroll around the Pre and see what everything does.

When closed, the Pre looks like a polished black stone, with very few protrusions to spoil the illusion.

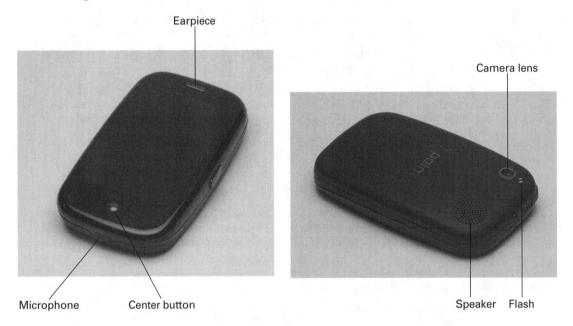

Earpiece

Camera lens

Microphone   Center button

Speaker   Flash

The sides of the phone, of course, are where the goodies are hiding. The left side is home to the volume control, and the right side includes a port for the combination charger/micro USB cable.

To remove the back, depress the back panel release, which is located on the bottom of the phone—you can insert your fingernail in the slot and then pull the back panel off. You don't need a tool, and you need only moderate pressure to liberate the back panel.

Finally, the top has the two of the most important controls on the phone: the power button and the ringer switch.

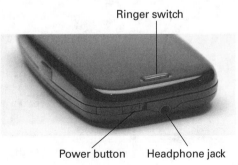

Ringer switch

Power button   Headphone jack

Turning the Pre On and Off

You know where the power button is—but do you really know how to turn your Pre on and off? As with most modern devices, there's a lot more to that simple little power button than meets the eye.

Saving Power in Standby Mode

You probably know that the power button doesn't really do what it claims. Rather than turning the Pre on and off, pressing the power button turns the *screen* on and off. That's important to remember, because the screen is a huge power drain, so you'll want to keep it turned off as much as possible to preserve battery life. When you turn the screen off, you can think of it as putting the phone in *standby*, or low-power, mode. (It also *locks* the phone, which prevents you from accidentally dialing your mom as the phone rolls around in your bag.)

Other Ways to Turn On the Pre

Pressing the power button is the most obvious way to turn on the screen and start using the Pre, but you can also turn it on in other ways:

- **Slide the keyboard open**   This turns on the screen and bypasses the unlock screen (unless you have a PIN- or password-enabled screen—see Chapter 4 for details on how to configure that).
- **Tap any key**   Please, no "which key is the *any* key?" jokes. If the keyboard is already open, the power button is tricky to reach because it's under and behind the screen. Just tap any key to "wake up" your Pre. When the keyboard is open, you can also press the Center button to turn on your Pre.
- **Take the Pre off the Touchstone charger**   Just as opening the keyboard turns on the Pre, taking the Pre off the Touchstone charger turns on the screen and bypasses the unlock screen. Check out Figure 1-1 for a look at the Touchstone.

FIGURE 1-1   The Touchstone charger holds the Pre magnetically and charges the phone without wires. The phone turns on automatically when you take it off the stand.

Disable the Radios in Airplane Mode

Despite the name, Airplane Mode isn't useful only when you're riding on an airplane. If you want to disable the Wi-Fi, Bluetooth, and cellular radios completely—temporarily turning the Pre into nothing more than a disconnected handheld organizer—you can turn on Airplane Mode by tapping the status bar in the upper-right of the Pre's display and then tapping Turn On Airplane Mode.

 Since this is the first time we've mentioned tapping, it's worth pointing out that you should always use the tip of your finger, not your fingernail. The Pre's touch screen requires contact with your finger to work.

You can use Airplane Mode when you really, really need to save every drop of battery life. Or you can use it when you're not allowed to use a phone, such as (you guessed it) when you're in an airplane—or, we suppose, at a top secret government research facility.

Turning Off the Ringer

Don't forget that you can turn off all sound by sliding the ringer switch to the off position. Does this save power? A little. Mainly, though, you'll want to do this when it's important that your "Helter Skelter" ringtone doesn't start playing in a movie theater, or so that your co-workers can't hear you playing a game when you should be working.

Completely Shut Down (or Restart) the Pre

You can turn the Pre off completely as well—for the ultimate in battery preservation. Suppose you're stranded in the middle of the desert with nothing but your phone and a unicycle. You need to ride the unicycle for many miles until you reach a coverage area to call for help. We recommend shutting down your Pre completely (and not playing Connect Four to pass the time) so the battery lasts long enough to get you rescued. Also, if your phone is acting strange, turning it off and then back on (also known as *resetting* or *rebooting* the phone) can solve a world of problems. See Chapter 12 for more troubleshooting help.

To shut down your Pre completely, press and hold the power button for several seconds until you see the screen shown here.

Tap Turn Off. Note that you can still cancel this or enter Airplane Mode. Be aware that if you do turn off the phone, turning it back on later will take several minutes—so be prepared to wait impatiently while the phone "boots." Obviously, this is something you won't want to do very often.

Revealing the Keyboard

This might seem pretty simple, but there's something of a trick to revealing the keyboard. To open the keyboard, just slide up the touch screen while holding the back panel. You can do it with one hand or two, but for best results, we suggest that you put the phone in your open hand and then slide the screen with your thumb (or, if you're using two hands, thumbs) smack dab on top of the screen—as shown in Figure 1-2. Don't worry about getting fingerprints on the screen. Slide it with a brisk, quick motion, and the keyboard will snap into place with a satisfying click.

FIGURE 1-2   The best way to open the Pre's keyboard involves a flicking motion of the thumb on the touch screen.

If you do it differently, you may encounter some problems. The keyboard wants to be slid out quickly, so, for example, if you do it too slowly or timidly, it won't feel quite right. More importantly, if you try to open the keyboard by pushing it open at the bottom edge, you'll find it's pretty sharp and you can actually hurt yourself. In fact, the gadget blog Gizmodo demonstrated that you can cut cheese with the edge of a Pre (see it for yourself at http://tinyurl.com/pbcejr).

Meet the Pre's "Desktop"

Unlike most phones, the Pre is a powerful computer capable of running several programs at once. As a result, it is kind of like a cross between a smartphone such as the iPhone and your desktop computer. In fact, the basic place where you see all your open programs is called the wallpaper (just like the desktop image in Windows), and it's on this wallpaper that all your programs (called apps) run. Here's the wallpaper with no programs running:

On the Pre, apps take the form of Activity Cards, or cards for short. When you're using an app, it usually runs at full screen, covering the wallpaper completely. This kind of makes sense, if you think about it: if the app weren't full screen, it would be hard to use on the small screen of a phone.

And in case you were wondering, pretty much anything you do with your Pre is its own app and therefore runs on its own card. The Phone is an app, as are your Calendar and Contacts. Using the camera opens the Camera app. And if you install a game or an app such as the *New York Times* or *Wall Street Journal*, they are apps with their own Activity Cards as well. Even the Settings is an app. Here are some typical apps (Email, Phone, and *New York Times*):

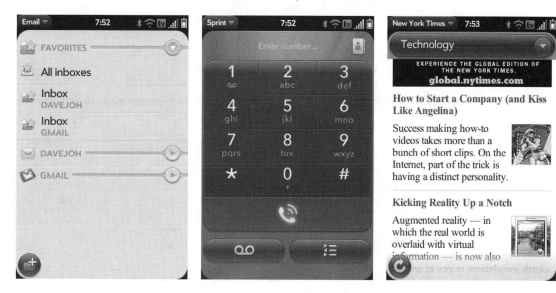

But here's the cool part: Apps don't always have to appear full screen on the Pre. You can switch from full screen to what Palm calls the *Card view*, where apps are shrunk into a series of what look like playing cards. You might have only one app running, or a dozen.

 Every app that's running consumes some memory and can potentially slow down your Pre a little. You might need to close some apps occasionally, and you might not be able to leave all the apps running all the time.

Once in Card view, you can sort through cards, close apps you don't currently need by "tossing" the card off the screen, rearrange the order of the cards, and choose a different card to switch to full screen. In this way, Card view is sort of like pressing ALT-TAB in Windows to change to a new program. Except on the Pre, you can use your fingers to shuffle and sort your apps, and then tap the next one you want to use (see Figure 1-3).

Meet the Parts of the Display

As you've now seen, the Pre is more than just a phone; it's a sophisticated computer with its own unique operating system. And while it's all pretty easy to use, wouldn't you know it, Palm created a whole new language—a variety of terms—to refer to the various bits on the screen. As we've already hinted, your Pre can work in a few different modes. Let's take a tour and see what everything is called.

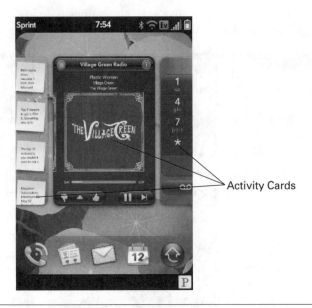

Activity Cards

FIGURE 1-3 In the same way that Windows lets you run multiple programs and switch among them, you can switch up apps on the Pre.

When the Pre Is Idle

With no applications running, here's what you'll see:

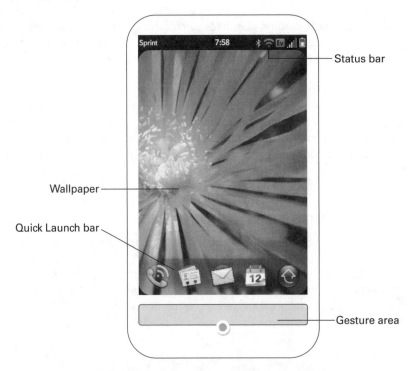

Status bar

Wallpaper

Quick Launch bar

Gesture area

To be perfectly clear, this is really just the Card view we told you about, except no cards are open to clutter the screen. Instead, you can enjoy the wallpaper image in its full glory.

The status bar tells you useful stuff such as the current time, remaining battery power, and signal strength. You can tap anywhere on the right side of the status bar to see the exact battery level and a menu with additional options for controlling the Wi-Fi and Bluetooth radios, plus Airplane Mode.

You can customize the wallpaper (see Chapter 4 for details) by displaying one of the default images, or you can use a picture you took with the Pre's camera. You can even select a photo from your computer or the Internet and use it as wallpaper. In any event, you'll see that wallpaper a lot, since it's the background for any applications you choose to run.

The Quick Launch bar is like a favorites menu—always available at the bottom of the screen. (We'll show you how to make it appear even when it's covered by another application when we talk about gestures later in the chapter.) This is where you go to start your four most commonly used applications. The last icon in the Quick Launch bar opens the Launcher, which shows you all your installed applications.

 Palm veterans who owned one of the old PalmPilot PDAs will no doubt recognize the Quick Launch bar as a carryover from those devices, which all used a similar set of "permanent" icons.

App menu

Finally, the gesture area is located below the screen. It is the black region located between the bottom edge of the screen and the Center button. The gesture area is really important—even though most gestures happen on the touch screen, there's one very special gesture that you can perform only here in the gesture area: the back gesture, which takes you back to the previous screen. We'll talk more about that soon.

When an App Is Full Screen

So that's what the Pre looks like when there's nothing going on. What if you tap an icon, which launches an application? Well, you see the screen shown here.

The wallpaper is covered by your application, and a drop-down menu appears at the upper-right corner of the status bar. Also, note that the Quick Launch bar is hidden.

Even when an app is running full screen, though, you can always get to the gesture area, since it's below the touch screen.

Gesture area

When the Pre Is in Card View

Ah, finally we get to the cool stuff. One of the awesome capabilities of the Pre is full multitasking. That means you can open several applications at once and switch among them whenever you want. They keep running in the background even when you're not looking at them, which can be really handy.

Let's try that out. With one application running on your Pre, press the Center button, which is the lone button below the display. You'll see the Quick Launch bar—as soon as you do, tap a different application. Here's how it looks with the Email Activity Card showing:

When you press the Center button, it toggles the view between the current application and Card view. As you can see, Card view depicts all your running apps as Activity Cards, and you can shuffle among them using swiping gestures, left to right or vice versa, onscreen.

Here's another little trick: You can make the cards smaller. To do that, tap and hold a card or tap under the cards (between the cards and the Quick Launch bar). The cards will shrink to half their size, revealing more of the wallpaper and letting you fit more cards on the screen at once.

You can toggle between the two card sizes each time you tap. Hang on to your hat, because we'll explain what else this view is good for when we talk about gestures.

When the Pre Is in Launcher View

Finally, the last major mode for your Pre is Launcher view. The Launcher shows a list of icons for applications installed on your Pre, and switching to this view—by tapping the Launcher icon on the far right of the Quick Launch bar—is a lot like launching an application, except that the Quick Launch bar stays visible.

Status bar

Launcher

Quick Launch bar

Gesture area

Did You Know?

How the App Launcher Pages Are Organized

The Launcher is composed of three separate pages; using the next and previous gestures, you can switch among these pages (see "Using Gestures" later in this chapter). When your Pre is shiny and new, the apps are organized so that the three pages roughly correspond to these categories:

- Built-in apps
- Extra apps and Sprint services
- Settings and preferences

After you start to settle in and feel more comfortable with your Pre, you're welcome to move around those apps and organize the three pages any way you like. Check out Chapter 4 for details on how to do that.

Dave vs. Rick: Top 10 Reasons to Own a Palm Pre

Welcome to the first of many odd little boxes in which we make lists, reminisce, argue with and insult each other, and generally sound off about all sorts of things only somewhat related to the Pre in a misguided attempt to entertain you. Here now are our top 10 reasons to own a Palm Pre:

Dave:

10. Awesome! Something new to lose!
9. It makes you look like a spy.
8. It's smarter than Rick. Actually, that's also true of your car keys.
7. I firmly believe that if something doesn't take batteries, it's not worth having.
6. Dude, seriously, the Touchstone charger is indistinguishable from magic.

Rick:

5. Affords huge variety of "Pre"-*fix* jokes. Get it?
4. It has a real keyboard. Take that, smarmy iPhone owners!
3. Secret built-in mirror replaces the mirror you normally carry around.
2. Touchstone charger came from the future.
1. If Rick likes it, it's gotta be good!

Using Gestures

Most of the time that you interact with your Pre, you'll be using gestures. After all, aside from the power and volume buttons, there's really only one button on the whole phone: the Center button. You already know that the Center button lets you switch back and forth between full-screen application view and Card view, where you can see and choose from among your running applications. But what of gestures?

Gestures are simply motions you make with your fingertips to control stuff you see on the screen. A gesture can be as simple as a tap—like clicking with the mouse on a computer—to start an application, or as fancy as "throwing away" an open application. The good news is that you need to know only a handful of gestures, and most of them are pretty much just what you'd expect, because they're based on how you interact with stuff on a computer screen or in real life.

Starting Apps and Managing Cards

This first set of gestures gives you all the juice you need to start and manage apps, which appear as Activity Cards, on your Pre's touchscreen.

	Gesture	What It Does	How to Do It
	Tap	Opens an app or menu, "clicks" a button, places the cursor in text	Quickly touch and release the touch screen.
	Back	Goes "up" one level in an app or takes you back to the last place you were viewing	Slide your finger from right to left in the gesture area. Remember that the gesture area is under the touch screen, not on the touch screen itself.
	Next, Previous	When in Card view, lets you flip among open cards (sort of like the Cover Flow view on an iPod)	Slide your finger from right to left across the touch screen to go to the next card or left to right to go to the previous card.
	Throw	When in Card view, lets you close an open app	Slide or flick a card straight up and off the touch screen.

Getting Around in Apps

This next set of gestures gives you all the tools you need to navigate around inside apps—scrolling, changing pages, zooming, and more.

	Gesture	What It Does	How to Do It
	Drag	Scrolls the screen up and down or left and right; lets you see more than fits on the screen, such as a Web page or list of contacts	Slide your finger across the touch screen in the direction that you want the screen to scroll.
	Double-tap	Zooms in for a magnified view of the screen—or zooms out of a zoomed view (might not work in all apps)	Tap the touch screen twice, rapidly, as if you were double-clicking a mouse. If you want to zoom into a specific part of the screen (such as in a Web page), double-tap at that location.
	Flick	Scrolls the screen up and down but with additional momentum, so it keeps moving after you lift your finger	Flick your finger on the touch screen in an up or down motion quickly, as if you're skidding a coin across a tabletop.

Pinch in/
Pinch out

Zoom in or out, like the
double-tap

Squeeze two fingers together
on the touch screen to zoom
in at that location, or pull two
fingers apart to zoom out.

Peek

Shows a portion of the next
page of an application

Drag your finger partially
across the touch screen, to the
left or right.

Working with Apps

This last set of gestures enables you to work with the Quick Launch bar and the App Launcher.

	Gesture	What It Does	How to Do It
	Launcher	When an app is running full screen, switches to Card view; also quickly opens the Launcher when in Card view	Flick up from the gesture area to the touch screen to open the Launcher or Card view. Flick from the touch screen down to the gesture area to reverse the process.

(continued)

Gesture	What It Does	How to Do It
Quick Launch	Drags the Quick Launch bar into the touch screen; useful for launching an application or Launcher when an application obscures the Quick Launch bar	Slowly drag up from the gesture area to the touch screen. Once you "pull up" the Quick Launch bar, you can slide your finger left or right to the icon you want.
Tap, hold, and drag	Rearranges apps in the Launcher or moves apps to the Quick Launch bar	Tap and hold an icon for a few seconds, and then drag it where you want to move it. (To move an icon to the Quick Launch bar, first move it back to the Launcher to make room.)
Drag-and-drop	Rearranges cards in Card view	Tap and hold a card for a few seconds, and then drag it left or right and release it at its new location.

Using Advanced Gestures

If you followed along with all those gestures, you probably noticed that the only way to switch to a different app is to leave full-screen view. The next and previous gestures—which let you browse Activity Cards—work only in Card view. And the confusingly similarly named back gesture works in the gesture area, but it doesn't let you browse apps. Bummer.

   If this is really bugging you, you'll be happy to know that you can change running apps without first switching to Card view—using a special advanced gesture. It's not difficult or death-defying to use, but Palm has it turned off by default for some reason.

To turn on advanced gestures, tap the Screen & Lock icon in the Launcher; then, in the Advanced Gestures section, flip Switch Applications from Off to On.

Now you can switch among running applications that are in full-screen view by dragging your finger across the gesture area (the same place you make the back gesture).

We turned on advanced gesture and, after using it for a while, decided we really didn't like it. It didn't always seem to behave the way we expected, so we turned it off and went back to the "factory default." Maybe Palm had it right by turning this off to begin with.

Managing Activity Cards with Gestures

Now that you've learned a bit about the various gestures at your disposal, let's use them. This is like using your newfound knowledge of bar chords to play a real song on the guitar. Or using your knowledge of bat swinging to play baseball. Or just make up your own comparison.

The following sections describe a few common situations.

Open a New App

Suppose you have an app open—say, the Phone—and you want to open the Calendar app. Piece of cake. Do this:

1. Press the Center button. This switches the Phone to Card view so you can see the Quick Launch bar.
2. Tap the Calendar icon. After a moment, the Calendar will open in full screen.

Switching Apps

Now suppose you found the information you wanted in the Calendar and want to switch back to the Phone to place a call. Do this:

1. Press the Center button. This switches the Calendar to Card view so you can see all the Activity Cards.
2. Tap, hold, and slide the Calendar card to the left or right to see the other cards running on top of the wallpaper (using the previous and next gestures). You should see the Phone card.
3. When the Phone card is in the center of the screen, tap it to make it full screen.

Closing an App You No Longer Need

As Uncle Ben once said, "With great power comes great responsibility." We know that both Lionel Luthor and the computer Will Smith fought in *I, Robot* abused their power; can you do better?

(Yes, in case you were wondering, those *were* the best examples we could think of.)

Here's what we're talking about: The Pre's multitasking ability allows you to open several apps at once, and that's a lot of power for a smartphone. In fact, it's possible to open so many apps that your Pre will noticeably slow down and exhibit performance problems. You might find that the Pre behaves sluggishly, and music might even stutter. That's why it's a good idea to keep just a few programs open at once, and close the ones you're not using (or don't expect to use again soon). If your Pre does start to bog down, closing one or two apps can solve your problem. Here's how:

1. If your app is currently full screen, press the Center button. This switches to Card view so you can see all the Activity Cards.
2. Find an app you want to close, using the previous and next gestures.
3. Tap, hold, and "toss" the card straight up, off the top of the screen (using the throw gesture).

Don't worry—you haven't deleted the app. You can always start it again later.

Rearrange Apps

We're not sure how useful this is, to be honest, but the Pre lets you arrange the Activity Cards in any order you like. This is handy, we suppose, if you tend to leave the same four or five apps running all the time, and you develop a "muscle memory" for what order they appear in when you're in Card view.

1. If your app is currently full screen, press the Center button. This switches to Card view so you can see all the Activity Cards.
2. Tap and hold the card in the center of the screen until you see it shrink to the mini-card size.
3. Drag-and-drop cards to arrange them in the order you prefer.

When you're done, tap the screen to return to the normal Card view. Or you can tap a card or press the Center button to switch to full-screen view.

Drag the Quick Launch Bar into View

Suppose you're using an app—you have the *New York Times* open, for example—and you need to make a phone call. You could press the Center button to put the app into Card view, and then tap the appropriate icon on the Quick Launch bar. Sure, you could do that—if you're lame. The cool, trendy, exciting way to do it is to drag the Quick Launch bar up, into view, and select the app you need with one, graceful gesture.

You might have seen this particular trick in TV commercials for the Pre. After all, it's a very cool-looking trick and makes you want to buy one just to play with the gesture. But even so, it's not obvious how to do it on your own.

Just place a finger in the gesture area (remember—that's the touch-sensitive strip below the touch screen) and move your finger up, into the touch screen. You'll see the Quick Launch bar bend and curve its way into view, riding on your finger.

You can now slide your finger left or right, and as you do so, you'll select each of the icons. When you hit the icon you want, just lift your finger and the app will start.

Yeah, it's a simple little thing, but it looks awesome and it's a ton of fun to do. If you're anything like us, you'll find yourself doing it not just when apps are running full screen, but also in Card view when you don't really need to use this little trick.

Using the Keyboard

Now that you have all the gestures down, you should have no trouble getting around the Pre. Of course, the Pre comes with something you won't find in a phone like the iPhone: a real keyboard. Let's take a look at that.

We already talked about the best way to open the keyboard—use a thumb or two on the touch screen to flick the Pre open in a brisk, confident motion. If your Pre is turned off, opening the keyboard will turn it on. Otherwise, opening the keyboard has no effect on your Pre or running applications. You can begin typing anywhere, and if an application is open that accepts text (such as Email, for example), the text will appear on screen. If not, your text entry will be interpreted as a search, and results will start flowing onto the screen—more about that in Chapter 4.

FIGURE 1-4   Entering text into a Pre using the natural thumb typing method

The keyboard is small, but even if you have fat, clumsy fingers like Rick, you should have little trouble typing. The easiest way to work with the Pre is to support it from behind with both hands and type with your thumbs, but you can type with other fingers as well if that's your preference (see Figure 1-4).

There are a few special keys on the keyboard:

Using the Orange Key

Press the ORANGE key to enter the various numbers and symbols that appear in the upper half of the keys. The ampersand (&) is above the A, for example, so you'd press ORANGE-A to enter it. When you press the ORANGE key, you'll see a small blue dot appear under the insertion point on the screen. The next key you press will add the upper key character to the screen, and then the typing mode will return to normal.

To enter a few upper key characters without pressing the ORANGE key before each one, double-press the ORANGE key first. After you do that, the dot under the insertion point turns black, and every key you press will enter the upper key character on the screen. When you're done, press the ORANGE key again and the dot will disappear. You're back in normal typing mode.

The ORANGE key also plays an important role in placing the cursor exactly where you want it in a block of text, as you'll see shortly in "Putting the Cursor Exactly Where You Want It."

You may hold down the ORANGE key while you type the next character, but you don't have to. Press the ORANGE key first, and when you see the black dot under the insertion point, you can press the next key by itself to enter the upper key character.

Using the Shift Key

The SHIFT key works just like the SHIFT key on your computer's keyboard. You can press it once to type a single uppercase letter and double-press it for "all caps" mode (caps lock), in which everything you type will appear in uppercase.

One press shows a blue arrow under the insertion point, while double-presses show you a black arrow.

The SHIFT key also plays an essential role in selecting text (such as for copying and pasting), as you'll see shortly in "Selecting Text for Copy and Paste."

You can switch from "orange mode" to "shift mode" (and vice versa) just by pressing the appropriate key. If you are typing in all caps, for example, press the ORANGE key to enter upper key characters.

Using the Symbol Key

You'll see a handful of symbols in the upper part of some keys, but what of all the less common ones you might need, such as the slash, greater than/less than, copyright, fractions, and emoticons? The Pre has got you covered. To see these symbols, press the—you guessed it—SYMBOL key, which is labeled *Sym*. This displays a scrolling list of 102 characters. Just use the drag gesture to scroll through the list and tap the character you need.

Putting the Cursor Exactly Where You Want It

Suppose you're typing a few sentences into your Pre—an email, perhaps, or an instant message—and you see something in an earlier sentence that you would like to correct. It's quite easy to position the cursor precisely anywhere on the screen, no matter how big your fingers are.

You might already have discovered that you can roughly position the cursor just by tapping within a block of text. The cursor will land under your finger, and it's very difficult to position it precisely, such as between two specific characters in a word. No problem. Just do this:

1. Tap in the block of text where you want the cursor to appear.
2. Press and hold the ORANGE key.
3. While continuing to hold down the ORANGE key, tap and drag your finger around the text to position the cursor exactly where you want it.

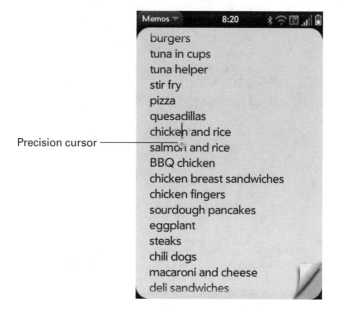

Precision cursor

You'll notice that you have precise control over the cursor in this mode, and a special symbol appears at the insertion point to indicate that you are in precision mode.

Selecting Text for Copy and Paste

For two years, Apple iPhone users clamored for something rudimentary that we utterly take for granted on our home computers: copy and paste. The iPhone finally got it, which is nice for users, we suppose. But the Pre allows you to copy and paste text quite easily as well. Here's how to do it:

1. Tap the block of text that you want to select.
2. Press and hold the SHIFT key.
3. While holding down the SHIFT key, tap and drag your finger in the text to make your selection. In general, you can't simply tap where you want the selection to end; instead, you need to tap at the insertion point and drag to the right or left, "pulling" the selection with your finger. You might need to lift your finger, return to the end of the selection, and drag some more several times until you get it all.

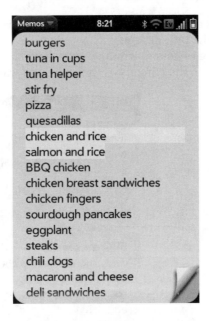

4. When the selection is complete, tap the application menu in the upper-left corner of the screen; then tap Edit and then Copy.
5. Position the cursor where you want to place the text.
6. In the application menu, tap Edit and then Paste.

If you are the sort of person who prefers shortcuts, you can copy text after it's selected by tapping and holding the left side of the gesture area and then pressing the c key. Then tap and hold the left side of the gesture area and press v.

Making Text Copyable

It's worth pointing out that you can copy and paste only text that is already "editable." That means you can copy text from an email, for example, but not from an article in the *New York Times*. There might be an easy work-around for that problem in many cases, though.

Take the *New York Times*: You can "share" an article via email, which puts the text in a special format so that you can copy it. So do this:

1. Open a *New York Times* article.
2. Tap the application menu; then tap Share, and then Email.
3. With the article in an email message, follow the steps in "Selecting Text for Copy and Paste," earlier in the chapter.
4. After you copy the text, you don't need the email anymore, so tap the Email application menu, and then tap Cancel.

Other Keyboard Tricks

The Pre's keyboard is pretty "smart"—it knows all sorts of tricks that make entering text and using the Pre easy. Here's a summary of the coolest stuff you can do:

Capitalization	The Pre will automatically capitalize words at the start of sentences and other "special" words.
Autocorrect	The Pre knows a slew of abbreviations and will autocorrect them for you—type *u* and it automatically becomes *you*, for example.
Undoing Autocorrect	If you don't want your Pre to capitalize or autocorrect a word you're typing, press the BACKSPACE key after the Pre makes the change and the word will revert to the way you originally entered it.
Delete	BACKSPACE usually deletes one letter at a time. To delete an entire word, press SHIFT-BACKSPACE (press and hold down SHIFT as you press BACKSPACE).
Caps Lock	Press SHIFT twice to type in all uppercase letters. Press it again to turn off caps lock mode.
Num Lock	Press the ORANGE key twice to type only numbers. Press it again to turn it off.
Bold	Highlight text, press and hold SYM, and press B. Then tap the blank symbol (the very last symbol, which is actually a blank space) to change text to bold.
Italics	Highlight text, press and hold SYM, and press I. Then tap the blank symbol to change text to italics.

Dave vs. Rick: What Could Your First Cell Phone Do?

Writing about the birth of the Palm is making us feel a little nostalgic, so we tackle the question, "What could your first cell phone do?"

Dave: Ooh! Ooh! I'll go first. My first cell phone could place voice calls. I bought it around 1993 when I was living in California, and on Saturdays we'd often drive an hour or so to Santa Barbara to wander the stores and go to the beach. So why did we get the phone? For emergencies, you might guess? Well, perhaps a little. But the main reason was so we could order a pizza for dinner on the way home and it would be ready for pickup as we rolled back into town.

I still have the phone, and I just dug it out of a box in the garage to take a look at it. It was the size of a hefty flashlight and could do absolutely anything you wanted as long as that thing you wanted was the ability to place phone calls. What about you, Rick?

Rick: What could my first cell phone do? That's like asking what my first record player could do. It played records! Seriously, if this is the best question you can come up with, it's going to be a loooong book.

2

Connect Your Pre to Your Data

HOW TO...

- Get started with Palm Synergy
- Create a Palm Profile
- Remotely erase your Pre
- Copy data to your Pre
- Work with Google
- Use the Data Transfer Assistant to migrate data from Outlook or Palm Desktop
- Keep Outlook in sync with your Pre
- Migrate data from your cell phone

Let's talk data. No, not Data, the beloved yellow-eyed android from *Star Trek: The Next Generation.* We mean the data that makes your world go round: contacts, calendar events, notes, tasks, and so on.

The Pre is arguably the most data-friendly smartphone in history, in that it's designed to aggregate information from a variety of sources. For example, you might have Microsoft Outlook on your PC, Facebook and Google accounts on the Web, and so on. Your Pre will effectively become the focal point of these data stores, the place where all your phone numbers, appointments, and the like come together.

 All this account synergy is the result of something Palm calls, well, Synergy. (We thought that term died in the early '90s. Ah, well.) Palm Synergy refers to the technology that brings together data from multiple online accounts and presents them in a simple, straightforward way. Any changes you make on your Pre or in one of your online accounts are automatically updated in the other location(s). So Synergy is not something you have to download or install or activate—it's simply a part of the Pre experience. And a darn good one at that!

Of course, you can enter new data on the Pre itself, as the situation warrants, and migrate existing data from programs such as Palm Desktop and services such as Yahoo!. It's entirely up to you how much data you want to keep on the Pre and where it should come from.

That said, merging data in your Pre is arguably the most confusing aspect of using a Pre. Consequently, this entire chapter is devoted to simplifying the merger of your data and your Pre. And it all starts with the Palm Profile.

Because chances are good that you've already performed the initial, one-time process of setting up at least one account (you can scarcely begin using your Pre without doing so), we're not going to rehash those steps here. They're covered pretty extensively in the user guide. Instead, we'll look at some additional synchronization options and solutions.

What Is a Palm Profile?

You probably have already set up a Palm Profile, as the Pre asks you to create one the first time you power up the phone. Remember? You typed in your email address and a password, and then Palm sent you a profile-verification email that looked something like this:

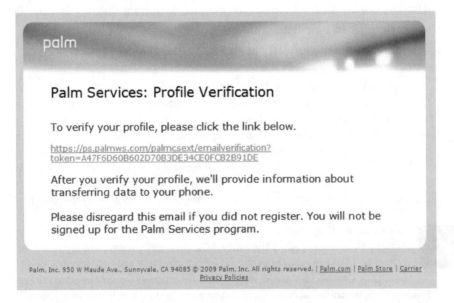

Your Palm Profile is really nothing more than an online record of basic details about you and your Pre (see Figure 2-1). It contains your name and email address, your phone number, and your Pre's device ID (which is akin to its electronic serial number). It also serves the very important purpose of backing up your apps, data, and settings, just in case you ever need to restore everything.

As you may have noticed (and as you can see in Figure 2-1), the Profile (as viewed online) includes one very important action button: Erase Device.

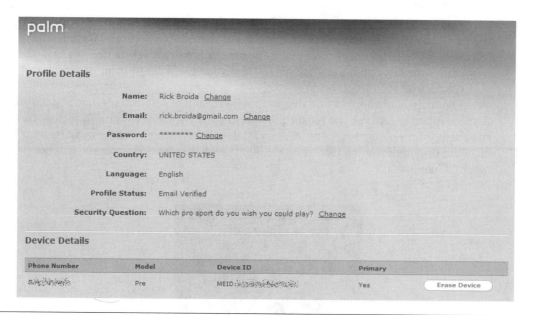

FIGURE 2-1   When you create a Palm Profile, you're effectively creating an online record that links you and your Pre. You're also creating an automated backup of your apps, settings, and data.

Remotely Erasing Your Palm Pre

Erase Device? Why on Earth would you want to do that? Well, let's say you work for NASA, and your Pre contains important documents concerning the locations of all the aliens that space-shuttle pilots have shot down over the years. (It must be true; we read it on the Internet.)

Now let's say your Pre gets lost—or stolen by the evil undersea Atlantisians who lured the aliens here in the first place (again: Internet). Man, are you in trouble. Or not, if you fire up your Web browser, load your Palm Profile, and click Erase Device. After entering a *secret government code* (okay, just a simple verification code), Palm will ask one more time if you want to do this:

When you click Yes, the Profile will send a remote trigger (via text message—see Chapter 3) to your Pre that automatically wipes the memory. It can take a few minutes for the trigger to reach the phone, at which point it resets itself to like-new, out-of-the-box condition. (This is the equivalent of a "hard reset" for anyone acquainted with PalmPilots and the like.)

Obviously, you shouldn't do this unless it's absolutely necessary, but rest assured: If you happen to recover your lost Pre (or replace it with a new one), the Palm Profile can easily restore your apps, settings, and data. In fact, after your Pre restarts, you'll have the option of signing into your Profile, at which point all your stuff will get restored like magic:

 Remotely erasing your Pre doesn't erase your data from its nondevice locations, such as Outlook and Google.

What Facebook Calendar Syncs with the Pre?

Facebook doesn't really have a calendar in the traditional sense, so you might be wondering just what data gets synced when you link your Facebook account with your Pre. In a word, *events*. Anytime you RSVP to an event with "attending," the details are synced with your Pre.

Copy Existing Data to the Pre

As we mentioned earlier, you can get data onto your Pre in two main ways: First, you can enter it directly using the built-in keyboard. That's fine for adding, say, a calendar entry while setting up an appointment with a friend or co-worker, or adding a new number to your contact list.

However, the best way to stock your Pre with data is to copy that data from one or more existing sources—namely, wherever you currently store your contacts, appointments, and the like. Following are some of those sources and how you can leverage them:

Source	Description	How It Can Work with the Pre
Palm Desktop	A desktop information-management program familiar to users of other Palm devices.	You can perform a one-time migration of your data to the Pre or use a third-party utility to synchronize Palm Desktop with the Pre.
Microsoft Outlook	A desktop information-management program commonly used in business and with Windows Mobile phones and devices.	You can perform a one-time migration of your data to the Pre or use a third-party utility to synchronize Outlook with the Pre.
Microsoft Exchange	A business tool that hosts Outlook data on a server.	The Pre can synchronize directly with Exchange servers.
Your old cell phone	Many users have an address book in the phone that was replaced by the Pre.	It may be possible to transfer the contacts from your old phone to your Pre.
Macintosh Address Book/iCal	The built-in contact/calendar apps used on Mac systems.	You can perform a one-time migration of your data to the Pre or use a third-party utility to synchronize Outlook with the Pre.
Google Calendar	Google's Web-based calendar, which also includes a contact manager.	The Pre can synchronize directly with Google Calendar.
Facebook	The mega-popular social networking site.	The Pre can synchronize directly with Facebook.
LinkedIn	The mega-popular business networking site	The Pre can synchronize directly with LinkedIn.

Let's take a closer look at these scenarios and talk about how you want to store and manage your data from this point forward. After all, the Pre is a life-changing device, so you might need to make a few changes in the way you operate.

For example, suppose you used Palm Desktop to sync your previous smartphone, a Palm Centro. Out of the box, the Pre doesn't sync with desktop software, so where does that leave Palm Desktop? What happens if you want to keep using the program as an information manager? *¡Ay, caramba!*

Fear not: You have options.

Did You Know?

How (and Why) to Sign Up for Google

If there's one thing almost every Pre user needs, it's a Google account. We suspect most people living on Earth already have one (and perhaps more than one), but if you don't, that's easily remedied. Just go to gmail.google.com and follow the instructions to sign up for a new account.

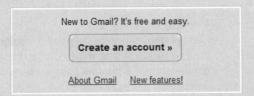

Signing up for Gmail (which is free, by the way) gets you not only a terrific email service (which you can use or not depending on your needs), but also access to Google Calendar, Google Contacts, Google Tasks, and just about every other Google service (including the excellent Google Docs, which offers browser-based word processing, spreadsheets, and presentations).

See, although your Pre data can exist in the digital equivalent of a vacuum (meaning it resides solely on your phone), there are many advantages to syncing it with Google. For one thing, it gives you an online backup of all your data. But even better, Google's Web-based apps are very handy. Suppose, for example, you want a month-at-a-glance view of your calendar. Google Calendar gives you that. Need to access your contacts and don't have your Pre handy (or, more likely, have a Pre with a dead battery)? You can sign into your Google account on any Internet-connected computer and view any of your calendar or contact data.

We particularly like Google Calendar because it lets you incorporate multiple calendars—not just your own, but also those of other calendar users. Thus, you could have one calendar that's yours, another belonging to your spouse, a third one for the kids, and so on. The Pre's Calendar app (see Chapter 5) lets you view any of these calendars (or all of them at once)—provided you have a Google account, that is.

So sign up!

Migrating Data from Outlook or Palm Desktop

Both Rick and Dave have years' worth of data accumulated in Outlook, and no doubt some of you do as well. Or perhaps you've been squirreling away your data in Palm Desktop. Either way, you'll want to copy that data to your Pre so you can keep it by your side (and, as a matter of course, add it to your online world).

The good news is that Palm has engineered a solution: the Data Transfer Assistant. This simple utility performs a one-time, one-way export of your data from Outlook or Palm Desktop to your Pre.

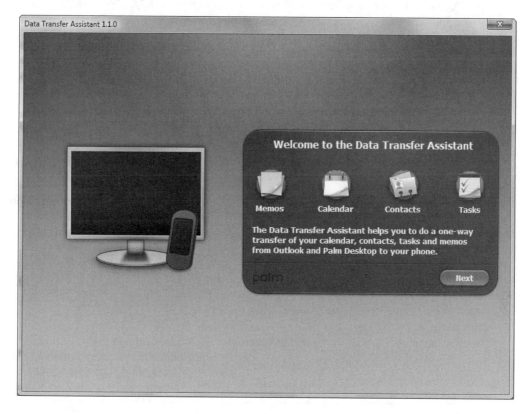

 Note What? A one-time export? No synchronizing? As we mentioned earlier, the Pre can't sync with these programs unless you install third-party software. See the section "Staying in Sync with Outlook or Palm Desktop" for more details.

Palm has very detailed, step-by-step instructions for using DTA (www.palm.com/us/support/downloads/pre/migration/dta_windows.html), so we're not going to rehash them here. But do read on if you plan to keep using either desktop program and want to keep your Pre in sync with it.

There's also a Macintosh version of the Data Transfer Assistant that requires you to export your Palm Desktop data to the Mac's iCal and Address Book programs first. Find complete instructions on Palm's support site at www.palm.com/us/support/downloads/pre/migration/exportical.html.

Staying in Sync with Outlook or Palm Desktop

It's only natural to want to keep using Outlook or Palm Desktop. After all, there's much to be said for having your contacts, calendars, notes, and the like accessible on your PC. In fact, we're a little disappointed with Palm for effectively severing ties with these applications, but we're not here to complain—we're here to help!

Actually, software developers such as Chapura, CompanionLink, and Mark/Space are here to help. They offer products that can sync your Pre with Outlook and/or Palm Desktop, the way nature intended.

Here are some third-party syncing products and descriptions:

Product	Price	Web Address	Description
Chapura PocketMirror	$29.95	www.chapura.com	Offers two-way synchronization between the Pre and Outlook's contacts and calendar.
Chapura Echo	$29.95	www.chapura.com	Offers two-way synchronization between the Pre and Palm Desktop's contacts and calendar.
CompanionLink for Google	$39.95	www.companionlink.com	Syncs Act!, GoldMine, Lotus Notes, Novell GroupWise, Outlook, or Palm Desktop with your Google account, which in turn syncs with the Pre.
The Missing Sync	$29.95	www.markspace.com	Syncs the Pre with Outlook, documents, music, photos, bookmarks, and just about anything else stored on your PC.

Migrating Data from Your Cell Phone

If your Pre represents an upgrade from an older phone (and for most people that's probably true), you probably have an address book—if not a calendar as well—you'd like to copy over to the Pre. After all, manually entering hundreds of names and addresses is nobody's idea of a good time.

The good news is that there's probably a way to extract the data from your old phone and move it to the Pre. The bad news is that because each phone is different, we can't cover every possible solution here. But we'll offer up a few examples so you can get an idea for what's involved.

Basically, if you already have a smartphone such as a BlackBerry or Windows Mobile device, you're golden: All your data is already being synced with Outlook, so just follow the instructions in the earlier section, "Migrating Data from Outlook or Palm Desktop."

Indeed, that's a good overall guideline: If you're already able to copy or transfer your contacts and appointments from your existing phone to Outlook, then you're halfway to where you need to be.

Okay, but what if you have a more traditional phone, such as a Motorola RAZR? That popular model doesn't sync with Outlook or, for that matter, any other program. However, that doesn't mean you're out of luck. Let's take a look at ways to extract data from most run-of-the-mill cell phones.

The following products help you get data off your phone and into your Pre:

Product	Price	Web Address	Description
BitPim	Free	bitpim.org	Freeware utility (available for Windows and Mac) connects your PC to your phone (via Bluetooth or USB cable) so you can retrieve your data. Lifehacker has an excellent tutorial on getting started with BitPim (http://bit.ly/STmdE), which isn't the most novice-friendly tool.
DataPilot	$29.95	datapilot.com	If BitPim doesn't work for you, try DataPilot. It's more user-friendly, and you can buy with it a USB cable specifically for your phone model.
Google Sync	Free	google.com/sync	Google's free utility is designed to sync contacts and appointments from Android phones, BlackBerrys, iPhones, Symbian phones, and Windows Mobile phones to your Google account (which would in turn sync with your Pre). It supports other kinds of phones too; check the site to see if yours is listed.
Sprint	Free	sprint.com	May be able to transfer your contacts from your old phone to your Pre. Visit a Sprint store to find out. (Assuming there's a Verizon version of the Pre by the time you read this, that company should offer a similar option.)

Rick vs. Dave: The App(s) We're Waiting For

As you'll learn in Chapter 10, the Pre can do a lot more than just check email and make calls. It can run countless programs, called apps, that extend its capabilities considerably. It's just a matter of time before the floodgates open, at which time we'll see hundreds, if not thousands, of fantastic new apps. Following are the ones we want ASAP.

Rick: The apps I want most are eReader, Kindle, and/or Stanza, all of which are e-book viewers that let you shop for and download books. You might scoff at the idea of reading on a screen as small as the Pre's, but don't knock it till you've tried it. After that, I'll be looking for RunKeeper, which leverages the Pre's built-in GPS to track your jogging time, distance, pace, route, and more—and then uploads all that data to a Web site where you can review your stats. All these apps are available on the iPhone, so I'm assuming they'll land in the Pre's App Catalog as well.

Dave: Actually, between the time that you wrote those words and I had a chance to reply, an app explosion has occurred in the App Catalog. Well, perhaps *explosion* is too strong a word—but there are now well over 100 apps, and it looks like many, many more will be added before long. Nonetheless, the apps I'm waiting for aren't there yet. I desperately want a TiVo scheduler for my Pre, so I can manage my television recordings away from home. And how about a Netflix app to manage my movie queue? And, of course, give me TripIt, so I can easily take my travel itineraries with me when I fly around the world with my girlfriend, Halle Berry. Last but not least, I want some sort of app that will help me meet Halle Berry.

3

Making the Call

HOW TO...

- Place a call
- Use the phone controls while in a call
- Take an incoming call
- Use the phone when it's locked
- Use voicemail
- Use a headset
- Mute the ringer
- Use speed dial
- Use call-related notifications
- Set a ringtone
- Multitask while on the phone
- Send text and instant messages

With all of the chatter about all the cool Web stuff you can do with a Palm Pre, it's easy to forget about the simple stuff—what you might call Pre's core competency.

You know, being a phone.

We'll be honest: If the Pre didn't get the basics right by allowing you to communicate with others, there would be no point in getting one of these things. So in this chapter, we'll take a tour of how to get the most out of your Pre as a phone and text-messaging device.

Placing a Call

Dave knows that there's really only one reason ever to use a phone: to order a pizza. (In fact, that's the main reason he got his first cell phone—to be able to call ahead for pizza. Yes, he knows it was dumb.)

Let's say you're ready to order that large pepperoni. Tap the Phone icon (the first icon in the Quick Launch bar), and you'll see this:

Direct Dialing

Your Pre works pretty much the way you'd expect any phone to work at this point. Want to make a call? Just tap the number on the dial pad on the touch screen. Here's pretty much everything you could ever want to know about direct dialing:

- If you make a mistake as you enter a number, tap the delete button to the right of the displayed phone number at the top of the dial pad. Or you can press the BACKSPACE key on the keyboard.
- To delete the entire number and start over, tap and hold the delete button or press and hold the BACKSPACE key.
- You can enter numbers either by tapping the touch screen or by pressing buttons on the keyboard. By default, the keyboard's letters don't do anything when the Phone app is open.
- When you're ready to place the call, tap the Dial button, which turns into the End Call button after you're connected. Tap it to hang up.

That's all there is to it.

Entering a Pause

You can "program" a pause into the way your Pre dials a number by entering the letter *p* within the number you're preparing to dial. Enter the *p* via the dial pad. For example, you could enter this string:

The phone will dial the number up to the *p* and then wait for your input. When you're ready to continue, tap the rest of the number.

Dialing 911

Here's how to enter the 911 emergency number:

- If your phone is turned on and unlocked, just start the Phone app, enter **911**, and tap the Dial button.
- If your phone is locked by a PIN or password, tap the Emergency Call button.

Search by Name Using the Dial Pad

The keyboard is disabled when the dial pad is open so that you can type only numbers, not letters that appear on the onscreen keys. But you can change that. Would you like to be able to type a person's name to search for his or her phone number in the Phone app? No problem.

Tap the Sprint menu in the upper-left corner of the Phone app screen, and then tap Preferences. In the area called When Typing in Dialpad, tap On next to Show Contact Matches.

Now you can type in a name using the keyboard so that the Phone app will automatically search your Contacts for matches and display their names and phone numbers.

Want to redial the last number you called? Tap the Dial button twice. The first tap places the last dialed call in the number area at the top of the screen, and the second tap dials the number.

How to...   # Add a Number to Contacts

It's easy to add a new number to your contacts list from the Phone app. You can do this in three ways:

- **In a call**   If you're in the midst of a call with someone who's not in your Contacts, tap the Add To Contacts button. This will allow you to save the number as a new contact or add it to an existing contact.

- **After a call**   Suppose you just got off the phone with someone who isn't in your contacts list and you want to add his or her information. Tap the Call History button in the lower-right corner of the Phone app, find the number in the list, and tap the Add To Contacts button to the right of the number (the little person with a plus sign). Then tap Add To Contacts and save the number as a new contact or add it to an existing contact.

(continued)

- **Before a call** If you enter a phone number in the number area at the top of the screen, you'll see the Add To Contacts button at the bottom. Tap it to create a new contact or add the number to an existing contact.

Dialing from Contacts

Dialing a number from memory is fine once in a while, but more often you'll want to let the Pre remember numbers for you—after all, memorizing things is for suckers.

We told you how to type name searches using the dial pad (see "Search by Name Using the Dial Pad"). If you don't make that change, though, the letters on the keyboard are disabled when the Phone app is running. So you can't ordinarily launch the phone and just tap out **Rick** on the keyboard to dial Rick's number. Some folks like it that way. (We assume Palm did a lot of testing and decided most people preferred to leave the keyboard turned off in the Phone app to reduce errors.)

You probably want the opportunity to search by name, though. For those occasions, you can tap the Contacts button at the top of the screen (actually, you can tap anywhere along the top). At this point, you have a couple of choices:

- *Browse for the name you're looking for by scrolling through the list.* When you find the name you want, tap it to send that number to the phone and immediately start dialing.
- *Type the name you're looking for.* You can type the first few letters of the first or last name, so **Ri** or **Br** will both return *Rick Broida* (if you're unlucky enough to have Rick in your Contacts list). We should point out that **ck**, on the other hand, won't give you *Rick*. You have to start typing at the beginning of a name.

If you have an Exchange Server account, wait a moment for your Pre to search the Global Address Book, and additional entries will flow in after a few seconds.

Dialing Without Starting the Phone App

You might be interested to know that you don't have to start the Phone app at all to use the phone. Try both of these options:

- *Tap Contacts in the Quick Launch bar next to the phone icon.* Either browse for the name you're looking for, or type the first few letters of the name. When you see the entry you want, tap it. Then tap the phone number you want to dial.
- *Don't start any app at all!* This is perhaps the easiest and best way to dial a contact's phone number, thanks to the Pre's Universal Search feature. With the Pre in Card view—either with no apps running or with the apps in Card view—just start typing. As you type, all sorts of search results will start to appear, including apps and contacts (see Figure 3-1). When you see the contact you want, tap it and proceed just as with any of the other methods we've discussed.

 If a phone number appears in a Web page or an email message, you can tap the number to dial it immediately.

FIGURE 3-1   Contacts entries appear after you start typing while in Card view; you can tap the entry and Pre will dial the phone number.

Dialing from the Call History

Another super useful tool makes placing calls really fast—the Call History button. Tap it and you'll see two categories: All Calls and Missed Calls. Browse the list and tap the entry you want—the Pre will send that number to the phone and dial it for you.

Deleting Your Call History

The Call History button is a fast way to call back people whom you're recently been in touch with. In fact, it's often faster to call people with the Call History button than any other method. Sometimes, however, the history gets a little "noisy," and you'd like to prune it a bit so the more important numbers stay within easy reach. After all, do you really want telemarketing calls to appear in your call history forever?

The good news is that you can delete individual entries from the call history or clear the entire history at once:

- **Delete an entry** To delete a single entry, flick it to the left or right, and you'll see an option to delete or cancel. Tap Delete to remove the entry permanently from the history.

- **Clear the entire history**   To start fresh, tap the Call History button, and then tap the app menu in the upper-left corner of the screen and choose Clear Call History.

Looking for a call log screen that shows you information such as the length of each call and the total call time? Don't bother. The Pre doesn't have a log (at least there's no long in the current version on the Pre's software).

Using the Phone Controls While in a Call

Now let's suppose that you've dialed the phone and you're in the midst of a call. Most of the time, that's all you need to know. If your contact has a picture, you'll see that, along with a timer that shows the running time of the call, along with some other buttons we'll get to soon. When you're in a call, you should see something like this:

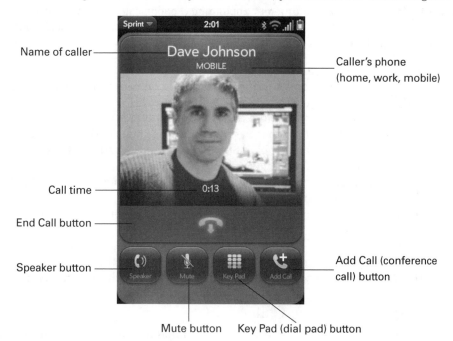

If you're not using a headset or the speakerphone, the phone's touch screen will turn off while the phone is pressed up against your face. That means if you pull the phone away to look at the screen, you might see a black display. Don't worry—nothing's broken. Wait a moment and the screen will light up.

Want to have fun? Try this experiment: While in a call, hold the phone in one hand and then slowly move your other hand, palm open, over the handset. When you get within about an inch of the Pre, you should see the screen go dark. Pull your hand away, and the display will light up again.

But why, you ask? Actually, it's kind of smart. Blanking the screen conserves battery life (since a bright screen is the fastest way to sap a cell phone's battery) and it also prevents your accidentally pressing buttons (such as the End Call button) with your ear or cheek.

So suppose you need to interact with your phone. If it's been pressed up against your cheek, give it a moment to come back to life. Then tap the button you need:

- **Contact picture** Tap the picture of the contact you're talking with and you'll be taken directly to his or her card in the Contacts app. There, you can refer to his or her personal information or you can tap Edit and modify the information. That's handy if someone says, "Hey! I just changed my email address!" You can switch to his or her contact and make the changes to information without ever leaving the call. You can get back to using the phone just how you'd expect: Press the Center button to switch to Card view, and then use the previous gesture to flip back to the Phone card.

 Whenever you're in a different app during a phone call, you'll see a notification in the lower-left corner that display's the contact's name or number. Tap it to go directly back to the Phone.

- **Speaker** Tap Speaker to switch to the Pre's speakerphone mode. You can place the phone on a tabletop and continue the call hands-free. To leave speakerphone mode, just tap the Speaker button a second time.
- **Mute** Tap Mute to, well, mute the Pre's microphone. You can then talk or do other things without the other party being able to hear what's happening on your end of the call. You can combine Speaker and Mute, incidentally, to participate in a conference call while multitasking—write email, have a conversation with someone else in your office—you'll still hear the call, but they won't be able to hear you until you un-mute the phone.
- **Key Pad** Sometimes you might need to enter additional information into the phone, such as when entering a password when calling your bank or walking through a phone tree ("Press 1 for English"). Tap Key Pad to access the dial pad and tap it again if you want to return to the view of your caller.
- **Add Call** This lets you set up a conference call, which we'll discuss next.

Dialing a Conference Call

You can connect multiple people into a single conference call with just a few taps on your Pre. Conference calls can be used for boring stuff like meetings—who doesn't love a good conference call to loop in marketing, design, legal, and sales for a 10 A.M. sync-up?

But it's also handy for connecting friends and family—"How about we all see a movie tonight? I'll conference in Jeff and we can pick a theater." Here's how to make the magic happen:

1. While in a call with someone, tap Add Call.
2. The first call will be put on hold, and you'll see the same screen you ordinarily see to make a call. Use any method you like to place the call—dial it manually, tap Contacts, you name it.

3. When the other party picks up, you'll see a split screen. The top screen call is the original, still on hold. The bottom screen shows the new call that has just gone through. Feel free to chat it up, but don't forget you still have that first caller on hold. When you get permission to conference your new call in, tap the Un-hold button in the top screen.

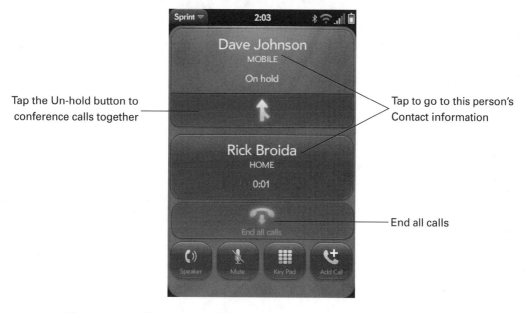

Tap the Un-hold button to conference calls together

Tap to go to this person's Contact information

End all calls

The screen will now consolidate into a single call, and you can talk to both parties at once. When you're done, tap the End Call button to hang up on both parties.

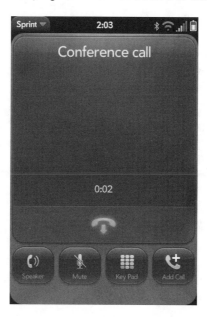

Note that you can conference with only two other parties at once—that's why it's sometimes called three-party calling. If you try to dial in a fourth party by tapping Add Call after you have a conference call set up, you'll see this message:

Taking an Incoming Call

Brrrring! Your phone is ringing. Congratulations; unlike Rick, that probably means you have at least one friend. (If it *is* Rick calling, Dave will show you how to ignore calls in a moment.)

The phone will behave slightly differently depending on what state the phone is in when the call arrives. It's not terribly complicated, but it's worthwhile to discuss the various situations in detail.

When the Phone Is On

You're actually doing something with your Pre. There you are, playing a game of Connect Four or reading the *New York Times*, when it starts ringing in your hands. *Ahhhghhghhh*! (At least that was Dave's reaction the first time his new Pre started ringing while concentrating on doing something else with it, like reading.) In any event, half the screen will display the incoming caller's name and number, along with options to answer or ignore the call.

Answer   Ignore

If you tap Answer, the Phone app will appear and your Pre will show the same call environment as if you placed the call. Choose to ignore the call, though, and it'll go directly to your voicemail, giving the caller an opportunity to leave you a message.

There's another option—you might do nothing at all. If you wait while the call rings through to voicemail (or if you're away from the phone and unable to accept the call when it comes in), the Pre will display this for about a minute after the phone stops ringing:

You can dismiss the notification or tap Call Back to dial the missed caller.

 You can silence the ringer for the incoming call by pressing the power button once. Or, you can ignore the incoming call by pressing the power button twice.

When the Phone Is Locked in Its Touchstone Charger

This is kind of cool. If a call comes in when the phone is sitting on its near-magical Touchstone charger (see Chapter 11 for details), you can do either of the following:

- *Leave it on the charger.* If you leave the Pre sitting on its charger, it'll automatically turn on the speakerphone. You don't even need to pick it up: just start talking.
- *Take it off the charger.* No need to even unlock the Pre—when the phone loses contact with the Touchstone, it'll unlock automatically and be ready to talk by the time it reaches your ear.

When the Phone Is Locked, Without a PIN or Password

More often than not, the phone will be turned off and tucked in your pocket when it starts ringing. To take the call, just drag the lock or phone icon up, the same as if you were unlocking the phone to use it normally. No need to do anything else—you'll be on the call right away. Another option: slide the keyboard open.

When the Phone Is Locked with a PIN or Password

Last but not least, if you're using the security option that requires a PIN or password to operate the phone, you'll be relieved to know that you don't have to enter your code just to take an incoming call. Drag the lock up, and you'll be in right away.

On the other hand, you won't be able to do much else until the phone is unlocked. You can use the Speaker, Mute, and Key Pad buttons, but to get to other apps or dial in a conference call, you'll need to tap Unlock and enter your code.

Unlock

Did You Know?

What's Your Phone Number?

What's your phone number? If you answer, "How would I know? I never call myself!" then here's a tip just for you.

Here's a fast way to find your phone number: Start the Phone app and then tap the app menu in the upper-left corner. Tap Preferences, and there it is: your phone number appears at the top of the screen.

Interpreting the Connection Status Icons

You've seen some fancy-looking status icons in the upper-right corner of your Pre's display—but what do they all mean? This is what you'll typically see:

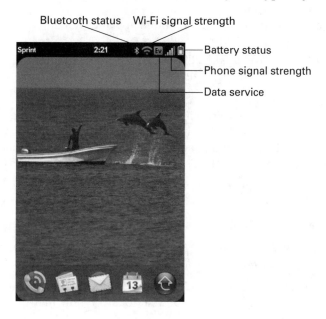

Depending on how you've configured your phone and where you are located, the specific icons you see might be a little different. Here are some other things you might see:

✈	Airplane mode is turned on—see Chapter 1 for details.
📶	The Pre is looking for a Wi-Fi network to connect to. The icon is gray while searching for a network and white when connected.
Searching...	The Pre is looking for a Sprint network to connect to. You'll see this when you first turn on the phone, before it has locked into the phone network or in an area where there is no service.
ᛒ	The Pre is in the process of connecting to a Bluetooth device.
🔋 🔋 🔋	The battery status might have a good charge or a low charge. To see the exact battery life remaining (in percentage), tap the status bar. The battery life appears in the menu.

Using Voicemail

Your Pre comes with a voicemail account that delivers missed messages to you whether your phone was turned off, you were on another call, you simply chose not to answer, or even if your battery died.

To get to your voicemail, tap the Phone app and then tap the Voicemail button.

 Here's a fast way to get to voicemail without starting the Phone app: Press and hold the E key, which is the speed dial key for voicemail.

The first time you use voicemail, you'll be prompted to set up a passcode and record your name and a message that others will hear when they call you. We recommend something short and sweet, but you might want to include a different way for people to reach you. Here's what Dave usually uses for a voicemail message:

Hi. This is Dave. I can't take your call right now. You can leave a message or e-mail me at dave@davejoh.com.

Rick's message is a little different:

Hi, this is Rick. Is this thing on? [garbled] What? [loud, unexplained noises] Hey, Brandine! I cain't work this newfangled chatterbox!

When you have voicemail, you'll see several indications, including a notification and a number on the Voicemail button that tells you how many messages are waiting for you:

To hear your voicemail, tap the notification, or first tap the Phone app and then tap the Voicemail button.

You can save voicemail messages for up to 30 days; after that, they are deleted from the voicemail system.

Using a Headset

So far, we've assumed you're using your phone the old fashioned way—you know, by holding it up to your ear like a caveman. But you can also plug in a wired headset—your Pre came with one (see Figure 3-2)—or use a Bluetooth headset.

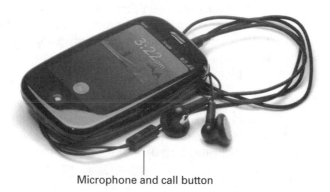

Microphone and call button

FIGURE 3-2   The Pre comes with a wired headset you can use for phone calls and to listen to music.

If you don't yet have a Bluetooth headset, you might want to use a wired headset. Any standard headset with a 1/8-inch jack will work just fine.

The one that came with your Pre has just one control—a button that you can use like the Place Call button on the Pre. The headset button will

- Answer an incoming call
- Answer call waiting
- End a call (or conference call) in progress

And, when you're listening to music, pressing it twice will skip to the next song.

Using a Bluetooth Headset

Equipped with a Bluetooth headset, you can talk hands-free, like a character from *The Jetsons* or any movie featuring businesspeople made in the last ten years.

Using a Bluetooth headset has a couple of advantages, actually. Allow us to list the most important ones for you:

- *It's safer.* If you're using your Pre in a car—and you're the driver—you should absolutely be using a Bluetooth headset. It's not safe to drive with a phone in one hand, propped up against your ear. In fact, it's illegal not to use a hands-free solution such as Bluetooth in many cities, so using a headset can save not just your life, but a hefty ticket as well.
- *It's more convenient.* Do you really want to hold a handset up to your ear all day? Of course not. Using Bluetooth, you can free up both hands for all sorts of stuff. Dave has used his Bluetooth headset to hold conversations while multitasking at his desk, while exercising on an elliptical machine, and while holding a cat. Try that with a Pre in one hand.
- *It's potentially healthier.* This one is arguable, because all the science isn't in yet. But a couple of admittedly inconclusive studies have suggested that cell phones can emit dangerous levels of radiation close to your brain, which could potentially lead to cancer and other long-term health problems. We don't want to buy into quack science or promote alarmist stories about the dangers of technology, but the fact remains that using a Bluetooth headset moves the cell phone safely away from your brain, and there's no downside to that even if it turns out that suspicions about cell phone radiation were unfounded.

Before you can use a new Bluetooth headset with your Pre, you'll need to pair them first. These days, with a new Bluetooth headset, that's a pretty painless process. To learn how to connect your Bluetooth headset to your Pre, check out Chapter 5. In fact, if you need to set up your headset, do that now. We'll wait.

Did You Know?

What Is Bluetooth?

Bluetooth is a somewhat oddly named standard that allows wireless devices to communicate over short distances. Most Bluetooth gadgets are called Class 2 devices and have a maximum range of about 33 feet, though other, less common, classes of devices have a range of as much as 100 feet (Class 1) and as little as 1 foot (Class 3).

The most common Bluetooth devices you're likely to encounter will be wireless headsets for mobile phones, but Bluetooth has all sorts of applications. You might find simple GPS receivers with no display or controls that send their navigation information to other devices via Bluetooth. There are also Bluetooth-enabled printers, mice, keyboards, and game controllers (like those that come with the Xbox 360).

So, where does Bluetooth get its name? It's named after the 10th century King Harald of Denmark, the dude (if we can, in fact, refer to anyone from the 10th century as *dude*) who united a hodgepodge of Danish tribes into a single kingdom—you know, in the same way that Bluetooth was intended to unite all sorts of mobile devices into a single portable area network (PAN).

Done? Great. To control the Bluetooth settings, tap the status bar in the upper-right corner of your Pre and then tap Bluetooth. This is where you can turn Bluetooth on or off.

For the most day-to-day convenience, we recommend that you leave Bluetooth turned on all the time. It does tend to drain your battery somewhat faster, so if you're really power conscious, you might want to switch Bluetooth on only when you really need it. But if you leave it on all the time, your phone will automatically connect to your headset whenever you turn the headset on.

To use your headset, switch it on and then place a call. The Pre, as we mentioned, should automatically recognize the headset and just start using it.

If, for some reason, the headset doesn't automatically connect to the headset, tap the status bar and return to the Bluetooth menu. Find your headset (if you have configured more than one Bluetooth device, you might have several items there) and tap it. It should connect.

Note that when you're in a call, the Phone app looks a little different. The Speaker button now says Audio, and you can tap it to switch among the Speaker, Bluetooth headset, and Normal, which means using the phone as an ordinary handset.

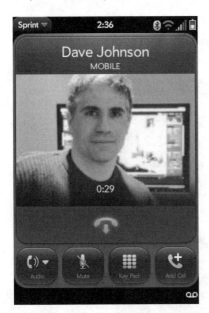 

 If you're in the midst of a call before you've turned on your Bluetooth headset, it's not too late. When you turn on the headset, your Pre will automatically switch over, even in the middle of a phone call.

Muting the Ringer

Even if you've chosen an awesome ringtone (Dave's current favorite is *Days of Elaine*, by The Decemberists), there are times when you don't want it to go off. Examples include when you're in a movie theater or church, at a meeting at work, and at your weekly get-together for The Campaign Against Cell Phone Ringtones.

No worries. Unlike some phones that require you to dig deep into your phone's menu system or press some keyboard shortcut to disable the ringer, the Pre has a built-in switch for that at the top. Snap it to the red position and the ringer is muted.

Using Speed Dial

As you can see, there are about a million ways to dial your Pre. You can tap in a number by hand, browse contacts, search for a name, or look at the call history. How would you like yet another way to get to your phone numbers? Yes, you say? Then how about speed dialing?

We all know and love speed dial—every desktop phone for the last 20 years has had a bank of buttons that you could program with your most frequently dialed friends, family, or co-workers. Many cell phones have some sort of speed dial as well, and the Pre is no exception.

Setting Speed Dial

The Pre, in fact, lets you assign a huge number of speed dial entries—almost every key on the keyboard can be assigned a name and number. Here's how to do it:

1. Tap the Contacts icon.
2. Browse to the contact that you want to turn into a speed dial entry and tap to open it.
3. Tap the Contacts menu and tap Set Speed Dial.

4. Tap the phone number that you want to assign to a speed dial entry on the keyboard. If your contact has multiple phone numbers (such as home and mobile), tap the one you want. If there's only one phone number, well, tap that one.

5. Tap the key in the list that you want.

Notice that the E key is preset to voicemail, and that can't be changed. As you set contacts to speed dial, you'll see them appear in this list, indicating that those letters are now reserved and can't be used for new entries.

If you want to change a speed dial entry, open the contact and go to the Set Speed Dial menu. You can choose to remove the speed dial entry entirely or just tap a different letter to change it.

At first glance, it might seem a little odd to assign phone numbers to letters on the keyboard. What good is that? But if you think about it, it's easy to come up with memorable speed dial assignments. You can use *H* for home and *M* for mom, for example. Use the first letters of your friends' names. Use whatever you can remember!

Making a Call with Speed Dial

Now that you've assigned a few contacts to some speed dial entries on your keyboard, it's time to make a call. To place a call using speed dial, start with the Pre in Card view—either with no apps running or with the apps in Card view—and then press and hold the appropriate speed dial key. The Pre will start dialing right away.

Here's another option: Tap the speed dial key (don't hold it down). Search should start and the top result will be the speed dial contact. Tap the entry to dial the number.

Using Dialing Shortcuts

Dialing shortcuts are a different sort of speed dial—they let you dial a number just by entering the last four digits. Doesn't sound useful? Then consider these situations:

- You work for a company in which all the numbers start with the same digits, and only the last four vary.
- Your family has four phones, and the store issued them sequential (or nearly sequential) numbers that all begin with the same digits.

In either case, you could dial *1234* and your Pre would automatically dial 425-555-1234 for you, assuming that you had created 425-555 as a dialing shortcut. Pretty cool, huh?

Here's what to do:

1. Tap the Phone icon.
2. Tap the app menu and then tap Preferences.
3. In the Dialing Shortcuts section, tap Add New Number.
4. Enter the digits that the Pre should dial automatically when you enter four digits, and then tap Done.

Did You Know?

Pre Hacking: Special Codes

While we're on the subject of speed dial numbers, you might be interested to know that you can enter a whole slew of other preset numbers and codes in the Phone app to get to special services and features.

This is just a little like hacking, because some of these codes let you do things that circumvent common sense protections that keep you from rendering your phone a nonfunctional brick of electronic components.

That said, here are a few very safe codes you can enter into your Pre:

*2 + Dial	Dials Customer Service
*3 + Dial	Dials Sprint Payment Services
*4 + Dial	Dials Sprint Account Information; an automated system tells you your current usage and account information
##477# + Dial	Displays the GPS Information screen; tap Get Fix to see detailed information about your location, speed, and altitude

If you're curious about other codes, check out a post at PreCentral.net (http://forums.precentral.net/palm-pre/184651-pre-specific-hash-codes .html#post1662866), which lists many more codes you can try.

Tip You can enter more than one dialing shortcut, and you can change the number of digits—anywhere from four to seven—that make up your shortcut.

Now when you dial a phone number, the Pre will always try to use a dialing shortcut. That means that when you enter the fourth digit, it'll automatically add the prefix numbers and stand by to dial in case you tap the Dial button. But fear not: If you enter another digit, the prefix goes away and you can continue entering all seven digits as usual.

Dealing with Call-Related Notifications and Status

Like a really diligent teenage sister, your Pre will take all sorts of notes for you about stuff you missed when you weren't around. No matter what happens when you are away from your Pre, you can catch up by looking at the notifications that stack up when you get back.

In a nutshell, notifications are the message bands that appear at the bottom of the screen and keep you in the loop about voicemails, missed calls, and the like. For a complete look at all the notifications you can get, see Chapter 5. But here are the phone-specific notifications you'll want to know about:

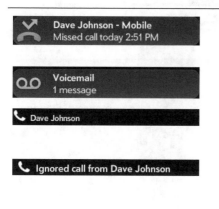	Tells you that you missed a call (but the caller didn't leave a voice message). Tap it to open the Phone app and call the person.
	Reminds you that you have voicemail. Tap it to open the Phone app and hear your voicemail.
	Remains on screen if you are actively on the phone while also using a different app. Tap the message to return to the Phone app.
	Appears briefly after you choose to ignore a call. It'll disappear on its own. If you tap it before it disappears, though, the caller's Contact card will open.

Setting a Ringtone

Let's be totally honest with each other. What we're about to share with you is a great power, requiring great responsibility and restraint. We're going to tell you how to turn any song into a ringtone. So, bottom line, if either of us ever encounters you and your Pre in a coffee shop and we hear it notify you about an incoming call by playing "The Macarena," we will seize your Pre on the spot and smash it to pieces.

 Note Our lawyers have instructed us to say that under no circumstances will we smash your Pre to pieces. Unless it's playing "Mmm Bop" by Hansen. No jury would convict us.

Setting a Global Ringtone

Okay, consider yourself warned (we're watching you). To change the standard ringtone that sounds the alarm whenever you get a phone call, you need to go to the Sounds & Ringtones app. Here's how to get there:

1. Tap the Launcher icon on the far right side of the Quick Launch bar.
2. In the Launcher, flip (using the next gesture) to the page with the Sounds & Ringtones icon. If you haven't moved it around yet, it'll be the second icon in the top row of the third page.
3. Tap Sounds & Ringtones.

Once you've opened the app, look for the Ringer Switch On section. This area controls your phone experience—what you'll hear, and how loud it is—when you have the ringer turned on. Tap Ringtone and you'll see a list of ten preset ringtone sounds.

To test a ringtone, tap the play button in the blue square. Be careful—if you tap outside the blue, you actually select the ringtone.

When you find the ringtone you want, you now know what to do. Just tap the name, outside the blue, and you'll be taken back to the Sounds & Ringtones main screen, and you'll see the name of the ringtone displayed as the selected ringtone.

Turning a Song into a Ringtone

That's great, but what if you want to hear the Decemberists' "Days of Elaine" as your ringtone? The Beatles' "I am the Walrus"? Bob Mould's "Whichever Way the Wind Blows"? It doesn't matter what your musical taste might be (that "Macarena" thing notwithstanding), because any song on your Pre can become a ringtone.

Your first challenge, of course, is to get some songs loaded onto your Pre. There are all sorts of ways to do that—you can email yourself a song, if you're desperate, we suppose. You can buy tracks from Amazon. You can drag tracks onto the Pre when it's connected to the PC in USB Drive mode. Or you might be able to use iTunes to sync your music library. (We say *might* because even as we wrote this very chapter, Apple released an updated iTunes that prevents the Pre from syncing. And by the time we edited the chapter a few weeks later, Palm had patched the Pre to work with iTunes all over again. For all the details on this soap opera, check out Chapter 8, which tells you everything (and more) that you ever wanted to know about music on the Pre.

For the moment, let's assume you already have some tracks on your Pre (skip ahead to Chapter 8, if necessary). To use one of those songs as a ringtone, just go back to the Ringtones screen and note the button in the bottom left of the screen. (That's a pair of eighth notes, for you musical trivia fans.) Tap it.

Now you'll see a list of all the songs on your Pre. Scroll around until you find the song you want, preview it by tapping the play button if necessary, and then tap the song title to select it. That's it!

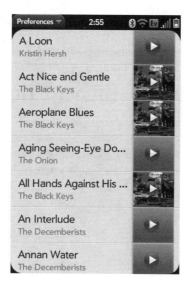

Setting a Ringtone for a Specific Contact

It's great to personalize your phone with a favorite ringtone, but it's downright awesome to assign custom ringtones to specific people in your contact list. Dave, for example, identifies incoming calls from his wife with the Lenny Kravitz version of "American Woman," while calls from Rick play Green Day's "American Idiot."

To do the same sort of thing yourself, you will have to open the individual contacts that you want to change. Do this:

1. Tap Contacts, which you'll find on the Quick Launch bar (unless you've moved it).
2. Find a contact for which you want to assign a custom ringtone, and tap it.
3. Tap Edit.
4. Tap Set A Ringtone.
5. Follow the process we outlined in "Setting a Global Ringtone" to select a preset ringtone or convert one of your own songs into a ringtone.

Custom ringtones for your contacts are the exception to the ringtone you set in the Sounds & Ringtones app. The global ringtone will always sound for any caller for which you have not specified an individual ringtone.

It should go without saying (though we'll say it anyway) that if you turn off the ringer, you won't hear any ringtone at all—you'll just get silence or a vibration, depending on how you've set the Ringer Switch Off section in the Sounds & Ringtones screen (see Chapter 4 for details).

Multitasking While on the Phone

Just because you're talking on the phone, it doesn't mean you can't do other stuff at the same time. The Pre is designed to allow you to run multiple programs at once, and therefore, you can talk on a phone call while also running other apps—and you can even use them while you're actively engaged in a call.

Using another app while you're using the phone: Just press the Center button to switch to Card view. From there, you can start new apps or switch to other apps already running.

Keep a few things in mind about multitasking with your phone:

- Unless you're using a Bluetooth headset, you'll probably want to turn on the speakerphone so you can take the phone away from your ear and look at the screen. It would be nice if the Pre automatically went to speakerphone when the phone was in Card view, but, well, you can't have everything.
- Don't toss the Phone app up off the top of the screen. That closes the app and, consequently, ends the call.
- When you're in the midst of a call, you can't use anything that requires an Internet connection. So while you can read and write email, you can't send or receive email. Likewise, you can't use an app that needs Internet access to do its thing, such as the *New York Times*. When you end the call, you'll get your Internet access back.
- You can simultaneously use the phone and send a text message. See "Sending Text Messages" a bit later for more details on that.
- To return to the Phone app, you can navigate to it using Card view, or just tap the Call In Progress status message at the bottom of the screen.

Communicating Using Text Messages and Instant Messages

Sometimes you'd rather send a text than talk on the phone. You might be in a public place, such as a restaurant or movie theater, where you can't talk out loud. Or your location is just too noisy—such as an airport baggage claim area. Or maybe you just need to send a short message and talking on the phone is overkill.

What's the Difference Between SMS and IM?

Text messaging, known officially as SMS, is a message protocol used by cell phones. Texts are sent using the same wireless network as voice—you don't need Internet access, for example, to have text messaging service on your phone. Messages are generally limited to 160 characters, and you can text anyone from your mobile phone, no matter what kind of phone they have or what cellular provider they're using. (For comparison, the sentence you are reading right now is just about 160 characters long, so SMS is obviously not intended to be a way to write your next novel.)

Instant messaging, on the other hand, is a text message service that operates over the Internet. Many IM services are out there, and few are interchangeable. You might have an account with Google (called Google Talk, and abbreviated GTalk), AOL Instant Messaging (abbreviated as AIM), Yahoo!, or MSN, for example, but you can't send a message from Google's IM to a friend who is using Yahoo! or MSN. They're closed services and can only talk to each other. That's why services like Meebo and Trillian are so popular—all the most common IM services are combined on the same screen, so you can talk to your friends or co-workers no matter what IM service they happen to use.

Whatever your reason, the Pre has you covered. The phone actually integrates text messaging—also known as SMS (short for Short Message Service) with instant messaging (which you probably know as IM), so you can send both kinds of messages from the same app.

Getting Started with Messaging

The Pre supports three specific varieties of messaging:

- SMS, which you get with your Pre's service plan, if it includes text messaging
- Google Talk
- AIM

To get a Google Talk account, you need to create an account at google.com. Once you create a Google account, your GTalk information is the same username and password you would use to log into google.com.

To get an AIM account, create your account at www.aim.com. You can choose to create a screen name from scratch or just use your email address as your screen name (see Figure 3-3).

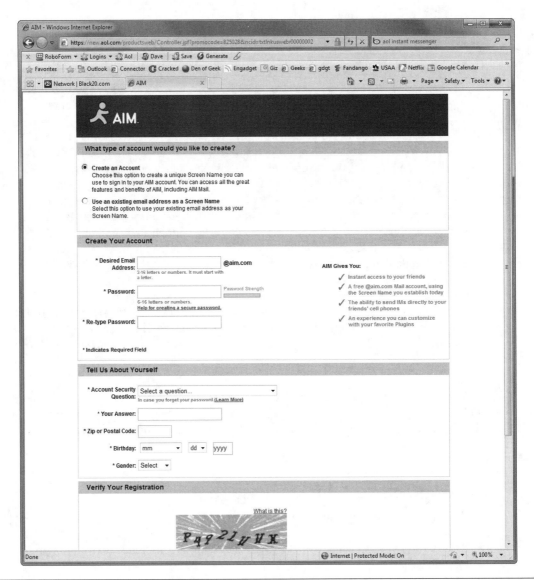

FIGURE 3-3   AIM is a free service you can get by signing up at www.aim.com.

Your GTalk account should be automatically configured for you when you enter your Gmail address in your Pre, but you can always add that information later. Likewise, it's easy to add an AIM account on your Pre by doing this:

1. Start the Messaging app (tap the Launcher icon and then tap Messaging).
2. Tap the app menu and then tap Preferences & Accounts.
3. Tap Add IM Account.

4. Tap the kind of account you want to configure—Google Talk or AIM—and then enter your username and password. Tap Sign In.

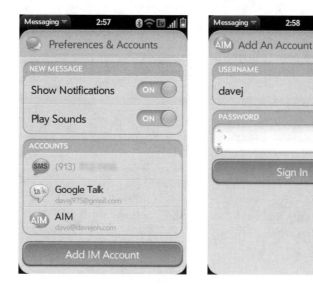

Sending Text Messages

Ready to send a text to someone? Just try this:

1. Start the Messaging app (tap the Launcher icon and then tap Messaging).

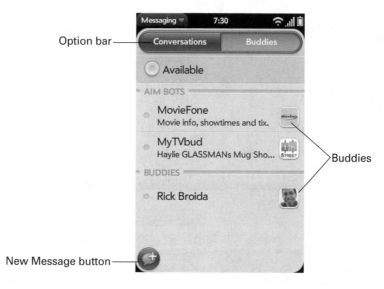

2. Tap the New Message button in the lower-left corner.
3. Enter the name or number of the person you want to text. You can search by name just as if you were placing a voice call, or tap the icon in the upper-right corner to browse your contacts. Notice that for each contact, you can choose to text a phone number (which means you're sending an SMS to their phone) or to their Google or AOL address—that's an IM, which will appear in their instant messaging client. If your contact is using a mobile phone with IM built in (like the Pre), they'll receive the IM on their phone. Otherwise, it'll go to wherever their IM client happens to live, such as on their computer.
4. Type the message and then tap the Send button (the paper airplane).

If your contact has both SMS and IM accounts, you can easily switch between the two at any time while remaining in the same conversation. To switch between SMS and IM, tap the menu button in the upper-right corner of the Messaging screen and choose the phone number or IM account that you want to use to send your messages. When set to a phone number to send an SMS, the menu button will display *Text*. When you switch to IM, it will display either *Google* or *AIM*. The conversation also keeps track of whether it's taking place in text or IM—just look for the icons, like these:

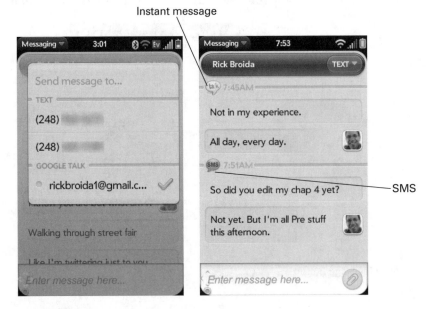

In general, you don't have to worry about whether you're in text or IM mode—it just works, either way.

> ### Did You Know?   Why Would You Switch Between IM and Text?
>
> That's a great question. It's all a matter of convenience. Here are two examples that show how this interoperable text and IM system is pretty cool:
>
> - Dave has a Pre, but Rick has a mobile phone for which he is paying a monthly fee for a limited number of text messages. Dave sends Rick a text message, and Rick sends back: "Switch to AIM, out of texts." With one tap, Dave can continue the conversation, but now via IM. Rick, however, is still too cheap to pay for unlimited texting.
> - Rick sends Dave a text from his Pre. Dave just arrives home and texts: "@home now, @PC. IM please." Rick can switch over to GTalk without losing any of the conversation, and Dave can now respond from his computer instead of his phone.

Choosing Conversations and Buddies

When you start the Messaging app, you'll notice that you have a choice of two modes, or categories, via the option bar at the top of the screen: Conversations and Buddies.

Continuing an Old Conversation

One cool thing about any messaging session—whether it's a text chat, an IM chat, or a combination of the two—is that it's persistent. Once you start a conversation, it'll stay on your Pre forever (unless you choose to delete it, which we'll show you how to do later).

To find a previous conversation, tap Conversations and then browse the list—conversations are listed chronologically, and you can see a snapshot of the final messages sent for each. When you find the conversation you want to continue, tap it. You'll then be able to read the entire previous conversation, switch the type of message (SMS or IM) if desired, and continue the conversation just by typing.

Chatting with a Buddy

The other choice at your disposal in the option bar is Buddies. Tap this option, and you'll see a list of all the buddies you have associated with your IM services. If you are a GTalk user, for example, you'll see your Google buddies listed; if you are both a GTalk and AIM user, you'll see your buddies for both services listed together. If you use AIM, you'll also see AOL's bots listed as well. (Bots are automated messaging programs from which you can get information, such as movie listings.)

Your Pre will display only buddies who are currently online and able to receive messages. But keep your eye on the color of their icon:

- Online buddies are green by default.
- Busy buddies are orange.

Also keep in mind that you can show your offline buddies in the list as well. Open the app menu and tap Show Offline Buddies.

Setting Your Messaging Status

By default, your Pre is always signed in to your IM services. If you have both a GTalk and AIM account, you're signed in to both, and it's not possible to sign out of one or the other selectively—if you sign out of one, you automatically sign out of both.

But you might not always want to be available to your friends. Just like on your PC, you can adjust your status so you can't receive text messages.

To set your status, do this:

1. Start the Messaging app (tap the Launcher icon and then tap Messaging).
2. Tap Buddies in the options bar at the top of the screen.
3. To choose among the default Available, Busy, and Sign Off options, tap the status button and make your choice from the menu.

4. To change the status message, tap in the text (such as Available) and type a new message. Then tap the checkmark on the right.

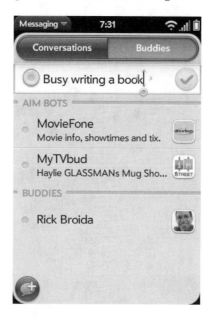

Notice that when you're busy, the status button turns orange, and when you're offline, it's white. Also, when you're offline, you cannot see any of your buddies.

Here's where it gets just a little tricky, though: If you tap Conversations and send a message, you get signed in automatically—but only to the service you're sending that message from. To make sure you're signed in to both services later, you can send a message using the other service, or you can tap the status button (which you'll notice is only half green) and choose the Available option to finish signing in to both.

Tip You can extend your Pre's battery life by signing out your IM services. If you don't need—or don't want—to chat with anyone, it's better to sign out than to set your status to busy, since a busy status still uses extra battery life to maintain an IM connection.

Deleting Conversations

It's cool that the Pre has such a photographic memory for messages, but it's entirely possible that you don't want to keep every conversation you've ever had forever. Getting rid of them is as easy as a swipe of your finger. Here's what to do:

- If you want to delete an entire conversation—all the back-and-forth messages over a period of time—start the Messaging app and tap Conversations in the options bar. Find the conversation you want to discard, swipe it to the left or right, and then tap Delete.

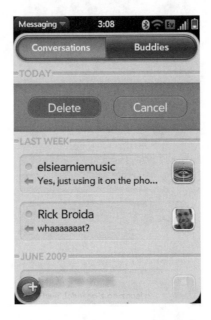

- If you want to delete only specific parts of a conversation, open the conversation and browse to the part you want to throw away. Then swipe the specific section to the left or right and tap Delete. You can pare down a long conversation one response at a time in this way.

Responding to a Message When You're Doing Other Things

Just like phone calls, text messages can arrive at any time, when you're not using your Pre at all or when you're actively using it for other things. If someone texts you, you won't get a big notification like when a phone call comes in though—you'll just see a status notification at the bottom of the screen, like this:

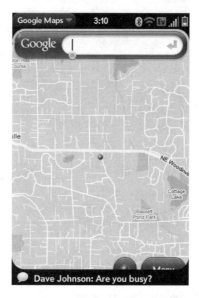

The message itself will appear for only a few seconds. After that, an empty notification will remain:

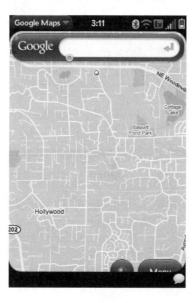

To read it or respond, you can tap the notification or just open Messaging. In Messaging, you can tell who sent you a message because both the new conversation and the buddy name will appear in bold, and you'll see an indication of how many new messages you have.

Dave vs. Rick: Top 10 Uses for Your Palm Pre

Dave: The Pre has so many features that it's kind of like an electronic Swiss Army knife.

10. Screen doubles as a flashlight when you drop your keys at night.
9. Write the Great American Novel while riding the bus to work.
8. Forget drunk dialing and drunk emailing: Pre's camera lets you drunk self-portrait yourself and see the results on Facebook the next morning.
7. Use Pre to show your grandparents photos of your kids and simultaneously confuse them with modern technology.
6. Use the keyboard to slice cheese for your next lasagna dinner (http://tinyurl .com/pbcejr).

Rick:

5. E-books, e-books, e-books. Nothing beats having a good book in your pocket everywhere you go.
4. The Evernote app. Your life is about to get ridiculously organized.
3. Google in your pocket. Seriously, how did we function as a society before Google?
2. Watching YouTube videos. Because seeing a cat play the piano never gets old.
1. It's also a tip calculator!

4

Customizing Your Pre

HOW TO...

- Customize the wallpaper
- Set a password
- Rearrange Activity Cards
- Arrange apps in the Launcher
- Modify the Quick Launch bar
- Find and set Pre preferences

By now, you've had some time to get used to your Pre. It's becoming a regular member of the family. If you're anything like Dave, you probably even bring it to the dinner table. So before we delve much further into all the cool stuff you can do with your new electronic pet/child/cousin, we should spend a few minutes looking at the various ways you can customize the Pre and truly make it an expression of your own personality.

Want a unique wallpaper? Check—you can do that. Want to protect your data from prying eyes? Password coming right up. You can also arrange the icons any way you like and put your most commonly used apps right on the Quick Launch bar, where you can get to them without opening the Launcher app. In fact, you can customize your Pre so much that it becomes kind of like a snowflake, as no two flakes are exactly alike (though your Pre won't melt at room temperature).

Setting a Custom Wallpaper

Let's start with the single most noticeable tweak you can make to your Pre short of changing it to a different color with some leftover house paint. Let's change the wallpaper.

At home, changing the wallpaper is a pretty big deal; you have to put a lot of planning into redoing the wallpaper because it's a semi-permanent modification to your home that involves trips to the store, glue application, and, at Dave's house, shouting. But you can change the wallpaper on your Pre ten times a day if you want to.

Using a Photo on the Pre as Wallpaper

Ready to give it a shot? Let's first see how to change the wallpaper to an image that's already on your Pre. The Pre comes with a dozen pretty wallpaper images right out of the box, and you can also use a photo that you took with the Pre's camera. Here's how:

1. Tap the Launcher icon on the far-right side of the Quick Launch bar.

Launcher

2. In the Launcher, use the next gesture to flip to the page that has the Screen & Lock app. If you haven't moved it yet, it will be in the upper-right corner of the third page.

3. Tap Screen & Lock.

4. In the Wallpaper section, tap Change Wallpaper.
5. Find the image you want to use—you can open All Images and browse the whole collection or go directly to a category like Photo Roll (which shows all the photos you've taken with your camera). To see the selection of images designed for use as wallpaper that come with the Pre, scroll to the bottom and tap Wallpapers.
6. To preview an image, tap it. If you like the photo and want to use it, tap Set Wallpaper at the top of the screen. If not, use the back gesture in the gesture area to try a different image.
7. When you've selected your wallpaper, press the Center button and toss the Screen & Lock app to close it.

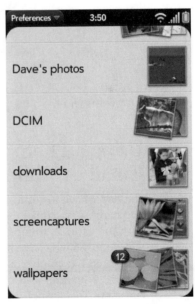

That's it—you now have new wallpaper.

Adjusting Wallpaper

You might appreciate knowing that, unlike some so-called smartphones, you can actually fine-tune the placement and composition of your photos while setting the wallpaper.

Suppose you have a great photo, for example, but it's the wrong aspect ratio for the screen, and you really want to show only a part of it anyway. No problem: When you preview the image, you can move the image around the screen and zoom in using the pinch gesture.

When you have the photo composed to your liking, tap Set Wallpaper.

Using a Photo from Email as Wallpaper

You don't have to settle for the handful of photos that came with your Pre and whatever you capture with the camera, though—any image you own is fair game. So what if someone emails you a photo that you'd like to plaster onto your Pre's touch screen? What then? Well, as you suspect, doing this is a snap. You simply need to get the photo from the email to a place where you can choose it as a wallpaper image. Do this:

1. Open the email message and you'll see the photos listed as an attachment (for details on using email, see Chapter 5).

2. Tap the attachment bar/paper clip icon to see a list of all the photos.

3. Tap a photo that you'd like to view on screen. Then tap Copy To Photos at the bottom of the screen. The Pre will copy the photo, store it on your Pre, and then close the photo and return to the email message.

4. Switch to the Launcher. You can press the Center button, for example, to switch to Card view, and then tap the Launcher button. Alternatively, you can pull up the Quick Launch bar from the gesture area and select the Launcher app.
5. In the Launcher, use the next gesture to flip to the page that has the Screen & Lock app.
6. Tap Screen & Lock.
7. In the Wallpaper section, tap Change Wallpaper.
8. Scroll down and tap Downloads to find the photo that you just saved from email.

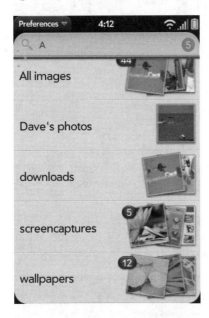

9. To preview the image, tap it. Then tap Set Wallpaper at the top of the screen.
10. Press the Center button and toss the Screen & Lock app to close it.

Using a Photo from Your PC as Wallpaper

You probably have a treasure trove of photos on your computer that you wouldn't mind seeing on your Pre occasionally. And these, too, can make the short journey to your Pre's touch screen.

You can do this in a couple of ways, and it doesn't really matter which way you choose—just use the method that's most convenient for you. You can email the photo to your Pre and follow the steps we just discussed, or you can connect your Pre and copy photos manually. Here's how to do that:

1. Plug your Pre into your computer's USB port. (For more information on how to do that, see Chapter 2.) As always, be careful when you connect the cable to the

Pre, since it's easy to insert it upside down. The side of the cable with the little divot should be on top, as should the narrower part of the wedge-shaped plug.

2. The Pre should ask you what kind of connection to make. Since you're copying photos from the PC, tap USB Drive.

3. On your PC, the AutoPlay window should appear. Click Open Folder to view files.
4. Drag the photos that you want to use as wallpaper to a folder on your Pre. You can use the DCIM folder, for example, or make a new folder and use that instead.

5. When you're done, you need to tell Windows to disconnect from the Pre. To do that, in the Notification Area of your PC, right-click Safely Remove Hardware and choose Eject Pre. Only then should you disconnect the USB cable from the Pre.

 If you unplug the Pre's USB cable without "ejecting" it in Windows first, you might corrupt some files, such as photos or music, on the Pre.

6. Tap the Launcher button.
7. In the Launcher, use the next gesture to flip to the page that has the Screen & Lock app.
8. Tap Screen & Lock.
9. In the Wallpaper section, tap Change Wallpaper.
10. Tap the All Images section to find the photo that you just copied from your PC.
11. To preview the image, tap it. Then tap Set Wallpaper at the top of the screen.
12. Press the Center button and toss the Screen & Lock app to close it.

Protect Your Pre with a Password

You wouldn't leave the front door to your house unlocked, would you? So why would you leave your phone unlocked and unprotected?

We'll be the first to admit that using a password is somewhat inconvenient. Scratch that—it's kind of a pain in the neck. But thanks to Synergy, your Palm Pre is a direct gateway virtually to your entire online life. Names, phone numbers, addresses—it's all on your Pre. Not to mention any other personal data you might happen to store there.

Rick and Dave don't agree on much, but they both agree that you should lock your Pre with some sort of password. That way, if your phone is stolen or lost, no one will be able to turn it on and extract personal information or run up your phone bill.

Set a Password

Here's how to password-protect your Pre:

1. Tap the Launcher icon on the Quick Launch bar.
2. In the Launcher, use the next gesture to flip to the page that has the Screen & Lock app.
3. Tap Screen & Lock.

4. Scroll down to the Secure Unlock section. Since you currently have no password set, it will be set to Off. Tap it to turn it On.

You can now choose to set a Simple PIN or a Password. The choice is yours—the PIN is a four-digit number that you'll enter by tapping a number pad that appears on the touch screen when you turn on the Pre. The password, on the other hand, can be any length and include any letters, numbers, or symbols. We've created passwords as short as 1 character and as long as 26 characters—the entire alphabet—and the Pre is happy to accommodate either (though we suspect you might get tired of entering a password that long every time you want to use your phone). You can also create a password using punctuation or anything from the SYMBOL key. That level of complexity means a thoughtful password is virtually unbreakable.

No matter what kind of PIN or password you choose, you'll need to enter it a second time to make sure you didn't enter any typos, and then it's set.

Picking a Secure Password

You might be wondering "How do I know if I've chosen a good password?" To some degree, choosing a good sequence is common sense. You don't want to choose something that's easily guessed, that's based on personal information (such as your pet's name), or that's too simple, such as a pattern like *1234*, *0000*, or *password*. Here are some tips for smartening up your password selection:

- Keep the digits in your password unique. Try not to repeat letters; use a combination of uppercase, lowercase, and numbers, and throw in symbols for good measure.

- The longer the better. You *can* choose a one-digit password (though PINs must always be four digits), but it's not a good idea. If someone spies you entering your password, they'll find it easy to figure out after they've stolen your phone.
- Don't use personal information. For example, avoid using your name, telephone number, address, and your cat's name. They are all easily guessed.
- Change your password every few months.

Want to know how "strong" your password is? Check out Microsoft's Password checker (http://tinyurl.com/ypc3dc). This Web site is designed to tell you how secure your password is for Windows logon and Web sites, but it works equally well for your phone.

One last note: Does all this talk about alphanumeric passwords mean you should ignore the PIN option? Not at all! A four-digit numeric PIN is a fine way to lock your phone, as it provides the convenience of simple and fast entry while imposing a barrier for anyone who should not be nosing around in your stuff. But remember to apply the same sort of logic to selecting your PIN—don't choose 0000 or 1234, for example.

Opening Your Protected Phone

After you set a PIN or a password, you'll need to enter that code when you turn on your Pre. To do that, you'll start, as always, by dragging the lock button up the touch screen.

If you chose the PIN option, enter the four digits.

If you chose the password option, enter the password using the keyboard.

Don't forget your phone's PIN or password; if you do, there's no way to turn on the Pre without wiping all the data and starting over. Even though some security experts advise against writing down your password, others believe that this provides insurance against choosing an unsecure password that's easily broken; if you write down even the most complicated PIN, you'll be able to find it when you need it. So we agree that you might want to write down the Pre's PIN/password and keep it in a secure place, at least until you have it firmly committed to memory.

Rearrange Activity Cards

One of the coolest aspects of using the Pre is that it multitasks: you can run several programs at once. Indeed, you might even treat your Pre like your desktop PC and just leave certain commonly used programs running all the time for easy access. And if you do, you might appreciate the fact you can actually rearrange them on the screen, so they appear in Card view in the order you prefer.

Though we touched on this briefly in Chapter 1, here's how to arrange running apps into a specific order:

1. If necessary, press the Center button to put the Pre in Card view, so you can see all the running apps as Activity Cards.
2. Tap and hold the card in the middle of the screen. After a moment, the cards will shrink to their smaller size. (You can get this same effect by tapping the touch screen in the space between the bottom of the cards and above the Quick Launch bar.)
3. While continuing to hold your finger on the card, drag it to the left or right to position it where you want it to appear in the card stack.

4. Tap and drag other cards around until they are all in the desired positions.
5. When you're done, tap under a card to restore the cards to the larger view, or press the Center button to leave Card view and make the selected app full screen.

Of course, your Pre won't remember any of these settings after you close the apps—the arrangement stays put only while these particular cards are open.

Arrange Apps in the Launcher

Now you know how to arrange cards so running apps are in exactly the right order to suit your discriminating tastes. That's cool, but let's be honest—how many apps will you be running at the same time? Three? Four? Maybe five? It's not that hard to flip through a handful of Activity Cards no matter what order they're in.

Your app collection is a different matter entirely, though. Brand new and right out of the box, your Pre comes with three dozen icons spread across the Quick Launch bar and three pages of the Launcher. After just a week or two with the Pre, Dave found that he had no less than 50 icons (see Figure 4-1) on his screen. There's some potential for some serious organizational issues here.

Thankfully, you can easily rearrange the app icons in the Launcher. You can group apps that have similar functions, put the most common ones at the top of the page, and

FIGURE 4-1   Finding a particular app can become challenging when you have a lot of apps installed.

put stuff you never use on the third page so you never have to tire out your little finger by flipping around to find the apps you need.

Here's all you need to do to arrange apps in the Launcher:

1. Tap the Launcher icon to open the Launcher.
2. Find an icon that you want to move to a different position on the page.
3. Tap and hold the icon until you see radiating white circles surround the icon. It's now ready to move.

4. Drag the icon to a new position.

You'll see the other icons flow around the icon you're moving and accommodate its new position.

You can follow the same procedure to move icons to other pages. You have three pages of icons to work with, so feel free to group icons logically or come up with any sort of organizational scheme you like. To move an icon to a different page, just tap, hold, and drag the icon to the edge of the page and wait a moment. The page will change, and then you can place the icon wherever you like.

If you're doing a lot of reorganizing, it might take a while to move a bunch of stuff among the three pages. But when you're done, all your apps will be easier to locate because you personally put them where you wanted them.

Modify the Quick Launch Bar

As you know, you don't have to open the Launcher to get to everything; you can use five icons on the Quick Launch bar as well for easy and immediate access to stuff you will use most often.

What you might not realize is that you can remove any of these icons—with the exception of the Launcher icon—and replace them with a different icon that you think you'll use more frequently. (You wouldn't want to remove the Launcher icon from the Quick Launch bar, because then there would be no way to open the Launcher!)

Take the Contacts icon, for example. That one didn't last an hour on Dave's Pre. Why? Dave knew that he could just as easily use search to find a contact and dial a phone number, so he had no need

Phone   Contacts   Email   Calendar   Launcher

to open the Contacts app directly. So he replaced Contacts with the *New York Times*, a free app he downloaded from the App Catalog (see Chapter 10 for the goods on that).

Dave vs. Rick: Apps in Our Quick Launch Bar

You know how some Web sites interview famous people to find out what music is on their iPod or what stuff they carry in their purse or wallet? Well, we don't have the budget for that sort of thing. So instead, we pose this highly illuminating question to each other: What apps are in your Quick Launch bar?

Dave: My Pre is configured to put my most treasured, important apps right at my fingertips. I've got my Quick Launch bar packed with the Phone, Email, Messaging, and the *New York Times*. I don't need Contacts, since I can get to any individual contact I need just as fast using Universal Search (which we talk about in Chapter 5, among other places). But I send email and text messages about as frequently as I use the Phone app—if not more so. And the "Grey Lady" is handy so I can see what the dominant liberal establishment mass media is up to. And so I can read David Pogue.

Rick: The moment there's a decent e-book app for the Pre (right now my only option is the less-than-stellar Shortcovers), you can bet it'll earn a permanent home in my Quick Launch bar. Other than that, I'm [*shudder*] with Dave: Phone, Email, and Messaging. Of course, my *New York Times* app is close at hand as well, if only so I can properly correct Dave when he whines about "the dominant liberal establishment mass media." Apparently he prefers government-run media. Or, worse, Fox.

Move Apps from the Launcher into the Quick Launch Bar

Ready? Good. Here's how to move icons from the Launcher to the Quick Launch bar:

1. Tap the Launcher icon to open the Launcher.
2. In the Quick Launch bar, tap and hold an icon (such as Contacts, for example) until you see radiating white circles surround the icon. It's now ready to move.
3. Drag it out of the Quick Launch bar and into the Launcher. Position it where you'd like it to live and then release the icon. Don't worry; you can always reposition it later.
4. In the Launcher, tap and hold the app icon that you want to move to the Quick Launch bar until you see those familiar radiating white circles surround the icon.
5. Drag the icon into the Quick Launch bar and position it where you want it to live.

You can use this technique to replace the first four icons if you want to. Though we guess you'll probably want to leave the Phone icon in the Quick Launch bar since, after all, you'll want to make phone calls.

You can drag icons into the Launcher and simply not replace them with anything. That's handy if you want a less cluttered Pre with only three or four Quick Launch icons, for example. Of course, that means you'll have to go to the Launcher to open stuff that you could have just as easily gotten to with a couple of fewer taps, but that's life: full of tradeoffs.

Arrange Icons in the Quick Launch Bar

Now that you know how to move icons around between the Quick Launch bar and the Launcher, it should come as no surprise that you can easily reorder icons in the Quick Launch bar as well. Want the Phone icon on the right, next to the Launcher icon? Rather swap the positions of the Calendar and Email icons? No problem. Just tap and hold any icon in the Quick Launch bar (except the Launcher icon—that one is firmly epoxied in place and will never move, no matter how hard you try), and then drag it to a new location after you see the telltale radiating circles.

 You can't drag icons out of the Quick Launch bar unless the Launcher is open. Nothing will happen if you try to drag an icon to the touch screen in Card view.

Setting Other Preferences

If you've read this chapter, you now know most of the important ways you can customize your Pre. Palm has sprinkled a variety of other customizations around the Pre, and there's really no one place—like the Control Panel in Windows—where you can go to find them all. Here is a fairly comprehensive list of things you might want to adjust:

Preference	Where to Find It
Silence your phone so it doesn't beep, blorp, or alarm you in a meeting.	Slide the ringer switch at the top of the Pre (see Chapter 1).
Adjust the volume of your Pre.	Press the volume buttons on the left side of the Pre.
Turn off all radio settings, including the phone, Wi-Fi, and Bluetooth.	Tap the right side of the status bar at the top of the phone (see Chapter 1).
Specify whether the phone will vibrate.	Sounds & Ringtones: Note the two different controls on this page—you can separately turn vibrate on and off when the ringer is on and when the ringer is off.
Set the ringtone and its volume.	Sounds & Ringtones
Turn system sounds on and off, and control their volume.	Sounds & Ringtones
Adjust the screen brightness and how long to wait before turning off the screen (30 seconds to 3 minutes).	Screen & Lock
Change the wallpaper.	Screen & Lock
Turn on advanced gestures.	Screen & Lock (see Chapter 1)
Set a PIN or password.	Screen & Lock
Choose whether to show notifications on the touch screen when the phone is locked.	Screen & Lock
Configure Wi-Fi.	Wi-Fi (see Chapter 6)

(continued)

Preference	Where to Find It
Configure Bluetooth.	Bluetooth (see Chapter 6)
Choose whether to allow the Pre to locate you using GPS automatically.	Location services (see Chapter 6)
Turn GPS on and off.	Location services (see Chapter 6)
Choose whether to allow the Pre to tag your photos automatically with location information using GPS.	Location services (see Chapter 6)
Change the name of your Pre (which might be used by some programs on the PC to identify your phone).	Device Information
Switch between 12-hour and 24-hour time (9 P.M. and 2100 hours, respectively)	Date and Time
Allow the Pre to use the date and time reported by our mobile phone network, or adjust the date and time yourself.	Date and Time
Update the Pre and installed apps with newer versions of software.	Updates
Turn automatic backups of your Pre on or off (they're on by default) or trigger an immediate backup.	Backup (see Chapter 12)
Choose a language for your Pre's display.	Regional Settings, Language
Uninstall an app.	In the Launcher, tap the drop-down menu in the upper-left corner and tap List Apps (see Chapter 10).

Dave vs. Rick: What We'd Change About the Palm Pre

The Pre is a pretty awesome gadget, but it's not perfect. What would we change about the Palm Pre?

Dave: Ah, this is easy. As you'll see in Chapter 8, I'm not especially happy with the way the Pre handles music and podcasts. Podcasting is a big part of my life. I ride the bus frequently, and I like to listen to various NPR shows and other programming as podcasts to pass the time. But since the Pre treats podcasts as regular music, you can't "mark our spot" in a podcast and come back to it later. That's really frustrating—so much so, in fact, that the Pre is (currently) pretty much unusable as a podcast player. Oh, Palm, how could you have so completely overlooked podcasting?

Rick: For starters: storage. The Pre can store music, movies, apps, documents, and so on—but it has only 8GB of space available. That's not enough for media junkies like me. Palm really needs to release a 16GB (or, better yet, 64GB) model, or at least outfit the Pre with a microSD slot so I can add all the storage I want. I wouldn't mind a speed increase, either, as the Pre seems sluggish at times—especially when I have more than a few cards open.

Also, I'd like it to record video, not just still photos.

5

Using the Pre's Built-In Programs

HOW TO...

- Use Universal Search
- Use Email
- Work with combined messaging
- Archive Gmail
- Use Contacts
- Work with linked contacts
- Use Calendar
- Work with layered calendars
- Use Memos
- Use Tasks
- Use Clock to set an alarm
- View Microsoft Office documents
- View PDFs

Right out of the box, the Pre can do more than most other mobile phones on the planet. What makes it so darn useful? Apps, baby, it's all about the apps. As you'll learn in Chapter 10, you can stock your Pre with all kinds of cool third-party programs. For now, however, we'll focus on the apps that are already installed. After all, you'll want to master what's in the box before you go beyond it.

 Certain built-in apps, such as Calculator, are so self-explanatory that we're not going to bother covering them here. Others, such as Photos, Music, and YouTube, are covered in other chapters. See the book's table of contents or index if you need help tracking down info on these apps.

Universal Search

Here's the old way of looking up Dave Johnson in your contact list: Find the Contacts icon, launch the app, then sift through your contact list until you find Dave amongst the 30 or 40 other Johnsons you have in there. (Poor guy and his commoner name.)

Here's the Pre way of looking up Dave Johnson: While in Launcher or Card view, just start typing Dave's name. Any such typing invokes one of the Pre's best features: Universal Search. This tool makes it quick and easy to find contacts, applications, and various kinds of data. For example, on Rick's Pre, this is what appears after typing just the first three letters of Dave's name:

Needless to say, tapping either of these search results will bring up the corresponding record in the corresponding app. Now let's look at an app-oriented example. Want a quick way to pull up the various Sprint apps on your Pre? While in Launcher or Card view, type **spr** and see what happens:

Presto! You see not only the apps with *Sprint* in their name, but also the built-in Sprint contacts. And therein lies the "Universal" aspect of Universal Search: It searches your entire Pre—not just a specific area—and presents you with all matching results.

Actually, Universal Search isn't fully universal. For reasons we just can't fathom, it doesn't search the Calendar, Memos, or Tasks apps. Hopefully, Palm will remedy this in a future WebOS update. The good news, for now, is that both Memos and Tasks have built-in search capabilities. So while you can't run a Universal Search for, say, all to-dos pertaining to your wedding anniversary, at least you can fire up Tasks and then start typing to narrow your list.

It's worth noting that searching for apps this way can actually be preferable to sifting through icons, especially if you have a lot of them. As you learned in Chapter 4, the Pre limits you to just three screens for apps and other icons. The more programs you install, the more Web shortcuts you create (see Chapter 7); and the more contacts you add to the Launcher (see the "Contacts" section later in this chapter), the harder it ends up being to find the icon you want. But a few taps of the keyboard can quickly hone you in.

There's more to Universal Search than just the apps and data stored on your Pre. For example, suppose you want to look up information on one of our favorite movies from summer, 2009: *District 9*. Note what happens when we type the word *district*:

Universal Search found no matching data in the Pre's apps or contact lists, so it reverted to its other mode: Web searches. Specifically, as you can see in this screenshot, the Pre gives you the option of searching Google, Google Maps, Wikipedia, or Twitter.

 What happens if you want to see these Web-search options when Universal Search *does* find matching Pre data (and subsequently displays only those matches)? No problem: Just tap once in the Find field. That will "toggle" the four Web-search buttons. You can tap Find a second time to hide them again.

You can find out more about these Web search options in Chapter 7. But they're pretty self-explanatory: Tap one to visit the corresponding site in the Pre's Web browser.

Email

Once you start using your Pre to send and receive email, anytime, anywhere, you'll wonder how you ever enjoyed life without it. In fact, it's so easy and so convenient, you may find yourself becoming addicted to email. (Just try not to turn into Dave, who routinely checks email during the most inappropriate times, like at the dinner table and during surgery.)

The Email app (see Figure 5-1) lets you work with multiple accounts, meaning you can check messages in Gmail or Yahoo!, send messages via your office's Microsoft Exchange server, and so on. The sky's the limit.

 Back in Chapter 2, you configured your Pre to sync with Google and/or Exchange. That means you've already got at least one email account already set up. This section proceeds from that assumption and focuses primarily on using the Email app. If you bypassed that sync setup for some reason, head back to Chapter 2.

FIGURE 5-1 Get ready to fall in love with the Pre's Email app, which makes it a snap to send and receive messages using your existing email account(s).

Let's start by taking a look at the main screen of the Email app, keeping in mind that yours will almost certainly look a bit different depending on what account(s) you've added.

All this may look a little intimidating at first, but it all starts to make sense after you explore the app a bit.

 Get acquainted with the expand/collapse button next to Favorites and each of your accounts. Tapping it shows and hides all the email folders associated therein. It helps keep the Email app uncluttered and easier to navigate, especially when you're working with multiple accounts.

Setting Up Favorites

At the top of Email's main screen is a section called Favorites, and it's exactly that—your "favorite" email folders. By default, the inbox for each account gets added to this section, which makes sense given that that's where all the action happens (in other words, all new email lands in your Inbox).

Of course, you might want to add other folders to Favorites or remove the inbox of a little-used account. To do so, just look for the little star icon next to any given folder for any account. One tap turns it yellow and adds it to Favorites. If it's already yellow, it's already part of Favorites—tap the star if you want to remove it.

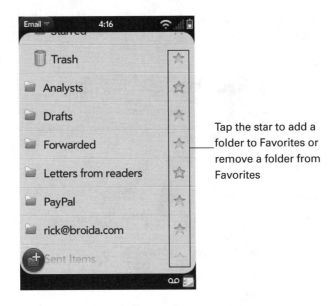

Tap the star to add a folder to Favorites or remove a folder from Favorites

Reading and Replying to Messages

Ready to read your email? By now you've probably figured out how: Tap the Inbox for the desired account (or tap All Inboxes to see all your inboxes in a single, combined view), and then tap the message you want to read. Here's an example of how your Inbox will look:

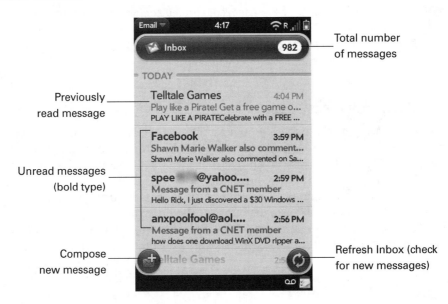

Total number of messages

Previously read message

Unread messages (bold type)

Compose new message

Refresh Inbox (check for new messages)

And here's an example of an actual email:

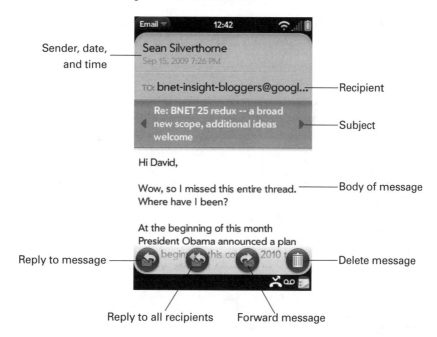

Sender, date, and time

Recipient

Subject

Body of message

Reply to message

Delete message

Reply to all recipients

Forward message

If you've ever used a desktop email program (and if you haven't, we must kindly ask you to put down this book and go take a Computing 101 class at your local library), all of this will seem very straightforward. About the only things that are out of the ordinary are the arrows on either side of the Subject area. Tapping the right one takes you to the next unread message, and tapping the left one takes you to the prior unread message (if there is one).

FROM field

TO field

Subject field

Email body

Address book

Add attachment

Send message

Composing New Messages

If you've ever written an email on your PC, you'll find the Pre experience remarkably similar.

Here's the lowdown:

1. While viewing the main Email screen or one of your inboxes, tap the New Message icon in the lower-left corner of the screen.
2. Tap the FROM field to choose which account you want to use to send this message. (This isn't necessary if you have only one email account on the device.)
3. Now it's time to choose your recipient(s). You might think this means tapping the little address book icon next to the TO field. That's definitely an option, but there's an easier way: Just start typing the recipient's name or email address. Matching address book entries will start to appear. When you see the one you want, tap it! Then repeat the process if you want to send the message to additional recipients.
4. Tap the Subject field and type a subject for the email. (Don't leave it blank—that's a violation of email etiquette!)
5. Tap the body area of the email and type your message.
6. If you want to attach something to the email (a photo, video, song, or document), tap the paper clip icon and then choose the media you want to attach.
7. When you're all done, tap the paper airplane icon to send your message! (Hopefully, this goes without saying, but you need to be connected to a Wi-Fi or cellular network to send mail.)

 Not ready to send the message just yet? Tap the Email menu (top-left corner) and choose Save As Draft. This will store the email in that account's Draft folder, where you can open it later, make any desired changes, and then send it on its way.

Deleting Messages

The Pre offers two options for deleting email messages you no longer want: You can tap the little trash icon while viewing a particular message. Or, while in Inbox view for any account, you can swipe your finger left or right over a message—keeping in mind that you *won't* get a deleted mail confirmation. This swipe gesture sends the mail straight to the Trash folder.

Adding and Deleting Email Accounts

So you've already set up at least one email account as part of the sync setup steps you performed in Chapter 2. Okay, but what if you're ready to add more accounts? Rick, for example, is rocking his Gmail, Windows Live Mail, Yahoo! Mail, *and* personal domain accounts. If you want to bring more email to your Pre, you've come to the right section.

How to...   Change Your Email Signature

While composing new mail, you might have noticed the following line appended to the bottom of your message: "Sent from my Palm Pre." This is known as an email *signature*, and although it's nice to let people know the origin of your email (it's actually a convenient explanation for why your message might be particularly brief), you might prefer to swap in a different message or remove the signature altogether.

Piece of cake. (Mmm...cake.) In the main screen of the Email app, tap the Email menu (top-left corner) and choose Preferences & Accounts. Tap the account you want to modify (the Pre lets you use a different signature for each one), and then scroll down until you find the Signature box. Tap it, erase the existing message, and type what you want (or leave it blank if you prefer). That's all there is to it!

Adding an AOL, Windows Live Mail (aka Hotmail), or Yahoo! Mail account to the Pre is remarkably easy. Here's how:

1. In the main screen of the Email app, tap the Email menu (top-left corner) and choose Preferences & Accounts.
2. Scroll down to the bottom of the screen and tap Add An Account.
3. Enter your email address and password, and then tap Sign In.

4. Wait a minute or two while your Pre signs into your account and fetches your mail.

That's all there is to it! Well, for those kinds of accounts, anyway. (Rick was also able to add his Comcast email account using the exact same steps.) If you run into trouble, head to the next section.

Adding Other Kinds of Email Accounts

If you have an email account from, say, your Internet service provider (ISP), or even your own domain, you may have to perform a few extra steps beyond entering your address and password. For example, you might need to change the settings for the incoming and outgoing mail servers (also known as Post Office Protocol, or POP, and Simple Mail Transfer Protocol, or SMTP, servers).

Here's how you can access these settings:

1. In the main screen of the Email app, tap the Email menu and choose Preferences & Accounts.
2. Tap the account in question, and then scroll to the bottom of the screen and tap Change Login Settings.

Unless you're technically savvy, most everything you see on the subsequent screen will look like Greek:

That's okay. All you need to do next is get in touch with your ISP or the company that hosts your domain and find out the specific settings for your email account.

Once you have that information, you should have no trouble making the necessary changes in this screen. It might be something as simple as changing the port number for your POP server or toggling the SMTP User Authentication switch.

Deleting Email Accounts

It's easier to destroy than to create, right? Well, if you want to delete an email account on your Pre, it's even easier than creating one:

1. In the main screen of the Email app, tap the Email menu and choose Preferences & Accounts.
2. In the Accounts section, tap the name of the account you want to delete.
3. Scroll down to the bottom of the screen and tap Remove Account.

 Removing an email account from your Pre also removes all messages from that account—but only on your Pre. The actual account is left untouched, with all your mail intact.

How to... **Synchronize Your Pre with Exchange**

Your Pre can synchronize with Microsoft Exchange, which means that you can access your work email, contacts, and calendar using your phone—as long as your IT department allows it. How do you know if it'll work? Well, you could email Dwight in IT and ask if it's okay for your Palm Pre to access Exchange, or you could check your company's policy posted on some SharePoint somewhere. But honestly? The easiest thing is to try setting up your Pre to see if it works. Odds are good that it will.

Set up your Exchange account the same way you'd set up any other kind of email account:

1. Tap Email, tap the App menu, and then tap Preferences & Accounts.
2. From there, tap Add An Account.
3. Tap the App menu again and choose Manual Setup.
4. In the Mail Type box, choose Exchange (EAS). Then enter your details—the name of the Exchange mail server, your domain name, username, and password, and you're done. (If you don't know your Exchange server or domain, you might have to look it up or ask IT about it.)

In a few minutes, you'll see your email and calendar information on your Pre.

Contacts

The Contacts app (see Figure 5-2) is arguably the lifeblood of your Pre—the place that stores the names, phone numbers, email addresses, and other information of all the people in your life. The good news is that it's a really simple app to use, and it offers a few nifty tricks you won't find in other smartphone address books.

 Note If you haven't yet mastered syncing with Google, Facebook, Microsoft Exchange, and the like, see Chapter 2. This section focuses squarely on using the Contacts app itself; we're assuming that you've already got at least some contacts synced from at least some sources.

When you start the Contacts app, you'll see your list of contacts in alphabetical order (sorted by last name). That's the default setting for Contacts; if you want to change it, do this:

1. Tap the Contacts menu in the top-left corner of the screen.
2. Tap Preferences & Accounts.

FIGURE 5-2 You'll probably spend a good deal of time in the Contacts app, where you can look up contact information, initiate calls, send text messages, and more.

3. In the List Order box, tap the arrow and then choose your desired sort order (First Name, Company & First Name, or Company & Last Name).

4. Use the back gesture to return to the contact list.

While you're viewing that Preferences & Accounts screen, feel free to check out the other options—all of which pertain to the accounts you linked up in Chapter 2. You'll probably never need to change anything, but if you ever want to, say, add or remove an account, this is the place to do it.

Sorry, but we're getting a little ahead of ourselves. So let's look at a few other basic ways to work with Contacts:

- Scroll through your list by using the up and down gestures (see Chapter 1 if you need a refresher).
- To find a contact quickly, type the first few letters of the contact's name.
- To view a contact, tap it.
- While viewing a contact, tap his or her email address to compose a new message. Tap SMS to compose a new text message (see Chapter 3). Or tap a phone number to place a call (see Chapter 3).
- To delete a contact, you can't just swipe the person's name in the contact list and then tap a Delete button (as you can with, say, a to-do in the Tasks app). Instead, you must first open the contact (by tapping it, natch), and then tap the Contacts menu button and tap Delete Contact.

Contacts you've synced to your Pre by way of Facebook can't be deleted on the Pre. You'll have to sign into your Facebook account on your PC and delete them there.

Adding and Editing Contacts

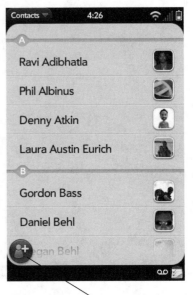

As we noted in Chapter 2, the easiest way to get contact data onto your Pre is to sync it from, say, Google or Facebook. Of course, there will be times (such as when you've just met someone) when you want to add new contact data right on the device. This is incredibly easy, but we'll walk you through the steps anyway, as there are a few areas of potential confusion along the way.

1. Tap the New Contact icon in the bottom-left corner of the screen.
2. Type the contact's name. (The Pre will automatically capitalize both the first and last names, so you don't need to mess with the SHIFT key.)

Tap here to add a new contact

3. If you want, tap the Account button opposite the Name field to assign that contact to one of your accounts. If you choose Google, keep in mind that the newly entered information will automatically get synchronized to your Google account.

4. Tap in any other field to enter additional information. For example, if this is a business associate, you might want to add a job title and company name. Alternatively, you can jump right to New Phone Number field and enter that. (The Pre will automatically switch to numeric mode, so you don't need to mess with the ORANGE key.)

5. Scroll down and tap other fields to enter additional information, such as email address, IM (instant messaging) address, and so on. Each Pre contact record also has fields for notes, birthday, spouse's name, children, and nickname. Keep in mind that all these fields are optional: You can enter as much or as little information as you wish.

6. When you're all done, tap Done.

Did You Know?

What Is a Contact Reminder?

One option you may notice when creating or editing a contact is the Reminder field. Any info you place in here appears when you email, IM, or receive a call from that contact. That's insanely handy. For example, if you want to add a reminder that an important business contact and his wife are about to have a new baby, you might add something like this: "Wife: 8 months pregnant." That way you can kick off the conversation by asking after the new baby, showing how thoughtful and conscientious you are and earning some goodwill.

Of course, keep in mind that these reminders will be visible to anyone who might be glancing over your shoulder or fiddling with your phone (the Pre tends to draw a crowd). So while you might be tempted to use a reminder like "Dork" for a contact like Dave, it's probably better to stick with practical, non-insulting messages.

Assign a Ringtone to a Contact

Dave is not fond of singer Amy Winehouse (because, as you'll learn in Chapter 8, he hates all music that is pleasant sounding), so Rick knew there could be only one choice for the ringtone that plays whenever Dave calls: "Rehab." See, the Pre lets you assign individual ringtones to individual contacts, which is not only fun, but also a kind of aural caller ID that lets you know who's calling just by the ringtone.

Although the process of assigning individual ringtones occurs in the Contacts app, we already covered it in Chapter 3: "Setting a Ringtone for a Specific Contact." So check there to learn how to do it. (Hint: Tap a contact to open it, tap Edit, and then tap Set A Ringtone. Tricky, huh?)

Add a Photo to a Contact

One of our favorite Pre features is the option to assign a photo to each contact. If you've already linked your Pre to your Facebook account, you've probably seen the end result: The Pre automatically fetches each contact's Facebook Profile photo along with the rest of the user data. Consequently, you may already have a contact list that looks something like the screen shown at the right.

Okay, but what if you're adding a new contact on the fly, or you've got some non-Facebook contacts that don't already have photos associated? No problem: The Pre makes it easy to add a photo to any contact record. Here's how:

Tap here to add a photo to the contact record

1. Whether you're in the process of creating a new contact or editing an existing one (see the next section), find the little "person" icon next to the Job Title field, and tap it.
2. Now you have a choice: Select an existing photo or snap a new one. To use an existing photo, tap Photo Roll and then tap the photo you want. To capture a new photo, tap New Photo and use the Pre's camera to photograph your subject. (See Chapter 9 if you're not yet familiar with using the camera.)

3. Next, drag with your finger to position the photo to your liking within the thumbnail frame. You can also use the pinch gestures to zoom in or out.
4. Tap Attach Photo and you're done! Now you'll see the tiny thumbnail wherever you view the contact in your list. And you'll see a much larger version of the photo when you call the contact or the contact calls you. Very cool.

Edit a Contact

Need to make changes or additions to a contact's information? It's easy: Just tap the contact to call up his or her record, tap Edit, and then make whatever modifications you want. When you're done, tap Done!

Add a Contact to Your Speed Dial

In Chapter 3 you learned all about Speed Dial and how to assign contacts to various keys on the keyboard. We won't rehash the instructions, other than to say that the assigning happens within the Contacts app (and, specifically, within the Contacts menu that appears when you tap the upper-left corner).

Add a Contact to the Launcher

Another form of "speed dial" is adding a contact to the Launcher, meaning that person gets his or her own icon right alongside your app icons. (You can turn Web favorites into icons as well; see Chapter 7 for details on that.) Here's how:

1. Browse to the contact you want to add to the Launcher and tap it to open it.
2. Tap the Contacts menu (upper-left corner) and then tap Add To Launcher.
3. Make any desired changes to the contact's first and last name, and then tap Add To Launcher.
4. Now open the Launcher and scroll down until you find your newly added contact icon. One tap is all it takes to bring up that person's contact record, at which point you can call, email, send a text message, and so on.

Note Want to remove a contact's Launcher icon? Follow the same steps outlined above, except that in step 2, you'll tap Remove From Launcher.

What Are Linked Contacts?

If you sync your Pre with multiple sources, it's almost a given that you'll have some overlap. For example, Dave is one of Rick's Facebook friends, and he's also a contact in Rick's Google account. Does that mean Rick's Pre will end up with two separate records for Dave Johnson?

No! Thanks to Palm's clever Synergy technology, the Pre will automatically link contacts from different accounts if it detects common data between them. So, in the preceding example, Rick's Pre will have just one Dave Johnson (which, let's face it, is more than enough), and that record will contain the *combined* data from the two accounts. That, friends, is seriously convenient and unequivocally awesome.

Remember that there's nothing you need to do to link contacts—the Pre takes care of it automatically. And you can spot a "linked" contact by the number that appears in the upper-right corner of the contact's record. A "2," for instance, indicates the contact is linked from two accounts.

Also, it's important to note that while contact data gets merged on your Pre, it stays in its original form in your various accounts. So you don't have to worry about all this linking messing up, say, your Facebook Friends list.

Finally, it's possible to link or unlink a contact manually, should the need arise. To find out how, see the *Palm Pre User Guide*.

Calendar

Organization, thy name is Calendar. Like most folks, we'd be hopelessly and permanently lost without ours, as we'd miss all our dates with supermodels (smartphone-book authors have to beat them away with a stick), appointments with the president, space shuttle launches (we're co-pilots), and so on. (Delusions of grandeur? Us? Nah.)

The Pre's Calendar app (see Figure 5-3) does a fine job of keeping track of where we need to be and when. It's the electronic equivalent of a day planner, but it does things no paper calendar can do. Let's start with what is arguably the second most valuable personal information app.

If you haven't yet mastered syncing with Google Calendar, Microsoft Exchange, and the like, see Chapter 2. This section focuses squarely on using the Calendar app itself and proceeds with the assumption that you've already got at least some Calendar data synced from at least some sources.

FIGURE 5-3 The Calendar app not only keeps tabs on your appointments, but it also syncs with Google Calendar and, if you want, other software and services.

Navigating the Calendar

Getting around in Calendar is a simple matter of tapping and swiping. For example, to switch between the app's three views, you just tap the three icons at the bottom of the screen:

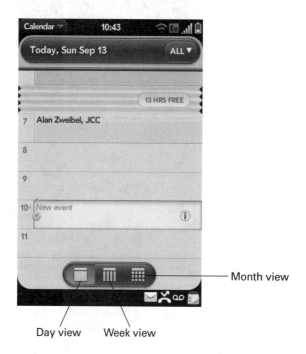

Month view

Day view   Week view

Within each of those views, you advance to the next day, week, or month by swiping your finger from right to left. To retreat to the prior day, week, or month, you swipe from left to right.

Finally, to go to a specific day or event, you simply tap it. What happens next depends on what view you're using. For example, if you're in a Day view and you tap an event, you'll open that event and all its details. But if you're in Week or Month view, tapping an event merely pulls up Day view for the day containing that event.

Tip Here's a quick way to get back to "today" in the calendar: Tap the Calendar menu and then choose Show Today. Presto! You'll jump from whatever date/screen you were viewing to the current date. Or, faster still, tap the date at the top of the screen to bring up the Jump To menu, and then tap Go To Today.

This all makes a lot more sense when you actually do it, so by all means take some time to poke (and tap) around in the calendar.

The Jump To Option

Want a quick way to jump to a specific date? Simple: Activate the Pre's Jump To option by tapping the date at the top of the screen:

Tap to activate Jump To option

This option is accessible from the Day, Week, and Month views. The Jump To box gives you two options (plus Cancel): Go To Date, which jumps to whatever date you've specified in the date selector, and Go To Today, which instantly returns to the current date (in whatever view happens to be selected).

Layered Calendars and Calendar Selection

One of the coolest (if not *the* coolest) things about the Pre Calendar app is that it supports multiple calendars. As you learned in Chapter 2, you can sync with up to four separate datebook destinations: Facebook, Google Calendar, Microsoft Exchange, and your Palm Profile.

Ah, but wouldn't two, three, or even four sets of appointments make for a big jumbled mess of a calendar on your Pre? It would, if not for the app's clever handling of those sets. Specifically, the Pre offers *layered calendars* that let you see all your calendars at once (with color-coded events to help differentiate them at a glance) or view them one at a time. And it's a simple matter to choose which view you want: Just tap the calendar selector button in the top-right corner of the screen.

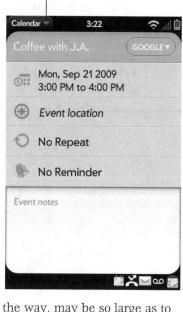

Calendar selector

By default, the app shows you All Calendars, but you can tap any of the others in the list (which, by the way, may be so large as to require a little up/down finger swiping to see all the entries) to see just the events for that individual calendar.

Adding/Editing Calendar Events

Let's say you're Rick (lucky you!), and you've just received a call from Jessica Alba, who needs help with her new Pre. You agree to meet for coffee at 3 P.M. Friday at the local Panera Bread. Obviously, that's an appointment you don't want to forget, so you whip out your trusty Pre and add it to the calendar. Here's how to create both real and made-up events like that one.

It's Wednesday. The aforementioned date—er, professional business meeting—with Jessica is on Friday. You have two options: You can bring up the Day view for Friday, and then tap the empty field next to 3 P.M. and type in a description of the event. Here's an example of how that looks:

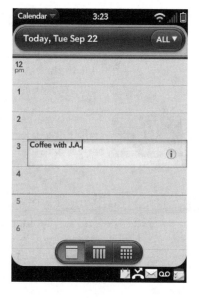

To fine-tune this event, tap the little encircled "i" on the right side of the field. Then meet us at the next section, "Modifying Event Details."

Your second option for adding new events works like this: While in Day view (for any day), you can tap the Calendar menu (upper-left corner), and then tap New | Event (or New | All Day Event if that's more suitable to the occasion). That will take you straight to the details screen, where you can specify all the event details (time, location, reminder, and so on).

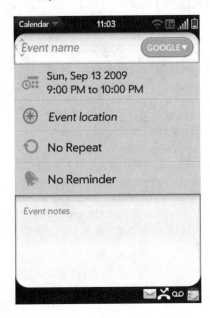

Which method should you use for creating new events? It's really up to you. If the event is far in the future, it's probably faster and easier to go the menu route than to navigate to the Day view for the day in question.

 Actually, you don't really have to go to the day of the event. You can tap any open spot in the calendar, on any day, and then go to the details screen and choose the correct date and time. Truth be told, that's the fastest method of all.

Modifying Event Details

It's the rare newly added appointment that won't require a visit to the details screen, which is where you tweak various, well, details. As you learned in the preceding section, you automatically land at this screen when you create a new event via the

Calendar menu, or when you tap the little "i" alongside a new created event in the Day view. Here's what you'll find there:

Let's talk about some of these details and how/ when/why you might want to modify them. (By the way, in case it's not obvious, just tap the detail you want to modify.)

- **Event name**   This is pretty straightforward: Type a name or description for your event: "Coffee with Jessica Alba" or "Dave's release from the mental hospital." Whatever you type here will appear in the calendar's Day view.
- **Calendar selector**   Tap this button to choose the calendar with which to sync this event. If you're a Google Calendar user, choose that. If you also or instead sync with Microsoft Exchange, that might be the better choice. And if you use neither, the event will, by default, sync with your Palm Profile, which is fine.

- **Date/time**   Tapping here brings up a different screen where you set the start and end dates/times for the event. If it's an all-day event, tap the box beside that option. (You'll notice that the time settings disappear.) And if it's a multi-day event (such as a trip), just set the end date for the final day of the event.
- **Location**   If a location is associated with this event, enter it here. It will appear in your Day view just below the event name—very handy.
- **Repeat settings**   Some events, such as birthdays and soccer practices, repeat on a regular basis. To avoid having to enter each and every instance of a recurring event manually, the Pre Calendar lets you set up a repeat option: Daily, Weekdays, Weekly, or Custom. The first three are fairly self-explanatory; if you choose Custom, you can specify the frequency of the recurrence and whether it should expire after a certain date or go on forever.

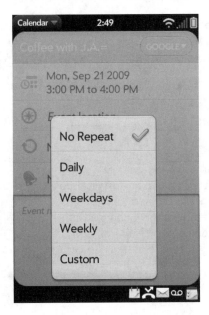

- **Reminder settings**   Tap here if you want your Pre to sound an alarm at a specified time prior to the event (or at the exact time of the event).

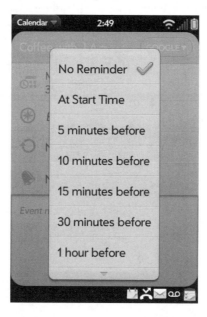

- **Notes**   If you need to include extra details about the event, this Notes field is the place. As with location, a snippet of the notes will appear in your Day view below the event name.

 When you're done setting all the event details, remember to use the back gesture to return to the main Calendar screen. There's no Done or OK button.

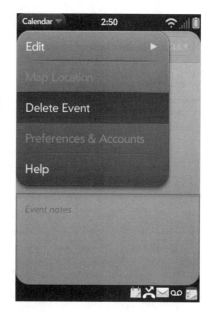

To modify the details for an existing event, just find it in the Day view and tap it.

Deleting Events

Need to delete an event from your calendar? Tap it to bring up the details screen, and then tap the Calendar menu followed by Delete Event. If it's a recurring event, the Pre will ask if you want to delete just that one instance (the one you tapped) or the entire series.

 You can't delete Facebook events from your Pre.

Calendar Preferences and Accounts

Does your week begin on Sunday—or perhaps Monday? Wish the Pre would automatically add a reminder for each new event? Need to add a new account to your calendar—or remove one? You can modify these and other settings in the Preferences & Accounts menu for the Calendar app. To access it, just tap the Calendar menu while in any view (Day, Week, or Month), and then tap Preferences & Accounts. The settings therein are fairly self-explanatory (and it's rare you'll need to mess with them), so we won't delve into them here.

Memos

If you've poked around the Pre's Memos app at all, you've undoubtedly noticed a few thematic similarities to the real world (see Figure 5-4). Corkboard, check. Thumb tacks, check. Colored sticky-note design, check.

Unfortunately, while Memos looks cool, it's little more than a glorified notepad. Tap New Memo, type whatever notes you want to keep, and then use the back gesture to return to the virtual corkboard main screen. And that's about the end of the Memos story.

 Memos randomly assigns one of four colors to each new note. If you want to choose a color yourself, tap the little page-curl in the bottom-right corner of the memo.

Our main complaint with the app is that it doesn't sync with Google, Outlook, or any other destination. (Granted, Google doesn't really have a memo equivalent with which to sync the Pre's data, but Outlook does have its Notes area.) What's more, you can't assign memos to categories, and there's no option to auto-sort them alphabetically.

FIGURE 5-4   The Memos app looks pretty cool, but it's limited in its capabilities.

Indeed, your only organization option is to tap and drag each memo to your desired location on the virtual corkboard.

The one silver lining is that notes aren't completely trapped on your Pre: You can email them. Here's how:

1. Open the memo you want to send.
2. Tap the Memos menu in the top-left corner, and then tap Email Memo.

3. The Pre switches to the Mail app with the contents of the memo already pasted into the body of a new message. Choose the recipient(s) from your address book, tap Send (the little paper airplane icon), and you're done!

 When you're done, just switch back to the Memos app as you would any other, by bringing up Card view and swiping your way there.

We're hoping Palm beefs up Memos in a future WebOS update or that some third-party vendor offers a more robust substitute. In the meantime, Memos is good for recording short, simple notes—and not much more.

 Want to find a memo in a hurry? While viewing the main Memos screen, just start typing. As with Universal Search, the app will dynamically filter your memos to display matching results.

Tasks

Rick likes nothing better than a good to-do list. (Dave continues to hope that his imaginary monkey-butlers will remember his important tasks, but here in the real world, it takes a to-do list.) The Pre offers a simple but effective to-do list in the form of the Tasks app (see Figure 5-5). It's limited in certain respects, but it should help you keep tabs on your current and future tasks.

FIGURE 5-5   The Tasks app lets you create multiple to-do lists, and it can sync with Microsoft Exchange (but not Google—yet).

To get started with Tasks, tap the little new-list icon in the lower-left corner of the screen. Because this is your first task, the app will ask to assign a list name—basically a category heading for one or more tasks to follow. You might choose something like "Personal," "Work," "Party Planning," or, if you're Dave, "Locations for Stalking Halle Berry."

Once you've typed in your list name, tap the new-task icon in the lower-left corner of the screen. You'll see a new field with "Task name" in gray letters:

Now type in the name of your task: "Pick up dry cleaning," for example. When that's done, you can tap anywhere else on the screen to finalize the entry, or tap the little "i" on the right side of the field to access the options for that task.

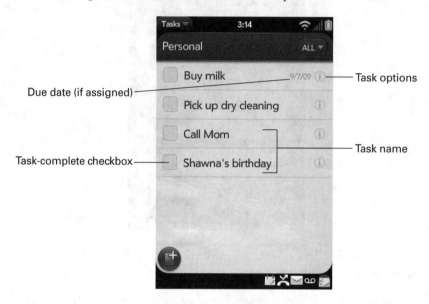

When you tap that little "i," you'll see the following screen with the following options:

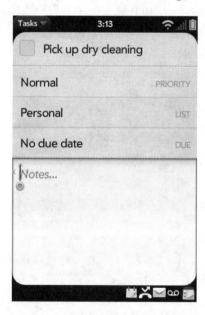

- **Priority** Tap here to set a High, Normal, or Low priority for the task. This will change how it appears in the task list. High-priority tasks appear in red, normal-priority tasks are black, and low-priority tasks are gray.
- **List** Tap here to assign the task to a list different from the one currently selected. For example, if you decided that "Pick up dry cleaning" belongs on the Work list instead of Personal, you can make that change here.
- **Due** Tap here to assign a due date to your task. As you'll see in the pop-up list that appears, your choices include Today, Tomorrow, In One Week, In One Month, and Other. Tapping the last option brings up a calendar where you can choose a specific due date.
- **Notes** In this field, you can type any notes that go along with the task. ("The cleaners on Fourth Street, not the one on Third Avenue," for instance.)

Completing and Deleting Tasks

Half the fun of having a to-do list is ticking off each item as you complete it. In the Tasks app, that's as simple as tapping the task-complete checkbox to the left of the item:

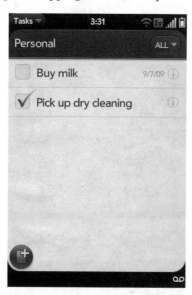

What if you want to restore a completed task? For example, suppose you picked up your dry cleaning, only to discover that you forgot to get your spouse's stuff. To restore that to-do, just tap the box again to remove the checkmark.

If you want to remove a task permanently from your to-do list, tap the left side of that task and swipe your finger all the way to the right. You'll see a Delete button:

Tap it, and the task goes to that great to-do list in the sky. Of course, you can tap Cancel if you change your mind.

Want to delete all your completed tasks in one fell swoop? Just tap the Tasks menu in the top-left corner of the screen and choose Purge Completed.

That's just one of the options in the menu. Here's a rundown of the others (those that aren't self-explanatory, anyway):

- **Set Due Date For All**   If all the tasks in a particular list need to be finished by the same date, you can assign that date with a few easy taps.
- **Mark All Completed/Incomplete**   Use this menu option if a list is particularly long and you want to mark the entire thing complete or incomplete. It'll save you having to check/uncheck each checkbox manually.
- **Delete List**   Done with, say, your Birthday Party list? Head here to delete the entire thing.
- **Hide Completed**   This hides all completed tasks from the current view.

Use Your Pre as an Alarm Clock

Your Pre can replace all kinds of real-world objects: your iPod (see Chapter 8), your GPS (see Chapter 6), and even your alarm clock (see this chapter, specifically this paragraph). Thanks to the Clock app, you can set alarms to wake you up in the morning, to remind you to pick up the kids from soccer practice, or to remind you of any other alarm-worthy event.

When you first tap the Clock icon, here's what you'll see:

Clock mode   Alarm mode

Yep, it's a clock—a cool digital representation of one of those old-fashioned flip-clocks you see in the movies. Prefer something a little more traditional? Tap the Clock menu in the top-left corner of the screen, tap Preferences, and then tap Themes. The default setting is Digital; tap Analog and the clock turns into this:

Of course, we're here to talk alarms, so let's get to it.

 If you have a Touchstone charger (see Chapter 11), you can leave the app running and use the Pre as a nifty-looking desktop clock. Normally, the Pre's screen dims after a few seconds on the charger, but Clock overrides the usual settings so that the screen stays fully backlit. Smart!

Setting Alarms

The Pre is unique among alarm clocks in that it lets you set up multiple alarms. Here's how to get started:

1. Tap the little alarm mode icon at the bottom of the screen. You'll see a blank Alarms screen.
2. Tap the "plus" icon in the bottom-left corner of the screen. Tap it to bring up the Alarm Preferences screen.
3. If you want, name the alarm ("Soccer Practice," for example).

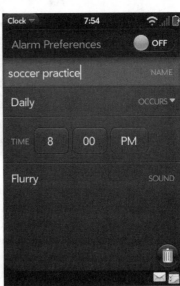

4. Tap Occurs to set the occurrence for the alarm: Ring Once, Daily, Weekdays, or Weekends. (If this is your morning wakeup alarm, for example, you'd probably want to choose Weekdays so it doesn't bug you on Saturday and Sunday.)
5. Set the time for the alarm. First, tap the hour, flick the numeric list up or down until you find the proper number, and then tap it. Repeat with the minutes (available here in increments of five—no 7:58 A.M. alarms for you, we're sorry to say). Finally, choose AM or PM.
6. Last, but not least, choose a sound for the alarm by tapping the Sound field. If you have any MP3s or other song files loaded on your Pre (see Chapter 8), you'll be able to turn them into ringtones to use as your alarm sound!

Once you've tweaked all the settings to your liking, a simple back gesture will take you back to the main Alarms screen, where you'll see an On/Off toggle for turning the alarm, um, on or off. If you want to delete an alarm outright, swipe your finger across it from one side of the screen to the other, and then tap Delete. Alternately, you can open the specific alarm and click the trashcan icon.

 Why not use the Calendar instead of the Clock app? After all, as you learned earlier in the chapter, appointments can have alarms. Well, truth be told, you can go that route if you prefer, but we think it's easier to use the Clock app for certain types of alarms—such as the one that wakes you up every morning. Plus, the Calendar doesn't let you use ringtones for your alarms. We'd much rather wake up to, say, Lily Allen than a series of beeps and boops.

If you ever want to make changes to an alarm's settings, just tap it to return to the Alarm Preferences screen. And, of course, to create new alarms, just tap that "plus" icon and repeat the process.

When the Alarm Goes Off...

If you're anything like Rick (and heaven help you if you are), the morning alarm produces a murderous rage—usually directed at the alarm clock. The good news is that the Pre has a Snooze button. The bad news is that you can't just smack the phone like you would a clock: You actually have to crack open at least one eye and tap the onscreen Snooze button. And you have to be awake enough that you don't accidentally tap Dismiss (the alarm-clock equivalent of "off") instead and go back to sleep for who knows how long.

Actually, tapping Dismiss might be good news, especially if you're the type who hits Snooze so often that you eventually end up late for work anyway. The Pre forces you to wake up enough to interact with it. And if you place it across the room before going to bed at night, you'll actually have to stand up if you want to hit Snooze.

 The Pre's Snooze buys you an extra 10 minutes until the alarm goes off again.

Document Viewers

Think about the four kinds of documents you use most in your day-to-day life. For us, they're the following:

- Microsoft Word files (also known as doc files)
- Microsoft Excel files (also known as XLS files)
- Microsoft PowerPoint files (also known as PPT files)
- PDFs

Wouldn't it be great if the Pre let you view these kinds of files? It does! (Really, would we have brought it up if it didn't?) Thanks to a pair of apps—Doc View and PDF View—you can open and read Word, Excel, PowerPoint, and PDF files right on your Pre.

Ah, but how do these files get on your Pre? There are two basic options. Let's take a look at both.

 Doc View is an early version of the DataViz app, Documents To Go, a familiar name to anyone who used a Palm Treo, Centro, or PDA. Currently, it's a viewer only, meaning you can't create or edit Word, Excel, or PowerPoint documents on your Pre. However, those capabilities are imminent in a forthcoming version of the app, which will most likely be available for purchase by the time you read this. Of course, if you're content with viewing alone, look no further than the bundled app.

Getting Documents onto Your Pre

Documents can land on your Pre one of two ways:

- **Drag-and-drop**   By connecting your Pre to your PC and enabling the USB drive, you turn your phone into the equivalent of a flash drive. From there, you can drag-and-drop your documents to the Pre. You'll learn everything you need to know about USB transfers in Chapter 6.
- **Email**   If someone sends you an email with a document attached, you can download the attachment and open it in the appropriate viewer. We talk more about this in the next section.

Using the Doc View App

After you've dragged and dropped some documents onto your Pre, all you have to do is tap the Doc View or PDF View icon, and then tap the document you want to open (see Figure 5-6).

When you open a Word document, you can scroll through it using the up and down gestures you learned in Chapter 1. You can also change the zoom level by using

FIGURE 5-6   The Doc View app lets you open (but not edit) Word, Excel, and PowerPoint documents.

the pinch gestures; the viewer will reformat the text accordingly so you don't have to scroll left and right, even if you zoom in to make the text larger.

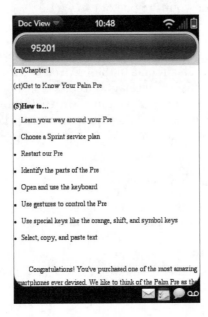

As for spreadsheets (Excel files), the viewer does indeed support left/right scrolling, as spreadsheets are by design vertical and horizontal animals. But the same pinch rules apply: You can zoom in and out as needed to view more or less of the sheet. You can also switch to other workbooks within the spreadsheet by tapping the arrows at the bottom of the screen.

When it comes to presentations (PowerPoint files), you move among slides by tapping the aforementioned arrows. If you want to jump to a specific slide, tap the numbers in between the arrows, type the number of the slide you want, and then press the ENTER key.

6

Using Your Pre on the Go

HOW TO...

- Keep a charge and conserve battery life
- Use your Pre as a flash drive
- Pack accessories for your Pre
- Use your Pre on a plane
- Use your Pre for navigation
- Use your Pre's Wi-Fi
- Use your Pre's Bluetooth

Some people find their Pre so useful that—imagine this—they put it in their pocket and take it with them when they leave the house! Daring, we know, and a whole new way to think about using your shiny black stone. And, as it turns out, the Pre is even designed for these kinds of "away missions." Its battery keeps it running all day away from a power outlet and its wireless connectivity is there to let you access the Internet and make phone calls from anywhere. The Pre even tells you the time so you don't need to wear a watch. Heck, if everyone finds out about this, carrying a mobile phone will become some sort of international craze.

Seriously, we know you already carry your Pre around town. But it's entirely possible you're not getting the most out of your Pre when you are on the go. And if you plan to take it with you on a trip, you should read this chapter. We have all kinds of suggestions for how to prepare your Palm for a grueling business trip or family vacation, as well as what kind of software you might need to make the trip go a little smoother. And how about a camping trip? Your Pre might not be the first accessory that springs to mind when you consider roughing it in the Rocky Mountains, but your trusty little handheld has a lot to offer in the wilderness, too.

Keeping a Charge

While it might be true that "the only good human is a dead human" (actually, that's true only if you're a gorilla from *Planet of the Apes*), we should also point out that a more relevant observation is that a dead Pre is no good to anyone—except, perhaps, as a doorstop or a paperweight. It's important that you keep at least a few spare electrons rolling around inside your phone when you're away from a wall outlet.

If you're far away from a power outlet, the message shown at right is the worst thing your Pre can choose to show you.

It means you have only a few minutes of power left. After that time, your Pre will shut itself off and the only way to get it back on is to recharge it.

You can do a few things to ensure that your Pre is ready to run when you need it.

Top off your Pre just before you go anywhere. As a rule, that means you'll probably want to leave the Pre on your Touchstone charger whenever you're not using it. (You *do* have a Touchstone, right? Sure, it's an optional accessory, and not a particularly inexpensive one at that, but you should consider it essential. Since there's no need to plug anything in, you're more likely to keep your phone charged.)

The Touchstone is great, but it does charge your phone more slowly than a trusty old USB cable. If you are in a hurry—and your Pre has a dangerously low charge—pull the cable out of the back of your Touchstone and insert it into the Pre directly. Or use your spare Pre USB cable—you've got one of *those*, too, right?

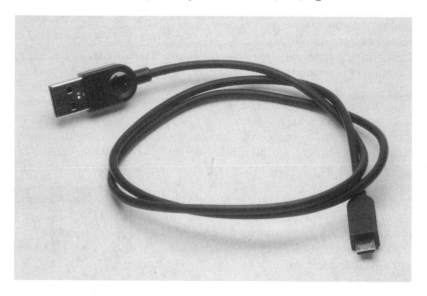

Your laptop will charge your Pre even if the laptop isn't plugged into an outlet. This one's something of a tradeoff. Think about it: You're away from a source of electricity, and you have to use your Pre, but its battery is almost dead. You've got your laptop, though, and it still has an hour of battery time left. What to do? If you need the phone more than the laptop, fire it up and tether them together with a USB cable and choose the Just Charge option on the Pre. When you have enough charge on your Pre to get the job done, shut down the laptop.

We also suggest that you get an extended battery or an extra battery. The standard Palm Pre battery is fine for most people, especially if you can charge your Pre at least once a day. But if you're a heavy duty user—or you spend a lot of time out of reach of a charging cable—you might want to upgrade your battery. As we wrote this book, we are aware of at least one extended battery for the Pre—the Innocell 1350 Extended Life Battery from Seido. It costs about $45 and you can find out more at http://tinyurl .com/nfo4wv. By the time you hold this book in your hands, more options will likely be available.

How to...   Make Your Battery Last

Your Pre comes with a lithium-ion battery, which will continue to give you great performance even after many hundreds of charges. To get the best possible performance from the battery, though, you should occasionally—once every week or two—run the battery all the way down till it quits and then charge it back to 100 percent. The rest of the time, it's fine to give the phone partial charges to keep it "topped off."

Conserve the Battery Life You Have

Let's say that your battery is topped off and you're on the road. What can you do to make sure that your phone lasts as long as possible before you can charge it again?

The most important thing to do—and really, this is usually all you need to know— is to minimize the time you are using the phone. This probably goes without saying, but your Pre will last longest when the touch screen is turned off—in other words, when the phone is in standby mode. Turn it on, do your thing, and turn it off again. Don't, as your mom might tell you, dawdle.

In addition, it pays to know that how you use your phone will have a significant effect on the battery life as well. Various features, such as using the Internet, listening to music, and watching video, all drain the battery at a different rate. In fact, we did a little unofficial battery testing to see how long our Pre handhelds lasted under various conditions. See the "How Long" Did You Know later in the chapter for a look at our results. If you need to save battery life to make some calls, and your battery is starting to run low, common sense says that you should pack away the headphones and avoid listening to music or watching NASCAR until you can charge it again.

You should be mindful of a few things when the battery starts to get low:

- You can turn off the Wi-Fi and Bluetooth radios to extend the battery life, especially if you don't really need them and tend to leave them on for convenience. To do this, tap the status bar in the upper-right corner of the touch screen, tap Wi-Fi, and then tap Turn Off Wi-Fi. Then do more or less the same thing for Bluetooth (tap Bluetooth and then Turn Off Bluetooth).

Note Here's a head scratcher. Palm recommends leaving the Wi-Fi on in some cases to optimize battery life. For example, if your cellular coverage isn't strong, data might be transmitted more efficiently via Wi-Fi instead of over the weak cellular network, which puts more strain on the battery. So turning off Wi-Fi isn't always the right thing to do.

- If you're even more desperate to conserve electrons, you can turn off all the wireless radios at once—Wi-Fi, Bluetooth, and voice. To do that, tap the status bar menu and then tap Turn On Airplane Mode. Of course, you won't be able to receive any calls until you turn off Airplane Mode.

- Shut it down completely. Hold the power button for about 6 seconds until you see the shut down options, and then tap Turn Off.

Don't shut off your phone completely unless you have to. If you're down to a 5 percent charge and you will need to call the president to warn him about an impending asteroid strike that will threaten all of humanity, but first you need to figure out the coordinates to aim the missiles, then it makes sense to turn off the phone completely to conserve the battery until you need it. But powering the phone on and off several times a day as a matter of habit is a penny-wise, pound-foolish sort of practice. It takes a nontrivial amount of power to "boot" your phone from scratch, so it probably consumes more battery life than you're saving by turning it off.

Battery Saving Tips for the Truly Dedicated

For the most part, our tips are all you need to stretch out your battery life between charges. But if you're looking for every possible way to eke out a few minutes of extra charge, here are some more tips for you:

- *Lower the brightness.* A bright screen is a beautiful thing to behold, and it makes your Pre easy to read in bright sunlight. But it takes a toll on your battery. Tap the Launcher icon and then tap Screen & Lock. Slide the brightness to the lowest level you (and your eyes) can tolerate.
- *Turn off the touch screen faster.* By default, the Pre turns off its touch screen after 2 minutes of inactivity, but you can reduce that to 1 minute or even 30 seconds. Right under the Brightness slider—mentioned in the preceding bulleted point—change the value in the menu to the right of Turn Off After.

- *Stop synchronizing your email.* The Pre goes online automatically to get your messages. You can stop that—or reduce the frequency—to conserve battery life. Tap Mail, then tap the app menu. Tap Preferences & Accounts. Tap an email account, scroll down to the Sync section, and tap Get Email. Change the value to Manual.

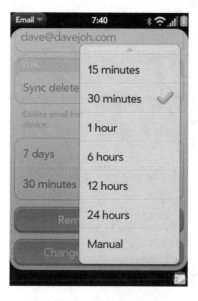

- *Turn off GPS.* Your Pre's GPS receiver is on by default, and that, too, uses battery life. Turn it off: Tap the Launcher icon and then tap Location Services. Set Use GPS to Off.

- *Be sure to sign out of your IM service to get the most battery life.* Tap Messaging, tap the Messaging app menu, tap Preferences & Accounts, and then tap your IM account and tap Sign Out. (Whew.)

How Long?

Curious about how long the battery is going to last? How about how long it takes to charge? We did some testing of our own, and here is a little guide to knowing what to expect from your Pre and its battery. First up is the time it takes to charge:

Time to charge on a Touchstone	3 hours
Time to charge with a USB cable	2 hours

And once the battery is charged, here's about how long it'll last:

Average use	1 day
Talk time	6 hours
Watching video	4 hours
Surfing the Web	5 hours
Listening to music	6 hours
In standby	4 days

Of course, no one ever uses a Pre for just one thing, so the average use is a pretty good guide to knowing what to expect—a day or two of reliable use that mixes phone calls, some Web surfing, a little music, and the occasional video. But know that if you fall sleep listening to music on your Pre, there's a pretty good chance that your battery will be low or dead when you wake up three hours later.

Using Your Pre as a Flash Drive

We are endlessly amazed by the little things in our modern technological world. Take flash drives, for example—tiny little widgets that slide into your PC's USB slot and can ferry around gigabytes of data. Just amazing. (We should clarify that Dave is also rendered speechless by the existence of donut holes, and Rick is strangely fascinated by shag carpeting, so maybe flash drives aren't so amazing after all.)

Flash drives have some obvious disadvantages, though. Being so small, they're easy to lose—and we've misplaced our share of them—and you pretty much need to remember to carry them around to begin with. In other words, they're something new to lose, and something new to forget.

That's why we love the fact that you can use your Pre as a flash drive. You can store up to about 6.8GB of data on your Pre, depending upon how much music and other stuff is already on the phone. Intrigued? Here's what to do.

Copying Files to Your Pre

Using the Pre's USB charging cable, connect your Pre to the PC from which you want to copy files. (We've said it before, and it bears repeating: Be careful to insert the USB cable into the Pre properly, with the divot on top. It's possible to insert the cable upside down, which isn't good for the cable or the Pre.) You'll see the following screen on the Pre:

1. Tap USB Drive. The Pre's screen will change to a static image. Set it aside, since you won't need to use the Pre for now.
2. You should see the AutoPlay dialog on your PC. Click Open Folder To View Files.

 If AutoPlay doesn't appear, you can do this manually: Click Start | Computer. In Devices with Removable Storage, double-click Palm Pre.

3. In the Palm Pre's open folder, drag any files that you want to carry on your Pre. You can copy files to existing folders or make new folders—you can use the Pre's internal storage any way you like.

When you're done, don't disconnect the USB cable—not yet, at least. In Windows' notification area (also known as the system tray), right-click Safely Remove Hardware and Eject Media.

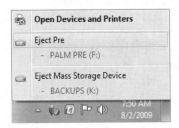

Click Palm Pre and wait for the balloon message that tells you it's safe to remove the Pre.

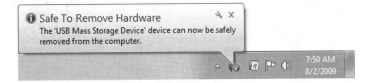

Now you can disconnect the Pre from your computer.

Copy Files to Another Computer

When you get to your destination, copying files to another PC works exactly the same as the process you used to get them onto the Pre to begin with.

Follow the same steps outlined in "Using a Photo from Your PC as Wallpaper " in Chapter 4 to connect your Pre to the PC, but this time, drag the files off the Pre and onto the computer's desktop or into whatever folders you'd like to store them. If you won't need the files again, you can delete them to reclaim some space on your Pre for other files later. Or you can keep a suite of important files on your Pre all the time— it's up to you.

And when you're done, don't forget to "safely remove" the Pre from the computer before you disconnect the USB cable.

Of course, don't forget to bring the USB cable with you when you travel. If you arrive at your destination with nothing but your Pre and an optimistic demeanor, you're going to be somewhat disappointed. On the plus side, you should already be in the habit of carrying a Pre USB cable in your backpack, carrying case, handbag, or whatever, since it lets you charge your Pre wherever you go. And don't forget that you can remove the cable from the back of a Touchstone and use it to connect the Pre directly to the PC—think of it like your own personal "MacGyver Moment."

Essential Files for Your Pre's Flash Drive

What sorts of files should you store on your Pre? It's kind of liberating to think about your Pre as a flash drive that's pretty much always in your pocket. If you might need to use some program or a set of documents in a computer when you're away from home or the office, you can store it permanently on your Pre.

That way, even if you need the files only once or twice a year—boom—having it on the Pre can be a real lifesaver. Here's what's on our Pres:

Dave: I keep PortableApps on my Pre (http://portableapps .com). This free app takes about 350MB of space on your Pre, and it lets you run a suite of essential office apps on any computer to which you can connect the Pre. The cool thing is that there's nothing to install on the computer: just attach your Pre, select Drive Mode, and then double-click PortableApps. You'll see a start menu appear on the PC with options that include the Firefox Web browser and the OpenOffice suite of apps. And the apps leave no trace of their existence when you pull the Pre out of the PC's USB port and put it back in your pocket.

I also have a folder on my Pre called Backups, where I keep recent backups of important files from my home computer—stuff like Quicken's data file. That way, in the event of catastrophe at home, I have the most current backups of my critical desktop apps.

Rick: Oh, sure, take all the good stuff. I agree that PortableApps is a handy productivity suite, but I prefer to use my Pre as an emergency system-recovery tool. I've stocked it with free but effective utilities such as ClamWin Portable anti-virus software (http://portableapps.com/apps/utilities/clamwin_portable), Spyware Terminator (www.spywareterminator.com), and Revo Uninstaller Portable (www.revouninstaller.com). If one of my computers ever starts acting funky, either due to a malware infection or damaged hardware, the Pre can help bail me out. You can find out more about this clever idea in the Business Hacks post, "Turn Your USB Drive into a System-Recovery Tool" (http://tinyurl.com/694stu).

Stuff for the Road

When you leave the house each day, you probably bring your Pre along for the ride. And if you're gone for only a few hours, or you're heading to the office, that's probably fine. But we have some humble suggestions for other essentials you might want to take on the road along with your Pre. (See Chapter 12 for more details about Pre accessories.)

- **Touchstone** If you spend a lot of time in two locations, such as work and home, we recommend owning a pair of Touchstones and keeping one at each place. Dave keeps one Touchstone on his desk at work and the second by the garage door at home. Touchstones are not inexpensive, but they make up for price with convenience. And if you have a Touchstone in both places, you always have quick access to the Pre's USB cable (just disconnect it from the back of the Touchstone) if you need to copy files to or from a PC.
- **USB cable** If you travel with your Pre and find yourself away from your home or office, a USB cable is a great accessory to bring along in your briefcase, backpack, or carrying case. It takes up almost no space, and you can use it as an emergency charging option to transfer juice from a nearby computer if your Pre is running low. You can also use it to transfer files, obviously.
- **Palm Profile Web site** You should know how to get to your Palm Profile Web site. You can get there by going to http://tinyurl.com/kors3m. It's not fun to think about, but if your Pre is ever lost or stolen, you'll want to be able to erase the phone remotely—and quickly—via the Web. You can also use this feature to reset your device if you ever forget your Pre's PIN or password. See Chapter 12 for details.
- **Spare battery** If you are routinely away from AC power for extended periods of time—a full day filled with heavy-duty phone usage, for example—then invest in a second battery. It's easy to replace on-the-go under pretty much any conditions except when you're scuba diving.
- **Bluetooth headset and charging cable** We can't recommend a Bluetooth headset enough for hands-free calling, and if you're going to be gone a few days, be sure that you can charge up the headset while you're away. If you like to listen to music or watch video while on the go, you might also want a Bluetooth stereo headset.

Using Your Pre on a Plane

We've mentioned your Pre's Airplane Mode a few times in this book, so it's about time that we introduce it to you formally. Reader, Airplane Mode. Airplane Mode, Reader.

Airplane Mode puts your Pre in a state that complies with current (2009) air safety rules—it turns off all the wireless radios in your Pre (phone, Wi-Fi, and Bluetooth) so that you can use your Pre to listen to music, read a book, play a game, or anything else that doesn't require a connection with the outside world.

To turn on Airplane Mode, tap the status bar in the upper-right corner of the touch screen and then tap Turn On Airplane Mode. It takes only a couple of seconds for the Pre to shut down the radios, and you're in full compliance for your flight. When you land, just repeat the process—tap the status bar and then tap Turn Off Airplane Mode.

 Curious about why Airplane Mode doesn't disable GPS? It's because your GPS receiver is exactly that—a receiver. It transmits nothing, so it cannot interfere with your plane's electronics.

Getting Around with GPS

Your Pre comes packed with 25th century space-age technology—a GPS receiver that lets your Pre pinpoint you within about 30 feet, anywhere on the Earth, thanks to signals sent by a constellation of navigational satellites circling the planet.

The Pre's GPS data can be accessed by any number of apps, making them "location aware." That means if you're looking for a restaurant, for example, a restaurant-finding app doesn't have to ask you where you are—it can simply read that information via GPS and automatically tell you which restaurants are near you.

Location-Aware Apps

The following apps can automatically use your location to help you make decisions or find points of interest:

- **Camera**   Tags your photos with latitude and longitude so you can (with the right software, such as the photo-shaping site Flickr) see your photos on a map.

- **Fandango** Uses your position to find the closest movie theaters.

- **Google Maps** Shows your position on the map.

- **Mobile by Citysearch**   Uses your location to help you find nearby restaurants, bars, banks, movie theaters, and other services.

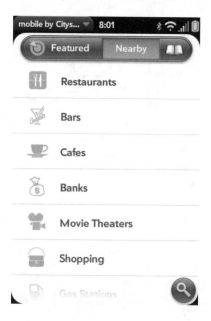

- **Where**   Like Mobile by Citysearch, Where finds nearby services.
- **Sprint Navigation**   Provides detailed turn-by-turn driving directions to help you navigate.

Did You Know?

What, Exactly, Is GPS?

Along with the Hummer and Patriot missile, GPS was one of the stars of the first Gulf War. By the end of 1992, anyone who watched CNN had at least heard of GPS. First conceived in the 1970s as a way to deliver precision navigation data to U.S. military forces and weapons systems from space, GPS (Global Positioning System) was designed, built, launched, and perfected through much of the 1980s. And though it was originally bought and paid for by the American military, GPS is almost a household word across the world and is used for driving, flying, hiking, surveying, and more by millions of people every day.

GPS is a navigation system, of course. It is based on a constellation of 24 Earth-orbiting satellites; they're distributed around the globe in six overlapping orbital planes. At an altitude of 11,000 miles, each satellite orbits the Earth exactly twice each day in an extremely predictable pattern. No matter where you are on Earth, if you can see the sky, a few GPS satellites are floating somewhere overhead.

And, believe it or not, GPS satellites don't actually tell you *where* you are. Each satellite, equipped with a highly accurate atomic clock, simply broadcasts its position and the time on a continuous basis. Any GPS receiver, such as the one built into your Pre, simply triangulates its position on the Earth by comparing the signal it receives from three or more satellites.

GPS receivers have become incredibly popular, especially since the military was ordered to disable Selective Availability (a feature intended to degrade the accuracy of the system for nonmilitary users in time of war) permanently back in the mid '90s.

If you want to learn more, and you've got money to waste, check out Rick's woefully outdated book, *How to Do Everything with Your GPS*. At least 24 percent of the material in there is still useful.

You can find many of these apps (such as Fandango and Where) in the App Catalog (see Chapter 10 for details)—others (such as Camera and Sprint Navigation) come preinstalled on your Pre. This, of course, is just a partial list; new apps are released all the time that take advantage of GPS information to help you find and do things in your general vicinity.

Turning GPS On and Off

By default, your Pre's GPS receiver is turned on and ready to provide location services to any app that asks. You don't have to stand for that, though; there might be times when you want to save battery life by turning off GPS, or you might not want your location to be tracked or remembered. It's easy to control your Pre's GPS abilities.

To get started, tap the Launcher icon and then tap Location Services (which, if you haven't moved it, is on the third page of the Launcher). You'll see the Location Services app.

Here, four switches let you control your GPS system:

- **Auto Locate**   This doesn't turn GPS on and off, but instead controls how easy it is for apps to use the location data your GPS is generating. When set to On, every location-aware app can automatically use your position without asking permission. That's convenient, but you might not always want your phone to "know" where you are. When set to Off, any app that wants to use your location must ask permission, like this:

FIGURE 6-1 When you allow geotagging on your Pre, latitude and longitude are embedded in your photos. When you use it with compatible software, such as the photo-sharing site Flickr, you can see where the photos were taken on a map. Flickr uses Google Maps.

- **Use GPS** This is the Big Hammer. This setting turns the GPS receiver on and off. We recommend that you leave it on all the time for convenience, but if you simply never use location services, you might as well turn it off to save some battery life.
- **Geotag Photos** When you use the Pre's camera, it embeds your location (in the form of latitude and longitude) into your photo's metadata. That means you can use Web sites like Flickr to show your photo's position on a map. Check out Figure 6-1 for a look at what geotagging your photos in Flickr is like.
- **Background Data Collection** Palm uses this setting to collect information to improve its navigation services. Nothing personal or identifiable about you is ever sent by the phone, so we recommend you leave this setting On.

Using Your Pre on a Wi-Fi Network

Have you ever driven past one of those top-secret military bases and seen all those domes and towers and fancy-looking structures bristling with all sorts of antennas? Well, your Pre is kind of like that (except it fits in your pocket and isn't surrounded

What, Exactly, Is Wi-Fi, and Why Do I Want It?

Wi-Fi is the wireless technology that has made the 21st century possible. How's that for hyperbole? Seriously, Wi-Fi, which stands for Wireless Fidelity, also goes by the high-tech name 802.11 (and its variations such as 802.11b and 802.11g). Wi-Fi connects compatible devices, such as most laptops and many mobile phones like your Pre, to wired networks. You can use Wi-Fi to connect your laptop to your home or corporate network, for example, which also gives it access to the Internet.

Wi-Fi has really made its mark on modern society through locations called hotspots. A *hotspot* is any location that offers Wi-Fi access to the Internet. You can find hotspots in many public locations, such as public libraries, parks, shopping malls, restaurants, and coffee shops. Some hotspots charge a fee for access, though the trend is definitely headed toward free.

We hear what you're asking: "If I have a Sprint Everything plan for data access already, and I can surf the Web, send email, and do all the other cool Internet-y things with my cell phone, why would I want to use Wi-Fi? Shouldn't I just leave it off, and get better battery performance?"

Well, that's a pretty long question, but we'll answer it for you anyway. Here are a few great reasons to use your Wi-Fi connection:

- Using Wi-Fi, you can use the Internet while you're simultaneously on a voice call. Without Wi-Fi, it's one or the other.
- Wi-Fi is sometimes faster. Depending on what kind of coverage area you're in, you might get better performance from Wi-Fi when watching Web video and performing other data-intensive jobs.
- You are outside a coverage area. You might be inside a building with no cell coverage—but the building has its own Wi-Fi coverage, for example. That'll get you email and Internet access, even though you can't place a voice call.

by a security fence). As you no doubt know, your phone has three different kinds of wireless abilities: Voice, Wi-Fi, and Bluetooth. You can turn on or off each of these independently or leave all three on for convenience. (That's what we do.)

Connecting to a Wi-Fi Network

Getting connected to a Wi-Fi network is pretty simple, but the process will vary depending on the type of Wi-Fi network you're interested in. For the most part, you need to know whether the network is *open*—where anyone can join—or if it's a *secure* network, which requires a password. Let's look at the process for connecting to both.

Connecting to an Open Network

Most free Wi-Fi networks that you'll find in public places such as libraries and restaurants will fall into this category. Your own home network might also be open. Do this:

1. Tap the Launcher icon to display the Launcher.
2. Tap Wi-Fi (should be on the third page of the Launcher if you haven't moved it).
3. Make sure that Wi-Fi is turned on at the top of the screen. (As we already discussed, you can also turn it on from the status bar menu when the Pre is in Card view.)

4. From the list of available networks (depending upon where you are, several networks might be listed), tap the one you want.

That's it. In the future, your Pre will automatically connect to this network whenever it's within the coverage area—you won't have to do anything special.

Connecting to an Open Network That Isn't Broadcasting Its ID

Wi-Fi networks broadcast their name, called a service set identifier (SSID), so that you can do exactly what we just did in the preceding section—choose it from a list and say "connect me to that network!"

A rudimentary security precaution taken by some people who operate networks is to disable the SSID. The network is still open, but common Wi-Fi–enabled gadgets like laptops and mobile phones can't connect to it because it doesn't appear in the list of available networks. No problem. If you know the name of the network, just do this:

1. Tap the Launcher icon to display the Launcher.
2. Tap Wi-Fi.
3. Make sure that Wi-Fi is turned on at the top of the screen.

4. Tap Join Network.
5. Type the name of the network.

6. Tap Connect.

Connecting to a Secure Network

Some Wi-Fi networks aren't quite so...err...open. Your own home network, for example, *should* be password-protected to keep strangers from using your Internet access for free or possibly even stealing data from your networked PCs. Likewise, Wi-Fi hotspots that charge a fee restrict access by securing the network with a password. Here's how to get access to one of these networks:

1. Tap the Launcher icon to display the Launcher.
2. Tap Wi-Fi.
3. Make sure that Wi-Fi is turned on at the top of the screen.
4. If you see the network you want, tap it. Otherwise, type the name of the network you want to join, and select the type of security the network uses (Open, WEP, Enterprise, or WPA-Personal).
5. Enter the security information, such as username and password. You might need to get this information from the person administering the network.

Disconnecting from a Wi-Fi Network

Once you're connected to a Wi-Fi network, you don't have to do anything out of the ordinary. Your Pre will attempt to use the Wi-Fi network first and fall back to the your 3G (normal mobile wireless) connection if you go out of range of the Wi-Fi network, or if some other problem prevents Wi-Fi from being used.

If you want to stop using the Wi-Fi connection, just turn off your Wi-Fi radio. You can do that from the status bar menu , or you can open the Wi-Fi app from the Launcher. As we mentioned earlier, your Pre will always try to reconnect to a network if the Wi-Fi is turned on and you're in range.

But what if you really don't ever want to connect to that network again? That's also easy to fix. First, make sure you're connected to the network—be in range of the network so the Pre will log onto it. Then do this:

1. Tap the Launcher icon to display the Launcher.
2. Tap Wi-Fi.
3. Tap the network from the list.
4. Tap Forget Network.

The next time you're in range of this network, the Pre will not try to connect to it automatically.

Why would you want to forget a Wi-Fi network? Well, here's a good one: Suppose you go to the library and find that its Wi-Fi network is extremely slow, rendering your Web browsing experience sluggish and unpredictable. In fact, your 3G connection is faster. Well, drop that Wi-Fi connection out of your life and just use 3G in that location.

> **Dave vs. Rick: Apps We Can't Live Without on the Road**
>
> When we wrote this book, a pretty limited number of apps were available for the Pre. Nonetheless, we still found favorites for those long bus, train, and plane rides. What apps could we not live without while we're on the go?
>
> **Dave:** Rick is probably going to pick some travel-related app like Where, but for my money, it's gotta be Pandora. Why? I can't live without music, and the Pre doesn't have enough room to hold all my tunes, so I rely on Pandora. Tell Pandora what kind of music you like, and it'll play more songs that are in a similar style or genre. It's a great way to find bands and artists that you never heard of but that will soon become favorites.
>
> **Rick:** The app I absolutely positively must have while traveling is Shortcovers, which lets me read e-books, Amazon Kindle-style, while traveling. I'm really hoping to see a Pre version of the Kindle software (there's already one for the iPhone), as I'm not wild about Shortcovers. I'm also eagerly awaiting a Pre version of the eReader app, which I've used as far back as PalmPilot days. The upshot: I love having a good book with me wherever I go, and the Pre makes that possible.

Using Your Pre with a Bluetooth Headset

If you've been reading this book chapter by chapter, like a novel (spoiler alert: Rick is the real murderer—Dave couldn't have done it, because he was busy caring for those orphans, remember?), then you'll recall we talked about the benefits of Bluetooth back in Chapter 3. Bluetooth is an awesome technology because it lets you wirelessly connect gadgets, as long as they're within about 30 feet or so of each other.

While all sorts of Bluetooth devices are out there—mice and keyboards, game controllers, and even printers—the most common application for Bluetooth is the classic cell phone headset. You can use two kinds of headsets with your Pre (see Figure 6-2):

- A traditional in-ear or over-the-ear headset/microphone for hands-free calling.
- A stereo headset for listening to music. Some stereo headsets will also work with the phone for hands-free calling.

Pairing Your Headset with a Pre

Regardless of which kind of headset you have, you need to start by "pairing" it with your Pre. This process is a one-time, 30-second step in which you electronically introduce your headset to your phone, let them do a quick mating ritual, and thereafter they always connect to each other automatically. Here's what you need to do:

1. If your headset is brand new, start by charging it for a few hours.
2. Turn on the headset and make it "discoverable." You might need to check your headset's user guide for details, but, generally, you make a headset discoverable by pressing and holding the power switch for about 6–10 seconds, starting it from the off position.

FIGURE 6-2 Hands-free headsets provide simple monaural audio and a microphone for phone calls, while stereo headsets are great for music—and some can also do double duty for phone calls.

3. On the Pre, tap Launcher and then tap Bluetooth.
4. Make sure that Bluetooth is turned on at the top of the screen.

5. Tap Add Device. Your Pre will display discoverable Bluetooth devices.
6. Tap the name of your Bluetooth headset.
7. If it asks for a passcode, enter it.

Now you're all set—your Pre has paired with the headset, so you can immediately start using it. When you later turn on the headset again, your Pre will automatically connect to it—as long as Bluetooth is turned on.

Is your headset currently connected to your Pre? There's a quick way to find out. Tap the status bar menu, and then tap Bluetooth. You'll see your headset listed with a friendly green checkmark if they're currently paired, connected, and working together.

Did You Know?

Your Headset's Pairing Procedure

Most Bluetooth headsets have only one or two buttons, so a lot of features are packed into very few controls. Be sure to read the user guide that came with your headset for the full scoop—luckily, most headsets all tend to work the same way. Here's a universal guide to pretty much all the headsets we've seen:

- From Off, press the power button briefly to turn it on. In this mode, the indicator light will flash slowly or stay lit.
- From Off, press and hold the power button for several seconds (generally 6 seconds or longer) to make it "discoverable" so your Pre and other phones can connect to it. In this mode, the indicator light will flash quickly or alternate two colors such as red and blue.
- From On, press and hold the power button for several seconds to turn it off.

Not all headsets use pairing codes—many will connect directly to your Pre without your needing to type anything. But if your Pre wants a passcode before it'll connect to a new headset, check the user guide for the code. Can't find the guide, or you're too lazy to ask your kid to bring it to you? Four zeros—0000—is a very commonly used passcode for headphones. Try it; it'll probably work.

Finally, you might be happy to know that your Bluetooth headset does not have an exclusive relationship with your Pre. You can pair the same headset with multiple phones and also pair the same Pre with multiple headsets. This is especially handy, because it means you can, if you're so inclined, keep different Bluetooth headsets at home and at work, for example, and you can also share a headset with your spouse or partner.

Troubleshooting a Bluetooth Connection

Having trouble getting your headset to pair to your Pre? Here are some things you can try:

- Make sure you're in range. You should be able to pair up to about 30 feet away from the Pre, but putting the headset within a foot or so of the Pre will help a lot.
- Make sure the headset is discoverable. Your headset's indicator light will probably flash in an unusual pattern when in this mode to let you know it's discoverable.

If you've previously paired your headset with the Pre but it won't connect later on, here are a few tricks to get them to make up and work together:

- Make sure your Pre's Bluetooth radio is turned on (tap Launcher, tap Bluetooth, and make sure Bluetooth is set to On at the top of the screen).
- Make sure your headset is turned on and the battery has a good charge.
- Press the call button on your headset.
- If the obvious stuff is working, then open the Bluetooth app and tap the headset in the list of devices to tell them to connect manually.
- Now we're getting into Funky Problem Land. One quick fix for a lot of headset woes is to make your headset discoverable and pair it with your Pre as if it has never been paired before.
- If even that does not work, try the Thor's Hammer of fixes: Turn off your Pre (all the way by holding the power button down for 6 seconds and tapping Turn Off), wait a moment, and turn it back on again. Then try all the same troubleshooting steps again.

If all else fails, your headset might be dead—see if you can test your Pre with a different headset.

Using a Headset

Now that you've paired your headset, you're ready to rock and roll—literally, if you plan to listen to music, or figuratively, if you plan to listen to jazz. Or make a phone call.

As we mentioned earlier, different headsets have different capabilities. You can tell what your headset is able to do with your Pre by checking out the symbol associated with the headset's connection status.

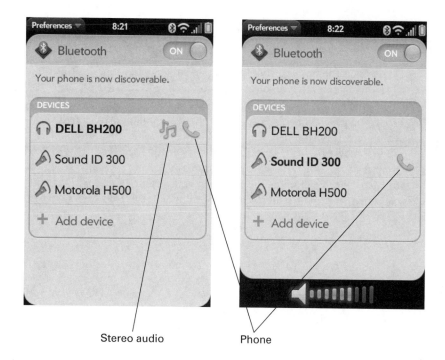

Stereo audio   Phone

As you can see, some headsets do only one thing, like handle the audio in a hands-free phone call. Other headsets, such as some stereo headphones, do both. If you have a stereo headset that handles both, that means it also has an integrated microphone for voice calls.

Once connected, you can use your Pre in the usual way, and audio will be directed to the headphones as appropriate. When using the stereo headphones, for example, all the audio from your Pre such as music, video, and other system sounds will play through the headphones.

If you're using a hands-free phone headset, all those stereo sounds will play through the Pre's built-in speaker (or through the wired headphones if you're using those) and only phone calls will be routed through the headphone.

If your stereo headset also supports phone audio, then you have the best of all worlds.

In most cases, you can also control the Pre using the headphone's built-in controls. On stereo headphones, for example, you can play and pause audio using the main play button on the headphones. Volume control should also work.

On hands-free headphone, you can end a call and redial the last call using the main control, as well as adjust volume.

Did You Know?

BING-411: An Essential Phone Number

If you're on the go, you should program this number into your Pre: 1-800-BING-411. This phone number, of course, connects you to the free, automated 411 services operated by Microsoft's Bing search engine.

This number connects you to a surprisingly comprehensive voice-operated search directory. You can search for businesses, and get traffic and weather reports, movie listings, stock info, and even the location of cheap gas stations. In most cases, Bing will read you information over the phone or optionally text it to your Pre. Combine BING-411 with your Pre's GPS and various apps, and you'll find that there's pretty much nothing you can't do with your Pre.

7

Your Pre on the Web

HOW TO...

- Access the Pre's Web browser
- Visit a Web site
- Use gestures to navigate
- Use navigation controls
- Rotate the page
- Bookmark a Web site
- Load bookmarked sites
- Reorder your bookmarks
- Import your desktop bookmarks
- Add Web sites to the Launcher
- Share Web pages
- Open multiple Web sites
- View your browsing history
- Tweak browser settings

Unlike the vast majority of smartphones on the planet, the Pre is really, really good at browsing the Web. It renders Web sites in such a way that you can actually read them, and it relies on simple gestures for scrolling, enlarging, and shrinking Web pages.

Of course, there's more to using the Pre's browser than just a tap here and a drag there. You need to learn how to work with bookmarks, how to add frequently visited sites to your Launcher for one-tap access, how to share cool sites with your friends, and so on. That's why we've devoted an entire chapter to the Web and how it fits in the palm of your hand. (Make that the Palm of your hand—hey, you knew we had to make that joke eventually.)

The Pre's browser app is called "Web." Pretty exciting name, huh? Much as we're loathe to keep referring to it as "the Pre's browser app," we're not going to call it "Web" (for obvious reasons), and we can't really name it "Frank" or anything like that. Palm's previous browser was called Blazer, a perfectly cromulent name. Couldn't the company have thought up something equally intriguing for the Pre's browser, like Zipper or Webby or Webster? Maybe Punky Brewster? Okay, now it's just getting weird. Well, what would *you* call it?

A Quick Note About Internet Connectivity

Like so many of the Pre's capabilities, the Web browser relies on an Internet connection. No Internet, no Web. Of course, as you know from reading Chapter 6, the Pre relies on two primary sources for Internet access: Sprint's wireless network and the Wi-Fi networks found in homes, businesses, and even some cities.

 By the time you read this, carriers other than Sprint may be selling and supporting the Pre as well. So we'd have to amend that previous sentence to include, say, "Verizon's wireless network."

This probably goes without saying, but you'll get the fastest connection from a Wi-Fi network. Of course, by default the Pre will access any Wi-Fi network that's in range, so you don't really have to do anything to ensure optimal performance as long as your Wi-Fi is turned on and connected. But you should be aware that Web pages might load a little slower than usual if you're not connected to a Wi-Fi network or if your Sprint connection is less than five bars. See Chapter 6 for details on how to use the Pre's Wi-Fi capabilities.

A Tour of the Pre Web Browser

To get to the Web, tap the Launcher app, and, if you haven't moved it, the Web app will be the second icon on the first page. When you first start the Pre's Web browser, you'll see a screen that looks like this:

Here you have two choices: You can tap one of the bookmarked sites (represented by thumbnail images), or you can start typing in the browser's address bar (see Figure 7-1). Because the former doesn't require much explanation (one tap and you're off to the selected site), let's focus on the latter.

As with any Web browser, you can type a URL (that is, a Web address, like www.rick-is-cool.com), press ENTER, and be on your way. So, for example, if you want to visit PC World, type **http://www.pcworld.com** and press ENTER. Or would you?

FIGURE 7-1   You can type a Web address into the browser's address bar or type a search term for Google or Wikipedia.

For one thing, you can skip the *http://* part and just start with *www*. The Pre's browser will automatically insert the *http* prefix. So now you're down to typing only **www.pcworld.com**.

But wait, there's more! Or, rather, less: You can skip the *www*, too. Just type **pcworld.com**, press ENTER, and you're off to the races. How's that for a time-saver!

Although you can leave off the *www* when entering Web addresses, you may want to substitute an *m*. For example, *m.gizmodo.com* takes you to that site's "mobile"

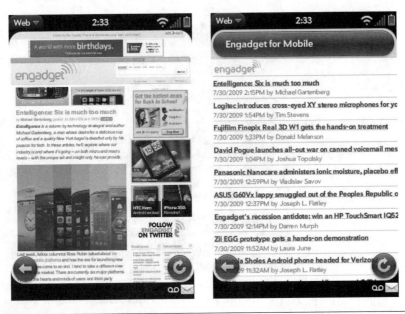

FIGURE 7-2 To see whether a mobile, Pre-optimized version of a site is available, try replacing the *www* in its address with *m* or *mobile*. Here you can see the standard and mobile versions of popular gadget site Engadget.

version, which is optimized for small, Pre-like screens (see Figure 7-2). Lots of sites work similarly, so experiment with adding an *m* prefix to Web addresses. That being said, some sites are smart enough to detect the presence of a smartphone browser like the Pre's and will automatically redirect you to the mobile version.

 If a mobile version of one of your favorite sites is available, consider bookmarking both it *and* the regular version. (You'll learn how to bookmark in the upcoming section, "All About Bookmarks.") Why bother with both? While the mobile version is optimized for small screens, it doesn't always have the full content of the "desktop" version. There may be times when you want to see the full content, even if it means a lot of scrolling and/or zooming.

Now that you know how to type in a Web address, let's take a look at how you'll navigate in and around Web sites. Get your fingers ready: It's tapping, swiping, and pinching time!

Navigating Web Sites

The Pre's Web browser isn't terribly different from Internet Explorer, Firefox, Safari, or whatever browser you use on your PC. Sure, it's smaller, and has fewer controls, and there's no mouse involved, and bookmarks don't really work the same way, but....

How to...   # Start Your Web Searches Without the Web Browser

When you want to search, say, Google or Wikipedia on your PC, your first step is usually to fire up your Web browser, and then type your search term(s) into the search box. As you've just learned, the Pre works similarly: You can run a search by starting the browser and then typing your term(s).

But there's a faster way.

Anytime the Launcher or Card view is visible, just start typing. As you learned in Chapter 5, this action invokes the Pre's Universal Search feature, which "rolls over" to Web searches when no match is found in the Pre's internal memory.

So, for example, suppose you want to search Google for "vegan chocolate-chip cookie recipes." You don't need to run the browser first; you can just type that at the Launcher or Card view screen, and then tap the Google button that appears.

As you can see, the Pre also provides other search-engine options, including Wikipedia and Twitter. So your search options aren't limited to Google.

Um, as we were saying, the Pre's Web browser is *very* different from Internet Explorer, Firefox, Safari, or whatever browser you use on your PC. But there are some fundamental similarities, such as links, back/forward buttons, bookmarks, and so on.

Gestures

Let's start with gestures, which take the place of certain actions that are normally mouse-driven. (If you need a refresher course on gesture functions and terminology, see Chapter 1.) You'll use four basic gestures with the Pre's browser:

- **Dragging**   Place your finger anywhere on the screen and drag it around to move the Web page accordingly. You'll drag mostly after zooming in on a page; it's not unlike scrolling up/down or left/right with your mouse.
- **Pinching out**   To zoom in, place two fingers on the screen and slowly move them apart (while keeping them in contact with the screen). You can do this with one hand or two, but we find that single-handed pinching works best.
- **Pinching in**   This works the opposite of pinching out, and is used to zoom out. Again, you place two fingers on the screen, but this time you slowly move them together.
- **Double-tapping**   Two quick taps of your screen zooms in on the location of the taps. If you're already zoomed in, two quick taps will zoom you out again.

Make sure to use the pads or tips of your fingers, not your fingernails. Anyone raised on PalmPilots probably used the latter, but the Pre's touch screen requires contact with your skin.

The best way to learn these gestures is to use them. So head to a site like pcworld.com, wait for it to finish loading (as reflected by the little blue-gray progress meter in the bottom-right corner of the screen), and then double-tap any spot on the screen to zoom in.

Next, try dragging around the page. Then pinch out to zoom in even further. Drag around some more. Now pinch in. Get the idea? Experiment!

Some sites optimized for iPhones will also work well on the Pre. For example, an iPhone-specific version of *The New Yorker* magazine (iphone.newyorker.com) also works with the Pre's Web browser. Type it in and enjoy some fine reading. And if you see other URLs with an *iphone* prefix, give them a try as well.

Navigation Controls

The Pre's Web browser has three onscreen controls that will prove familiar to anyone who's ever touched a desktop browser: back, forward, and stop/refresh. They appear in the bottom corners of the screen:

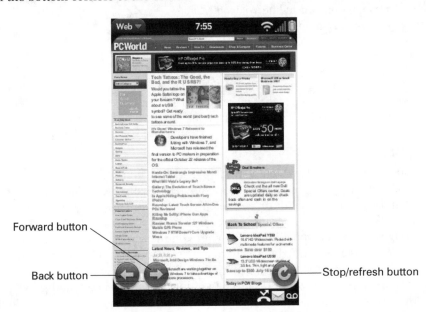

Tapping the back button takes you to the previous Web page, just like in a desktop browser.

You can also use the back gesture (you know, the one that happens *below* the screen) to go to the previous page.

Tapping the forward button takes you ahead one page, but the button appears only if you've previously tapped the back button. (In other words, you won't see the forward button if you have no place to go forward to. This will make more sense as you use the browser.)

The stop/refresh button has two functions. If you tap it while a page is loading (during which time it shows an *X* in the middle), that will stop the page-loading process. If you tap it after a page has loaded (or has been stopped from loading), it will refresh (that is, reload) the page. Again, this is pretty much identical to how desktop browsers work, though many of them have separate stop and refresh buttons.

Links

A link, of course, is an underlined (and usually blue-colored) snippet of text that, when clicked, takes you to another Web page. In the case of the Pre, you don't click with a mouse—you tap with a finger. A successful tap will produce a gray box around the entire link, and a second later you'll be off to the linked page.

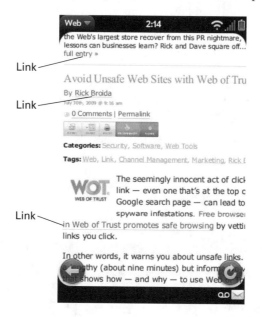

 While the Pre is pretty good at registering taps on links, you may want to zoom in a bit so you're sure to hit the right spot.

Landscape Browsing

Most computer monitors are wider than they are tall, yet Web sites are still designed with a "portrait" orientation. That means the Pre's taller-than-it-is-wide screen is actually perfect for viewing Web pages.

Well, sort of. It *is* pretty small, which is why you almost always need to zoom in when you want to read something. And when you do, it quickly becomes desirable to have a screen that's wide rather than tall.

No problem: Just turn the Pre sideways. As you can see in Figure 7-3, the screen quickly pivots accordingly. That's because the device has a built-in tilt sensor that determines orientation and rotates the screen to match. This works in a few other apps as well, including Photos and various third-party apps.

All gestures work the same whether the Pre is in portrait or landscape mode. To use the keyboard, however, you obviously need to be in portrait mode. At some point, Palm may add a soft (that is, onscreen) keyboard to work around this, but for now there's no easy way to enter data when your screen is sideways—unless you're proficient at sideways typing.

It doesn't matter if you turn your Pre left or right; the screen will rotate accordingly. (You can even turn it upside-down if you want, though this is no different from the standard portrait view.)

The Address Bar

When you use a desktop Web browser, the address bar (you know, the place where you type Web addresses) remains onscreen the entire time. And when you first start the Pre browser, the address bar is pretty much the first thing you see. But after you

FIGURE 7-3 Tip your Pre sideways to view Web pages in landscape mode, which is often better for viewing text and photos.

tap a bookmark or type in a URL and land on a Web site, you may have this reaction: "Hey! Where'd my address bar go?"

Don't worry, it's not gone—it's just hiding. And you can bring it back in two ways:

- *Start typing.* Just as Universal Search lets you load up Web pages straight from the Launcher or Card view, so does it appear when you start typing while viewing a page. The moment you start typing a Web address, search term, or whatever, the address bar appears. (An exception is if you've placed your cursor in a Web form, in which case any typing you do will produce text in that field.)
- *Drag down.* The address bar is still at the top of the screen, but the Pre hides it by default so you can see more of the actual Web page you're viewing. To access the bar, just drag your finger down (which has the effect of scrolling the page up) until it appears, and then tap it.

If you change your mind and want the address bar to disappear again, just drag or swipe up to scroll back down the page.

All About Bookmarks

A browser without bookmarks is like a peanut butter and jelly sandwich without bread: messy, annoying, and just plain hard to eat. Obviously, the Pre's browser lets you bookmark Web sites for future reference, but we'll be honest: It's a bit messy and annoying. For one thing, there's no way to sync your desktop favorites with your Pre favorites (not yet, anyway—Palm may well add this capability in a future operating system update). And it's not particularly easy to sort bookmarks, which insults Rick's compulsive need for order.

Still, with a little know-how and a few tricks, you can make the most of browser bookmarks. We'll start with the startup page.

 We tend to use the terms "bookmarks" and "favorites" interchangeably. Internet Explorer uses the latter to describe sites you save for later, while Firefox and the Pre's browser use the former. Tomato, tomahto.

The Browser Startup Page

As you learned at the beginning of the Web browser tour, the Pre browser's startup page shows the address bar up top and some thumbnail images below (see Figure 7-4).

FIGURE 7-4 The browser startup page shows the address bar and six preinstalled bookmarks—but the bookmarks get replaced over time with your most recently bookmarked sites.

These images represent six preloaded bookmarks for popular destinations, including Amazon, ESPN, and Sprint's rather lame news portal. However, this is not the actual browser-bookmark screen.

Instead, the startup page (the page that first appears when you first launch the Web app) contains links to up to 12 of the most *recently bookmarked* sites. (We say "up to 12" because until you start using the browser, you'll see only those preloaded six.) This may seem a little weird at first, and possibly a bit annoying, but it's actually quite convenient: Any site you bookmark is a site you probably plan to visit again soon, and the startup page facilitates that.

 Google's popular Chrome browser offers a similar feature, showing you thumbnails of the nine most recently *visited* sites each time you open a new tab.

Our only real complaint with the startup page is that you can't reorganize the thumbnails. That sort of makes sense given that it isn't a static page: It changes every time you bookmark another site. But we'd still like to be able to drag the thumbnails to different spots, perhaps to make the list alphabetical or put our three most-visited sites up top.

While we're waiting on Palm to cook up that feature, let's look at something much more important: how to create bookmarks in the first place.

Rick vs. Dave: Our Favorite Sites to Visit on the Pre

As all computer users know, the Web is a treasure trove of useful information, interesting reading, and everyday fun. Here's a list of the sites we visit most often on our Pres.

Rick: Obviously, I'm a huge fan of The Cheapskate blog on CNET (www.news.com/cheapskate), but that's because I'm the author of it. My other faves:

1. **Gizmodo** (m.gizmodo.com)—If there's a better site to find the latest gadget news (and some of the Web's funniest headlines), I haven't found it.
2. **TV Squad** (m.tvsquad.com)—A longtime favorite, this site serves up a generous daily helping of TV news, reviews, interviews, and the like.
3. **Slashfood** (www.slashfood.com)—A fantastic blog for food lovers.
4. **USA Today** (iphone.usatoday.com)—What can I say? I like easily digestible news.
5. **There, I Fixed It** (www.thereifixedit.com)—A laugh-out-loud (and frequently gasp-out-loud) collection of photos showing jury-rigged and "fixed" objects.

Dave: Wow, I'd never seen There, I Fixed It before. What an awesome site! Finally, Rick, you have proved yourself valuable to me in some small way. I suspect you'd like me to say, "Hey, folks, you should also check out Business Hacks, a cool site with tips, tricks, and tools for being more productive at work," since both Rick and I contribute to it. But I'm not a fan of shameless self-promotion, so I won't be bringing it up. Anyway, here are some of my favorites:

6. **Black 20** (www.black20.com)—My favorite site for funny videos. Be sure to watch every episode of Network. Just be warned: It has some adult language, so if that's not your bag....
7. **Garfield Minus Garfield** (garfieldminusgarfield.net)—Then you might like this site instead, which is the daily Garfield comic strip with the signature cat airbrushed out. The result is a strip about an apparently psychotic Jon Arbuckle who's desperately lonely and talks to himself.
8. **Engadget** (www.engadget.com)—Engadget is like Pepsi to Gizmodo's Coke. I prefer Pepsi.
9. **Snopes** (www.snopes.com)—Did your mom send you yet another highly improbable e-mail about Bill Gates giving you $5 for every email you send? Snopes is *the* destination for debunking myths, legends, and hoaxes.
10. Of course, my favorite site of all is **PC World's Digital Focus** (pcworld.com/blogs/id,6/digital_focus.html). It's a weekly column of digital photography written by a smart, funny, and good-looking dude.

Creating New Bookmarks

Let's say you visit a site you want to bookmark for later. It's an easy, desktop-like process:

1. Tap the Web button in the upper-left corner of the screen.

2. Tap Add Bookmark.

3. Review the title for the bookmark. If it's okay, tap Add Bookmark. If not, place your cursor in the Title field and make any necessary changes. For example, when bookmarking my Cheapskate blog, the title that appears is "The Cheapskate - CNET News." I elected to delete the latter half, largely because it seemed extraneous.

That's all there is to it. (Needless to say, if you change your mind about the bookmark, you can tap Cancel.)

If the title is so long that it won't fit in the Title field, you're probably wondering how you can move your cursor to the end. Simple: Tap once to place your cursor anywhere in the field, then hold down the ORANGE key and drag your finger to the right. Keep dragging until your cursor reaches the end of the title. (You may have to lift your finger, put it down, and drag again if it's a particularly long title.)

Using Bookmarks

Now that you've created a bookmark, how do you find it again? And, for that matter, how do you open any bookmarked site? This is so easy, we're not even going to number the steps: Tap the Web button, and then tap Bookmarks. Voilà! The Bookmarks page:

To open a site, just tap the bookmark.

Want to load a bookmark without visiting the Bookmarks page? While in the browser, just type the first few letters of the bookmark's name. Yep, it's Universal Search in action again! As you type, you'll see not only matching bookmarks, but also matching sites from the browser's history. (More on that in the upcoming section, "View Browser History.")

Organizing Bookmarks

While you've got the Bookmarks page open, let's look at some of the housecleaning chores you might want to do there. For example, there's no way to alphabetize your bookmarks automatically, but you can do it manually—or arrange them in whatever order you like.

Changing Bookmark Order   Want to put Rick's Cheapskate blog at the top of your bookmark list? Of course you do! Such shameless self-promotion must be rewarded. To move any bookmark to any position in the list, just tap and drag: Put your finger on the bookmark, and then slowly drag it up or down the screen. You'll see the other bookmarks move out of the way as you go. As you near the top or bottom of the screen, the list will scroll accordingly. Lift your finger when the bookmark is where you want it. Plop! It drops into place. Wash, rinse, and repeat with other bookmarks until the list order is to your liking.

Deleting Bookmarks   Want to delete a bookmark? It's a cinch: Just flick it to the left or right side of the screen, and then tap the Delete button that appears "underneath." Tap Cancel if you change your mind.

Renaming Bookmarks   If a bookmark title is so long that it doesn't fit on the Bookmark page, or you just want to rename it for some reason, you can easily make a change. Just tap the little "i" (short for "information") that appears on the right side of each bookmark. Then follow the same instructions you learned in "Creating New Bookmarks."

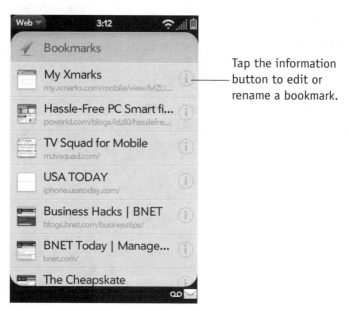

Tap the information button to edit or rename a bookmark.

 You can also use this screen to make changes to a site's address, if necessary.

Accessing Desktop Bookmarks

As you learned in Chapter 2, the Pre does a terrific job syncing certain kinds of data. Unfortunately, Palm has yet to devise a way for it to sync desktop bookmarks you've created in Internet Explorer, Firefox, or whatever browser you use on your PC. Fortunately, there's a simple solution: Xmarks.

Xmarks (www.xmarks.com) started out as Foxmarks, a Firefox add-on that allowed you to sync your bookmarks with other PCs. Then it became Xmarks, adding support for Internet Explorer and Safari. To this day, it's one of Rick's favorite services, and not just because it's free. Xmarks syncs both bookmarks and Web passwords between the desktop at home, the laptop at work, the netbook that goes on trips, and so on.

So how does that help Pre users? Simple: Xmarks also syncs your bookmarks to the Web, meaning you can access them from any browser—even one that doesn't have the Xmarks add-on installed, like the Pre's. Here's how to get started with the service:

1. Head to Xmarks and download the appropriate add-on for your browser.
2. After installing it, you'll walk through a few steps to create an Xmarks account. Make sure to make note of your username and password.

3. Once your account has been created, Xmarks will sync your bookmarks to the Web (where they remain private and password-protected, of course).
4. Load the Pre's browser and go to mobile.xmarks.com. Sign into your newly created account.
5. Bookmark the Xmarks site.

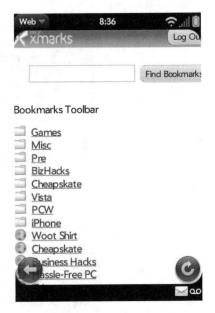

Presto! You've got easy access to all your desktop bookmarks. And whenever you add, remove, or change them on your PC, the mobile Xmarks site will be updated accordingly. The software keeps everything in sync.

Xmarks isn't the only game in town. Social-bookmarking site Delicious (www.delicious.com), which was formerly known as Del.icio.us, also offers Firefox and Internet Explorer add-ons that sync your bookmarks with the Web, and there's a Preoptimized mobile version of the Delicious site (m.delicious.com).

But we were giant fans of Xmarks even before we got our Pres, so that's how we're rolling. We can't recommend the service highly enough. Once you try it, you'll wonder how you ever got along without it.

Did You Know?

What the Pre *Can't* Do on the Web

The Pre's Web browser is pretty cool, but it can't do everything a desktop browser can. For example, if you were hoping to head to Hulu.com to watch episodes of *The Daily Show, 30 Rock,* and the like, you're outta luck: The Pre's browser can't handle Flash-based video (yet), which is the kind you find on the majority of streaming-video sites. Same goes for audio: You can't listen to music from, say, your favorite artist's MySpace page. (Of course, there are lots of other ways to listen to music on your Pre; find out all about them in Chapter 8.)

Also out: Web-based games. (And, let's face it: The Pre's screen is really too small for those kinds of games anyway.) Also also out: Any site or service that requires a special plug-in.

Of course, these limitations may not exist forever. We suspect that Palm will add Flash support to the browser at some point in the future, at which time you'll be able to get your Hulu on and do even more on the Web than you can already.

Opening Multiple Browser Cards

You know how your desktop Web browser lets you open multiple windows at a time so you can view multiple sites? You can accomplish the same thing on your Pre. When you want another browser "window," just open a new card. To do so, tap the Web button, and then choose New Card. Presto: a new instance of the browser appears, right at the startup page for easy navigation.

You can open as many browser cards as you want, keeping in mind that the more cards you have open, the slower your Pre will run. We recommend limiting yourself to three or four browser cards, maximum.

Add Web Sites to the Launcher

Sure, bookmarks are great for accessing your favorite sites, and Universal Search lets you load favorites just by typing in the first few letters of their names. But there's an even faster way to merge onto the information superhighway (wow, there's an antiquated term—how old *is* Dave, anyway?): You can actually turn a bookmark into a Launcher icon.

That's right! Now you can visit Rick's shamelessly self-promoted Cheapskate blog (www.news.com/cheapskate) with just *one* tap of the screen. Here's how to make it happen.

Load the site you want to immortalize with a Launcher icon. (It doesn't *have* to be Cheapskate. Rick's Hassle-Free PC blog for *PC World* is fine, too.)

1. Tap the Web button.
2. Tap Page, and then tap Add To Launcher.

3. Make any desired changes to the title, keeping in mind that only the first handful of words (roughly four to seven words) will fit beneath the bookmark's icon.
4. Tap Add To Launcher and you're done!

Here's what the Launcher looks like with a few choice bookmarks added to it:

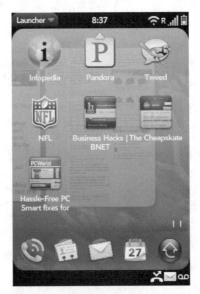

Obviously, you'll want to use Launcher bookmarks sparingly, as it's pretty easy to over-clutter the screen with icons. But this is really a great way to put your favorite sites just a tap or two away.

Share Web Sites with Friends

Want to tell some friends about this great Web site that showcases awesome technology bargains? Well, who could blame you! The Pre makes it a snap to share any site you've visited in the browser. Here's how:

1. Tap the Web button.
2. Tap Page, and then tap Share.
3. The Pre creates a new email with a link to the site and a thumbnail image of it.

4. Choose the recipient(s) from your address book (or type in an email address), add any message you want, and then tap the Send icon.

Pretty easy, huh?

View Browser History

Ever wish you could go back in time? Or at least find that cool Web site you visited yesterday, but now you can't remember its name or address? For all standard time-travel needs, we're partial to the build-a-time-machine-out-of-a-DeLorean approach. But for going back to your Web past, all you need is your browser's History feature.

See, like most desktop browsers, the Pre's browser keeps tabs on where you've been. Don't be alarmed—this is actually a very handy feature. To access it, just tap the Web button, and then tap History:

As you can see in Figure 7-5, the browser keeps a chronological list of all the sites you've visited, starting with the most recent. To see older entries, just scroll down the list (by flicking your finger up the screen, of course). To revisit any of these archived links, just tap one.

FIGURE 7-5 The Pre's browser lets you go back in time, so to speak, by keeping a list of all the sites you've visited. You can tap any site to return to it.

Clear Browser History

Every now and again, you may want to erase your browser's history. We can think of two possible reasons for this:

- The history file takes up space, and you need to free up some extra storage on your Pre. (It won't get you much, but, hey, every little bit helps.)
- You want to remove any trace of embarrassing Web sites you've visited, like Hello Kitty or Fox News.

Whatever the reason, you can erase the history with just a few taps. In fact, once you've loaded the history, as described in the preceding section, just tap the Web button and tap Clear History:

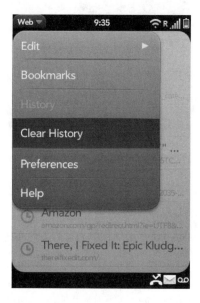

Because this is a permanent move, you'll see a warning message asking you to verify the action. Tap Clear History again to make it so, or tap Cancel if you want to reverse course. Keep in mind that the moment you erase the browser's history, it will start building a new one as you visit more sites.

Tweak Browser Settings

Finally, we come to the browser's Preferences, where you can tweak a handful of settings. It's unlikely you'll ever need to change the default settings, but you did buy this book to learn *everything* about your Pre, right?

To access the settings, tap the Web button, and then tap Preferences. You'll see this screen:

Let's run down the various settings therein:

- **Block Popups** If you've ever encountered pop-up windows in your desktop browser, you know how annoying they can be. That's why the Pre blocks them by default, though if you're having trouble using a particular site because it requires a pop-up window, you may want to turn off Block Popups temporarily. Just slide the little blue lever to the left, thereby changing the Yes to a No.
- **Accept Cookies** Mmm, cookies. Oh, sorry, not those kind. Browser cookies are tiny files that store information, such as the username and password you use to sign into various Web services. On the desktop, browser cookies often get a bad rap for being a security threat, but they're really not. That being said, if you don't want your Pre to retain that kind of information, set the slider to No.
- **JavaScript** JavaScript is a programming language that enables various Web features. We're hard-pressed to imagine a reason you'd want to turn this off.
- **Clear History** The Clear History button performs the same action you just learned about in "Clear Browser History."
- **Clear Cookies** Mmm, cookies. Oh, sorry, we're still thinking of the chocolate-chip variety. If you've decided to turn off Accept Cookies, you'll then want to remove the cookies already stored on your Pre. One tap is all it takes. (Well, two, really, if you count the subsequent verification tap.)
- **Clear Cache** If the browser seems sluggish, you may want to try tapping the Clear Cache button. It empties out all the other stuff your browser stores throughout its day.

8

Your Pre as a Jukebox

It's time to put the iPod in a drawer. Your Pre can do nearly everything an MP3 player can do (see Figure 8-1), and it can do some things even better. In this chapter you'll learn how to use the Pre's Music app, how to stock the device with your favorite tunes, and even how to use it as the world's coolest pocket radio. We'll also look at other audio options, such as podcasts and audiobooks. And we haven't forgotten music-enhancing accessories, such as headphones, earphones, and speaker docks.

Turn Your Pre into an MP3 Player

You can listen to music on your Pre in two basic ways. You can load MP3 files on the device itself, much as you would with an iPod or other MP3 player. Or you can leverage the Pre's Internet connection to stream music from the Web—not unlike listening to a radio. In this section, we focus on the former option: turning your Pre into the equivalent of an MP3 player.

FIGURE 8-1   Plug in a pair of earphones and your Pre does a fantastic impression of an MP3 player.

 If you're already familiar with MP3s and/or you already have a library of them, you can skip ahead to the section "Copying MP3s to Your Pre."

What's an MP3 Player?

Before we can answer that question, we need to answer this one: What's an MP3? You've probably heard the term before, but perhaps you've never really understood it. Here's the technical definition, as provided by Wikipedia:

> *MPEG-1 Audio Layer 3, more commonly referred to as MP3, is a patented digital audio encoding format using a form of lossy data compression. It is a common audio format for consumer audio storage, as well as a de facto standard of digital audio compression for the transfer and playback of music on digital audio players.*

Uh, what? Lots of words, there, but they don't make a lot of sense to laypeople like Dave. Here's a simpler definition of MP3:

> *An MP3 file contains digital audio, usually music.*

That's really all you need to know. Anyone over the age of 35 can think of an MP3 as the digital equivalent of a 45 rpm vinyl record, but in MP3's case, the song has been turned into bits and bytes. An MP3 player, therefore, is any device capable of playing those kinds of files.

Of course, when most people think of MP3 players, they think of iPods—but lots of devices can play MP3s, including computers, cell phones, and even some GPS navigation systems. And, of course, your Pre.

 While MP3s are the most popular and widely used digital-audio format, another format is also worth mentioning: AAC (Advanced Audio Coding). The Pre can play AAC songs just like it plays MP3s, which is good news for anyone acquainted with Apple's iTunes Store—which sells only AAC-formatted tracks.

Where Do MP3s Come From?

There are two primary sources for the MP3s you'll load on your Pre:

- **CDs** Remember those? The process of converting audio CDs to MP3 files is called *ripping,* and you can do this on any PC that has a CD-ROM drive (or, for that matter, CD burner, DVD drive, and so on) and the right software. Read on to learn how to squeeze hundreds of your CDs onto your Pre.

- **Online music stores** These days, we buy most of our music online. You've probably heard of Apple's iTunes Store, which is where iPhone and iPod owners buy music for their devices. Although Apple employs a different file format for its music (AAC, not MP3), the Pre can play those files. However, we generally prefer to get our tunes from a different source that's built into the Pre: Amazon MP3. You can purchase songs right on your device, or you can buy them on your PC and copy them over. Read on to learn more about both options.

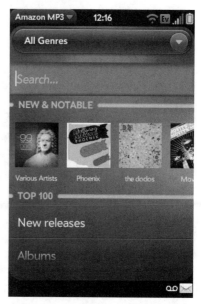

Got a bunch of old LP records and/or cassettes lying around? You can rip those too. A little Googling will help you find all the information you need to make it happen.

How to Rip CDs

Ripping a CD is easy—all you need is the right software. Fortunately, Windows has a perfectly good tool built right in: Windows Media Player. (Mac users can do the job with iTunes, but for purposes of this chapter, we're going to focus on Media Player.)

Before we get started, bear in mind that ripping takes time. How much time depends on the speed of your computer and CD/DVD drive, but plan on at least a few minutes for each disc. If you have a substantial collection of CDs—say, 50, 100, or even more—you might need to block out an afternoon to rip the entire thing.

 This is a great job for kids. Pay a teenager a quarter per CD (or whatever rate you think is fair) to transfer your music collection to your PC.

Here's how to rip a CD using Windows Media Player. (Our instructions and screenshots are based on version 11. If you have an earlier version, most of the steps will be similar, if not identical.)

1. Start Windows Media Player.
2. Click the Rip button.
3. Click the tiny arrow below the Rip button to reveal a drop-down list of options.

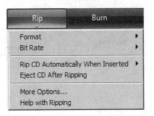

4. Click Format, and then MP3 (because we want WMP to turn the tracks into MP3s, not another digital-audio format).

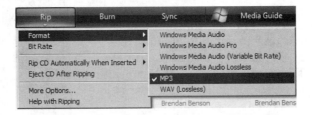

5. In the same menu, click Bit Rate, and then click 256 Kbps. (The higher the rate, the better your MP3s will sound—and the larger your files will be. Fidelity snobs like Dave would insist on 320 Kbps, the highest bit-rate setting, but Rick thinks most users will be perfectly happy with 256 Kbps. And remember that your Pre

has a finite amount of storage space, so smaller files equate to more music you bring along.)

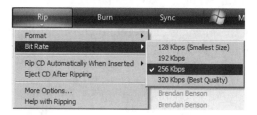

6. Insert your CD into your computer's CD or DVD drive. Windows Media Player should start the ripping process automatically. If it doesn't, click the Start Rip button.

When the process is completed, you'll be able to locate your newly ripped MP3s in the Music folder (or My Music if you're using Windows XP).

Now pop out that CD, pop in the next one, and keep on rippin'! We'll discuss how to get your newly ripped MP3s onto the Pre later in this chapter.

Note   This was a very basic overview of CD ripping in WMP. If you want a more detailed explanation of the process, you can find it online. Just search for "how to rip CDs in Windows Media Player," or visit this handy how-to guide at About.com: http://tinyurl.com/d6zrq2.

Did You Know?

How Many MP3s Can a Pre Hold?

In an ideal world, your Pre would have enough storage space to hold every song you own. In reality, it has only 8 gigabytes (GB), and some of that space gets allocated to apps and data. Needless to say, we're sad that Palm decided not to outfit the Pre with a microSD memory-card slot, which would let you significantly expand the available storage. Maybe future models will have that feature; they'll almost certainly have more internal memory.

In the meantime, let's figure out just how many MP3s will fit on your Pre. It's all about math: The average MP3 ripped at a bit rate of 256 Kbps (Rick's preferred bit rate) requires 6MB of space. That means if you have 100 MP3s, they'll consume roughly 600MB of your Pre's memory.

Extrapolated even further, you could fit around 1000 songs (or 100 albums, assuming 10 songs per album) into 6GB of Pre storage. That would leave you a couple gigabytes for apps, photos, and other stuff. Of course, if you don't care about other stuff, you can probably squeeze close to 1300 songs onto your Pre.

On the other hand, if you're more of a casual music listener, or you'd rather devote your Pre's storage to other things, you can always stream music instead. Find out more in the upcoming section "Listen to Streaming Music."

How to Buy Music from Online Stores

CDs are *so* 20th-century. These days, it's faster, easier, cheaper, and even more environmentally friendly to buy your music online.

Faster, because the music is delivered to you almost instantaneously. No waiting a week for a disc to get shipped to your mailbox. No wasting time (and gas) driving to and from your local music emporium. (Assuming you even *have* a music emporium in your area. Most of them are now Orange Julius franchises.)

Easier, because there's no ripping involved: The music arrives on your PC in MP3 form.

Cheaper, because the average MP3 album costs $8 to $10, while CDs still sell for anywhere from $12 to $18. What's more, you can buy individual MP3s, usually for 99 cents apiece. With CDs, you have to buy the whole album—even if you want only a song or two.

More environmentally friendly? It's true. CDs are tangible goods, requiring manufacturing, materials, transportation, storage space, and so on. Digital downloads require none of these things; they're just bits and bytes transferred and stored electronically. (Come to think of it, the same goes for e-books. More on that in Chapter 10.)

You can buy MP3s for your Pre from several sources. Let's start with the most obvious: Amazon.

The Amazon MP3 App

Believe it or not, an MP3 store is built right into your Pre. You've probably discovered it by now: The Amazon MP3 app connects you to Amazon's eponymous Web store (see Figure 8-2). You can use the app to browse and search the store, listen to 30-second song snippets, and purchase music—which gets downloaded to your Pre on the spot. (Talk about instant gratification!)

You can also buy MP3s online from other places (see the upcoming section, "Other MP3 Stores"), but we think the majority of users will be happy with Amazon. It has great selection, competitive prices, and the convenience of being built into your Pre!

Let's get started with the Amazon MP3 app. To get to it, tap the Launcher and navigate to the second page, and the app should be on the top left if you haven't moved it. When you first start it, here's what you'll see.

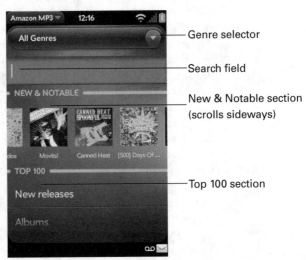

Genre selector

Search field

New & Notable section (scrolls sideways)

Top 100 section

FIGURE 8-2   Amazon's Web-based MP3 store offers a huge selection of music. You can download songs to your PC and then copy them to your Pre, or use the Pre's Amazon MP3 app to download songs directly.

You interact with the Amazon MP3 app in two main ways: browsing and searching. For example, you might want to browse the albums listed in the New & Notable section, which you can do by swiping your finger across the album covers (first left, and then right to go back). In fact, this is a great way to get familiar with how the app works. Tap any album cover, and you'll see a screen much like this:

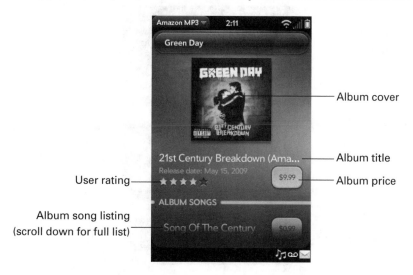

This screen offers several options:

- **Buy the album**   When you tap the album price button, it transforms into a Buy button. Tap that, and you can purchase—and download—the album right on your Pre. You'll need to provide your Amazon account email address and password as instructed. Don't have an Amazon account? Head to the site on your PC and create one.

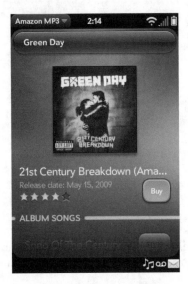

- **Listen to song samples**   Not sure this is the same cool track you heard on the radio? Like the Web-based Amazon MP3 store, the Amazon MP3 app lets you play a 30-second snippet of any song. Just tap the song name (not the price button) to start listening; you'll see a progress bar move across the name as it plays. Tap the song name again to pause playback.

- **Buy individual tracks**   You'll have to scroll down a bit to see the full track list, but otherwise this works just like buying an album: Tap the price button next to the track name, tap the Buy button that appears in its place, and then supply your Amazon account info.

There's just one tiny wrinkle when it comes to downloading music to your Pre: You must be connected to a Wi-Fi network. If you're not within range of one, the Pre can't download the selected album or songs, as you can't download songs over Sprint's cellular network.

If you want to see music downloads in action without spending any money, try grabbing some of Amazon's thousand-plus freebie tracks. Although there's no easy way to find them from within the Amazon MP3 app, you can peruse the listings on Amazon's site (http://tinyurl.com/ nqbeya), and then search for any particular track within the app. Try Apples in Stereo's "Energy," a bubbly little pop track. Search for it, "buy" it (don't worry, it's a freebie), and then switch over to the Music app to play it.

Above the New & Notable section you'll see a genre selector and a search field. The latter is pretty self-explanatory: Type the name of a song, artist, or album, and then tap the magnifying glass icon (or press ENTER) to run the search. The results screen will look something like the screen at right.

As you can see, search results are typically divided into three sections: Artists, Albums, and Songs. Tap any listed item to see more. Eventually, you'll reach a song and/or album page where you can sample and buy tracks.

 Note As with all Pre apps, don't forget about the back gesture: it returns you to the screen you were viewing previously. See Chapter 1 if you need a refresher course in gestures.

How to... Copy Amazon MP3 Purchases Back to Your PC

Just because you buy a song on your Pre and download it to your Pre doesn't mean it has to stay on your Pre. Indeed, you might just want to copy that song to your PC for listening while you're at work. Or copy it to your spouse's Pre—or even to another MP3 player. (This is the beauty of unprotected downloads—you're free to use them as you please.)

Whatever the case, you can copy your Amazon MP3 purchases from Pre to PC in two easy ways. The first is USB mode: Connect your Pre to your PC with the included USB cable, and then tap USB Drive from the menu that appears on the Pre's screen. From

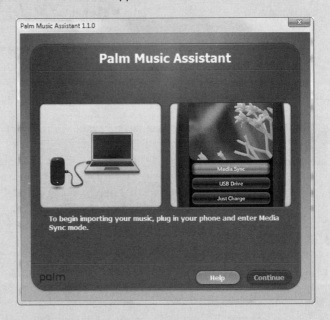

there, you can simply open the Pre's AmazonMP3 folder on your PC and drag the tracks to a music folder on your PC. For more on using the Pre's USB Drive option, see Chapter 6.

Your second option, which is a little more automated, is the free Palm Music Assistant utility for Windows (http://tinyurl .com/lop2sd). This program serves a single purpose: to copy Amazon MP3 purchases to your PC and add them to your iTunes library. (iTunes? Yep. See the upcoming section, "The Pre and iTunes: On Again, Off Again.")

The very simple instructions for using Palm Music Assistant are spelled out on the same screen where you download it, so we won't rehash them here. It suffices to say that if you buy music on your Pre and decide to use iTunes for music management, this utility is well worth your time.

The Genre Selector The genre selector appears at the top of the Amazon MP3 app's main screen. When you tap it, you'll see this list:

 It's not immediately obvious, but you can scroll up and down this list as you would any other.

It's important to note that choosing a genre affects everything that appears below the selector. For example, if you choose Alternative Rock, the New & Notable section will change to reflect what's new and notable in the alt-rock genre. Likewise, when you tap into any of the Top 100 sections (New Releases, Albums, and so on), you'll see selections only for the selected genre.

What's more, any search you run will deliver results based on the selected genre. While selecting a genre can be helpful for certain kinds of searches, we tend to leave the selector on All Genres most of the time.

Other MP3 Stores

Amazon MP3 isn't the only game in town. If you're looking for other sources for music, check out these sites, all of which sell unprotected MP3s (except for iTunes, which sells unprotected AACs).

- **Amie Street (www.amiestreet.com)** This mostly indie music store offers a "dynamic" pricing system, meaning every song debuts with a low price (or even no price) that goes up as more people buy it—but never more than 98 cents.
- **eMusic (www.emusic.com)** Long before iTunes and Amazon started selling DRM-free music, eMusic led the charge with unprotected MP3s. Once an indie-only destination, eMusic has added the likes of Arcade Fire, Bruce

Did You Know?

What About iTunes?

Apple famously put digital song downloads on the map. And, to this day, iTunes is the world's largest music store. If you've ever owned an iPod or iPhone, you've probably purchased music from iTunes. Which begs the question: Can you play your iTunes purchases on your Pre?

No. And yes.

See, as we discussed earlier, the Pre can play the AAC-formatted songs sold by iTunes. (It can also play songs ripped from CDs in the AAC format.) However—and this is a big however—if you purchased any songs prior to April 2009, they may be saddled with Digital Rights Management, or DRM, a form of copy protection that Apple has since abandoned. (Good riddance.) Unfortunately, while DRM-protected songs will play just fine on an iPod, they won't play on your Pre—not without a little tweaking, anyway.

Your best bet is to take advantage of an option built into iTunes: Upgrade to iTunes Plus. This automatically replaces any DRM-saddled tracks in your library with DRM-free equivalents. The upgrade will cost you a few bucks (exactly how much depends on how many affected tracks you have in your library), but it's definitely the fastest and easiest solution.

The Upgrade to iTunes Plus option removes the DRM protections from songs you've purchased.

The other option is to burn your protected songs to CDs, and then rip them back to your library in MP3 or unprotected-AAC format. That's both time-consuming and slightly damaging to your songs, however, as the process of uncompressing and recompressing them degrades their overall audio quality. But it won't cost you anything, other than the price of some blank CDs.

You might still have another question about iTunes: Can you use it to sync your existing song library and/or playlists to your Pre? Surprisingly, yes! That excellent question requires its own section, "Syncing Your Pre for the First Time," a bit later.

Springsteen, and the Dixie Chicks to a catalog of more than 6 million songs. But tunes aren't sold *a la carte*: subscriptions start at $11.99, which gets you 24 downloads per month. You can get audiobooks here, too.

- **iTunes (www.apple.com/itunes)**   Yep, you can buy music from the same store that caters to iPods and iPhones. You will, however, need to install the iTunes application on your PC. That's not necessarily a bad thing, as you may be able to sync your Pre with it directly. Find out more in the upcoming section, "Syncing Your Pre for the First Time."
- **Lala (www.lala.com)**   Lala is only part music store. While you can buy MP3s at competitive prices, you can also stream any song or album free of charge—one time. (Alas, this is PC-only streaming for now; there's no way to do it on your Pre.) Want to listen to your personal song library on other computers? Lala lets you do that, too. Neat service.
- **Napster (www.napster.com)**   MP3 fans will remember Napster as the file-sharing service that sparked the MP3 revolution—and quite a few lawsuits. These days, Napster is a legitimate online music store with an interesting subscription option: $5 per month buys you five MP3s per month, plus unlimited music streaming on your PC. You can buy additional music *a la carte*, but you must be a subscriber to do so.
- **Rhapsody (http://mp3.rhapsody.com)**   The MP3-store branch of Rhapsody's music-subscription service offers a wide selection and average prices ($9.99 for most albums, $1.29 for most tracks).
- **Walmart (http://mp3.walmart.com)**   While 99 cents is the average price per MP3 these days, Walmart's online store sells many new and top-100 tracks for 94 cents, and many albums for $8 to $9. You can also find a good selection of older albums for under $7.

Rick vs. Dave: Our Favorite Bands

We have vastly different tastes in music. Consequently, we tend to argue about it more than any other subject. Of course, we'll try to keep it cordial for you.

Rick: While Dave tends to favor harsh, blaring guitar riffs and singers with raspy, unpleasant voices, I enjoy music that actually sounds good. Admittedly, I have fairly mainstream tastes, as you'll see from my list of favorite artists:

- *Coldplay.* I don't know what it is about Chris Martin's voice, but I can listen to Coldplay's catalog all day, every day, and never get sick of it.
- *Brendan Benson.* A terrific solo artist before he joined forces with Jack White as part of The Raconteurs, Brendan (I call him by his first name because we're buds— at least in my head) belts out some of the best power-pop hooks and lyrics in the biz. Just try to keep your head from bobbing along during "Spit It Out."
- *Green Day.* I consider *American Idiot* to be one of the greatest punk-rock albums of all time. There's not a bad track on it. And the rest of Green Day's catalog ain't bad, either.

(continued)

- *Amy Winehouse.* Despite being a train-wreck of a human being, Winehouse created one of my all-time favorite albums: *Back to Black.* Soulful and sexy, it's the best Motown collection that didn't come from Motown.
- *Lily Allen.* I realize this choice squanders any last bit of man-cred I may have had, but I really dig her Brit-pop hooks and acerbic lyrics.

Dave: Rick's musical palette is similar to my 16-year-old daughter's. Actually, scratch that—my daughter actually has excellent taste in music, but Rick is interested only in the sort of saccharine-sweet, by-the-numbers, radio-friendly bubblegum churned out by soulless music marketing machine drones that many people also find appealing. But that's okay. That said, here are some of my favorites:

1. *The Beatles.* Modern music starts and ends with these four lads from Liverpool. They redefined popular music and created musical tapestry that 40 years later is still being explored and reinterpreted by musicians.
2. *Kristin Hersh.* As the chief architect of Throwing Muses, she is the very embodiment of alternative rock. Kristin's music is challenging and mesmerizing—every note is unique, every chord is interesting—and the lyrics speak to me in a way that seems almost supernatural.
3. *White Stripes.* All hail to Jack and Meg White for making the blues relevant again. I could listen to the White Stripes nonstop for weeks and not get tired of their low-tech, garage rock sensibilities. And Jack has simply got to be the best lyrical storyteller alive today.
4. *Velvet Underground.* "I'm Waiting for the Man." "Heroin." "All Tomorrow's Parties." "Pale Blue Eyes." "I'll be Your Mirror." "The Murder Mystery." *Wow.*
5. *Black Rebel Motorcycle Club.* An awesome combination of psychedelia, blues, and garage-rock grunge. Awesome.

Copying MP3s to Your Pre

Though you may download the occasional song or album from Amazon, for the most part you'll want to stock your Pre with MP3s stored on your PC. You can go about this in several ways, including dragging and dropping MP3 folders in disk mode, syncing your Pre with a third-party program, and using Palm's Music Assistant utility.

Each option has its pros and cons, so let's examine them in turn—starting with, believe it or not, Apple's iTunes.

The Pre and iTunes: On Again, Off Again

As you may know, iTunes (see Figure 8-3) is the music-management software used to sync Apple's iPods and iPhones. It also provides the gateway to the iTunes Store, where you can buy and download music. Surprisingly, Palm engineered the Pre so that it can work with iTunes, meaning the latter effectively recognizes the former as an iPod. Consequently, you can use iTunes to copy songs, playlists, podcasts, photos, and even videos to your Pre.

Did You Know?

Why Not Use USB Mode and Drag My Music to My Pre?

If your Pre can double as a USB flash drive (as discussed in Chapter 6), why not just drag your music files and folders to the phone instead of mucking around with iTunes or MediaMonkey?

Why not, indeed! This process, sometimes known as *sideloading*, accomplishes more or less the same thing as syncing with iTunes: It copies your songs to your Pre. And the Pre's Music app is smart enough to find music on the device regardless of how it got there. So if you'd rather not go to all the trouble of installing iTunes or another program, you can just sideload your music and be on your merry way.

However, there's a difference between copying and syncing. iTunes, MediaMonkey, and the like give you a way to *manage* your music, not just copy it. These programs let you create playlists, sort your music collection by any number of criteria, and so on. They also make it *way* easier to move music on and off your Pre.

For example, let's say you have two playlists, each one with about 7GB-worth of music: Top-Down Classics and Classical Favorites. It's a rainy day, so instead of driving around with the top down, you're headed to the coffee shop to curl up with a good book. With iTunes, it's a simple matter to remove Top-Down Classics from your Pre and replace it with Classical Favorites. Without iTunes (or a similar music manager), you'd have to do a ton of dragging and dropping. iTunes also has the advantage of showing how much space is available on your Pre.

Bottom line: If you plan to keep the same chunk of music on your Pre for weeks or months at a time, sideloading is fine. If you want an easy way to swap out songs, artists, albums, playlists, and more, a music manager is a must.

Name:	Palm Pre
Capacity:	6.69 GB
Software Version:	1.0
Serial Number:	XXXXXXXXXX
Format:	Windows

FIGURE 8-3   iTunes may have been built with iPods and iPhones in mind, but it does a fine job managing music on the Pre.

This may come as a shock, but Apple is none too pleased about Pres using iTunes. (The company prefers to reserve the iTunes "ecosystem" for Apple products. Go figure.) In fact, shortly after the Pre's introduction, Apple released an iTunes update (version 8.2.1.6, if you're interested) that disabled Pre syncing. Shortly after *that*, Palm released WebOS 1.1, which restored the capability. As of this writing, it's Apple's move. Time will tell whether iTunes/Pre syncing remains a viable option. We hope so, as iTunes really is a great way to manage and sync your media.

iTunes isn't your only option for Pre media management—see the section, "An iTunes Alternative: MediaMonkey"—but we do think it's the best. So let's take a look at how you'll use the program with your Pre.

Before we get started, however, we should note that iTunes is such a "big" program, with so many features and options, we could easily fill a separate book on it. In fact, someone already did: Check out *How to Do Everything: iPod, iPhone & iTunes, Fifth Edition* by Guy Hart-Davis (McGraw-Hill/Professional, 2009) if you want to become a master of the app. In this book, we focus on Pre-specific areas, mostly because our editors would kill us if we tried to add another 200 pages.

Installing iTunes

If you don't already have iTunes installed on your computer, you'll need to install it. Don't worry, because it's free, and although Apple asks for an email address, you don't even need to provide one. You can download iTunes here: www.apple.com/itunes.

After downloading the installer, run it, and then follow the setup instructions. It's all pretty straightforward.

If you're already using a different music manager (such as Windows Media Player), you may be tempted to uncheck the option Use iTunes As The Default Player For Audio Files during setup. We recommend enabling this option, as it'll make your life easier when syncing your Pre.

The first time you run iTunes, it will ask if you want to add MP3, AAC, and/or WMA files to your iTunes library. Feel free to let it do so, keeping in mind that it will search for these files only within Windows' default music folder. That's fine if that's where you store them, but if you keep them elsewhere, you'll have to add them to iTunes manually. Here's how:

1. In the Library section, click Music.
2. Choose File | Add Folder to Library.
3. Navigate to the folder that contains your music. (In Rick's case, for example, it would be C:\MP3s.)
4. Click OK, and then wait while iTunes imports all your songs. (This could take awhile depending on how much music you have.)

With step 4 done, it's almost time to connect your Pre. But, first, you might want to create a playlist or two. In fact, we consider this a fairly essential next step.

The Importance of Creating Playlists

A playlist is exactly that: a list of songs you want to play. They're incredibly useful for divvying up songs based on mood, tempo, artist, and just about any other criteria you can think of. If nothing else, a playlist is great for corralling all your favorite tunes—for those times when you want to hear just the cream of your own crop, not your entire library.

Where the Pre is concerned, a playlist has more practical value: You can use it to cull your music collection to a viable size. See, as we discussed back in "How Many MP3s Can a Pre Hold?", your Pre has only a fixed amount of storage space. You can't copy a 20GB music collection to a Pre with only, say, 6GB available. And that's where playlists come into, well, play.

What you can do is create a playlist that fits the confines of your Pre. Then, instead of syncing your entire library (which flat-out won't work due to the Pre's limited memory), you can sync just that playlist.

You'll also want to use playlists to manage any podcasts and/or audiobooks you want to bring along. We'll talk more about that in the section "Podcasts and Audiobooks." In the meantime, here's how to create a playlist in iTunes:

1. Choose File | New Playlist. Or press CTRL-N on your keyboard. Or click the little plus sign in the lower-right corner of the iTunes window. Same result.
2. You'll see "untitled playlist" appear in the Playlists section. Type in a descriptive name and press ENTER.

That's it! Bet you thought it would be a lot more complicated, huh? Now that you've created your playlist, you'll want to add songs to it. Here's how:

1. Click the Music option in the Library section.
2. Find the song, album, or artist you want, and drag it to the newly created playlist and drop it. Repeat as desired.

Tough, huh? Keep in mind that you're not actually moving songs; you're merely designating them as part of that particular playlist. The songs themselves stay exactly where they are on your hard drive. (And when they get copied to your Pre, as described in the next section, that's exactly what's happening: copies are being made. You're not *moving* the music from PC to Pre.)

The other great thing about playlists is that they can overlap. In other words, suppose you create one playlist called Rock Favorites and another called Blues Favorites. It's no problem to put, say, Brian Setzer into both playlists. Playlists can include whatever songs you want, even if those same songs are already in one or a dozen or a hundred other playlists.

That said, things can get a little confusing when it comes time to sync your playlists—so let's move on to that exciting process.

Syncing Your Pre for the First Time

To sync your Pre with iTunes, you're going to need two things: your USB cable and a good 10 minutes of undivided attention (for the first sync, anyway). Let's run through the process, stopping along the way where we need to explain things.

1. Start iTunes. By now you should have added some music to your library and created at least one playlist of tunes you want to sync to your Pre (unless your library is small enough that the whole thing will fit).
2. Plug your USB cable into a USB port and then into your Pre.
3. Tap the Media Sync button on the Pre's screen.
4. After a few seconds, iTunes should recognize the Pre, at which point you'll see it listed in the Devices section. It will also immediately start copying over your entire music library—assuming the Pre has enough room to hold it all. If it does, just wait for the process to finish, and then disconnect your Pre and fire up the Music app. If it doesn't, you'll see a message indicating your Pre can't be synced. That's okay—it's why you created a playlist, remember?

If your Pre can't accommodate your entire music collection, you'll need to configure iTunes so it copies only selected playlists—such as those you set up in the preceding section. Here's how:

1. Make sure that Palm Pre is highlighted under the Devices section. If not, click it.
2. Click the Music tab near the top of the iTunes window. You'll see that All Songs And Playlists is enabled.
3. Click the Selected Playlists radio button (the little circle).
4. Choose one or more playlists in the box below.

5. Click the Sync (or Apply) button (at the lower-right corner of the screen) to copy the selected songs to your Pre.

When iTunes has finished syncing (wait for the "OK to disconnect" message in the status window), you can disconnect your Pre, run the Music app, and start enjoying your new MP3 player. See "Using the Music App" for more details. Or stick around to learn about adding podcasts and audiobooks to your Pre.

Podcasts and Audiobooks

Even Dave can't listen to music 24/7 (though he does like to drift off to Miley Cyrus at night, and his alarm clock plays Hansen's "MMMBop" in the morning). Fortunately, the Pre can serve up spoken-word audio when you're ready for a music break.

Specifically, it can play podcasts—which we like to describe as "radio shows to go"—and audiobooks. In fact, iTunes is a great source for both: Just browse your way into the iTunes Store and click the Audiobooks or Podcasts links to see what's available.

Before we go any further, however, we need to make you aware of a few important caveats:

- *As of this writing, the Music app lacks an auto-resume feature.* That means if you stop listening to an audiobook or podcast somewhere in the middle, you can't automatically pick up from where you left off. You can fast-forward to try to find the right spot, but that's a slow and frustrating process.
- *As of this writing, the Music app doesn't differentiate between audiobook/podcast files and music files.* Consequently, if you like to shuffle-play your music, you'll inevitably hear some of your spoken-word programs mixed in with your tunes—not a welcome situation for most listeners. (Fortunately, playlists offer a workaround for this problem—see "Playlists Save the Day" for details.)
- *While iTunes' podcasts are compatible with the Pre (meaning you can copy them over as easily as you copy music), its audiobooks are not.* Consequently, you'd have to burn any audiobook purchases to CDs, and then rip them back to your PC in MP3 or AAC format—major hassle. So major, in fact, that we're going to focus mostly on podcasts in this section, as they're a more viable option for the Pre. You *can* listen to audiobooks, but until Palm adds auto-resume and support for iTunes' audiobook files, we think it's more trouble than it's worth.

Because we're such huge fans of podcasts, we're hoping that Palm has worked out at least some of these issues by the time this book reaches your hands. In the meantime, here's how to subscribe to a podcast in iTunes and then add it to your Pre.

1. Start iTunes.
2. Click the iTunes Store link in the left column.
3. Click the Podcasts link in the iTunes STORE box.

4. Browse the selection until you find a podcast that looks interesting (we highly recommend *This American Life*), and then click it to load its description page.

5. Click the Subscribe button.

By default, iTunes will immediately download the most recent show, but you can get more by clicking Podcasts (in the Library section of the iTunes interface), clicking your newly subscribed podcast, and then clicking Get Next to each older show you want to download.

 Some podcasts, such as *This American Life,* limit you to the current week's show, meaning you can't download the back catalog.

Now it's time to sync your podcast(s) to your Pre. Here's how:

1. Make sure that Palm Pre is highlighted under the Devices section. If not, click it.
2. Click the Podcasts tab near the top of the iTunes window.
3. Check the Sync box, and then click the pull-down menu next to it.

4. Choose a timing method for podcast synchronization. For example, you might want to bring along all episodes of your podcasts, or opt for 3 Most Recent to help save storage space on your Pre.

5. Click Sync (lower-right corner) (or click Apply) and wait for your podcasts to get copied to your Pre.

 The average 1-hour podcast consumes a little less than 30MB of storage space, so you can carry lots of them without making much of a dent in your Pre's memory. Rick routinely walks around with upwards of 20 podcasts in his pocket—four episodes each of his five favorite shows.

Playlists Save the Day   Although the Pre can't yet distinguish between podcast audio files and music files, it *is* smart enough to funnel all podcasts into an automatically created playlist called—hold on to your hats—Podcasts. That not only makes podcasts much easier to find within the Music app, but it also helps keep them segregated from your music.

While you can't just fire up the Music app and tap Shuffle All (you'll get an unwanted mix of music and podcasts), you can create a playlist containing all your music (as explained earlier in the chapter) and shuffle-play *that*. Problem solved!

PrePod: A Homebrew Podcast Alternative   Given the Pre's limitations when it comes to podcasts, you'd think that third-party software developers would step in with a solution. And you'd be thinking right: PrePod is a third-party app that will download your favorite podcasts directly to your Pre, and then let you listen at your leisure— complete with auto-resume!

PrePod is free, but you won't find it in the App Catalog—not yet, anyway. That's because PrePod is a "homebrew" app, meaning it requires a bit of hoop-jumping to install. You can find out all about homebrew apps in Chapter 10.

Rick vs. Dave: Our Favorite Podcasts

We're podcast junkies. We listen to them almost as often as we listen to music. Here's a rundown of our favorites.

Rick: This might be one area where Dave and I agree a little bit, though I suspect his choices will be of the highly geeky, non-informative variety—unlike my entertaining and/or brain-enriching picks:

- *This American Life*
- *A Prairie Home Companion*'s News from Lake Wobegon
- *The Moth*
- NPR: *All Songs Considered*
- *The New York Times* Book Review

Dave: Interesting list, Rick. But unlike you, I don't listen only to stuff that's been officially sanctioned by *The New York Times* and NPR. (If I am ever forced to listen to more than 5 minutes of Garrison Keillor, I would gladly beat myself to death with my own Pre.) I couldn't pare my list down to five.... Here are the six I listen to frequently:

- *Wait Wait... Don't Tell Me!*
- *Circuits with David Pogue*
- *The Mike Rosen Show*
- *Ask a Ninja*
- *The Skeptic's Guide to the Universe*
- *The Onion* Radio News

Tip For now, PrePod really is the best way to listen to podcasts on your Pre, as it circumvents the problem of iTunes-supplied podcasts getting mixed in with your songs, and it bookmarks your playback spot so you can return to it later. Granted, there's some extra work involved in adding your favorite shows, but once that's done, you're all set.

An iTunes Alternative: MediaMonkey

We've always loved anything with "Monkey" in the title. (Just mention The Monkees to Dave and he'll fall down laughing.) And we've always loved MediaMonkey (www .mediamonkey.com), a music-management program that's a fine alternative to iTunes. Granted, it doesn't have a built-in music store, but if all you want is a simple way to organize your music library and sync it with your Pre, MediaMonkey is definitely worth a look. In fact, you can look at it in Figure 8-4.

There's one important difference between iTunes and MediaMonkey: The former relies on the Pre's Media Sync mode, while the latter uses USB mode. There's not

FIGURE 8-4   MediaMonkey helps you organize your music library, create playlists, and sync songs to your Pre.

much real-world difference between them: Media Sync was implemented primarily so the Pre could trick iTunes into thinking it (the Pre) was an iPod.

MediaMonkey is free. Although a $19.95 Gold version is available, that's probably overkill for most Pre users. We've found the free version more than up to the task.

Note   The Pre can sync with just about any music-management program that supports USB-mode devices. We've used it successfully with Winamp and Windows Media Player. So if you're not an iTunes fan and don't want to make the switch to something like MediaMonkey, your favorite app may work just fine with the Pre.

Using the Music App

Now that you've loaded up some music, it's time to learn your way around the Music app, which is located on the first page of the Launcher app (provided you haven't moved it).

There's nothing too complicated here, but we'll run through some basics in case this is your first time using an MP3 player.

Shuffle all audio files on the player

View your music library sorted by artist

View your music library sorted by album

View your music library sorted by genre

Open the Amazon MP3 app

View all your songs in alphabetical order

View your playlists

Let's take a closer look at each of the options on the Music app's main screen:

- **Shuffle All**   One tap and all your songs start playing in random order. This is a great way to listen to music—unless you have podcasts on your Pre, in which case they'll become an unfortunate part of the mix. That's why we're fans of the aforementioned PrePod app, which effectively keeps podcasts separate from your music so you can shuffle-play with ease.
- **Artists**   Want to see all the songs by Green Day? Or Coldplay? Tapping this option gives you an artist-sorted view of your music library. Tap an artist to see a full list of songs—and a Shuffle All option that will randomly play just the songs by that artist.

- **Albums**   No surprise here: It's your music library sorted by album title. Tap any album to see its song list. Tap any song to start the music playing, or tap Shuffle All if you want to hear that album in random order.

- **Songs**   All your songs in one big list, again with a Shuffle All option up top. Again, don't be surprised to see your podcasts on this list—unless you've downloaded them with the PrePod app, that is.

- **Genres**   Looking for classic rock? R&B? Soundtracks? Here's the place to sort your songs accordingly. However, the usefulness of any genre-based list depends on how your songs and albums are "tagged," and in our experiences, genre tags

are impossible to manage effectively. For example, what's Coldplay? Pop? Pop/
Rock? Adult Alternative? Heck, some might call it Easy Listening. Bottom line: We
rarely bother with the Genre option.

- **Playlists**   This is the place to access whatever playlist(s) you created in iTunes,
  including podcasts. Note that when you tap through to see a playlist's contents,
  you'll get the ubiquitous Shuffle All option followed by a random-order song list.
  Within a playlist, you don't have the option of sorting by album, artist, song name,
  and so on.

- **Amazon MP3**   Here's your quick ticket to the Amazon MP3 app. You can access
  it from here or from the Launcher; same result.

In any music list, you can quickly search for an artist, album, song, or whatever, by tapping out the first few letters on the Pre's keyboard. That's a music-specific implementation of the Pre's Universal Search feature (see Chapter 5).

Play Controls

Listening to music on your Pre is pretty much the same as listening to music on any other audio player. It has onscreen controls for pausing, fast-forwarding, and so on. You can toggle shuffle-play on and off, and you can quickly skip ahead to other songs. Let's take a closer look at the Music app's controls.

Here's an example of how things look after the music starts:

If some of these controls aren't immediately clear, well, you've come to the right page in this book:

- **List view**   Tap this icon to see a list of all the songs currently queued for playback. As you'll see, a progress meter slowly scrolls across the current song, along with count-up/countdown timers on the right side. If you ever need to fast-forward or rewind a song, this is a good way to get a visual read on the "location." This is also a great way to skip ahead to a specific song in the queue: Just tap it to start listening.
- **Album cover view**   If you want something a little more colorful, the Pre can show the album cover for the current song. You can swipe your finger left or right on the album covers to switch quickly to the previous or next song, respectively, in the queue.

In this view, the entire screen (most of it, anyway) doubles as a play/pause control. You can tap the album cover, the song name, or anywhere else with no button or other control.

- **Shuffle toggle** You already know about the Shuffle All option, but you can also activate or deactivate shuffle-play while listening to your music. Just tap the icon to toggle shuffle on (blue) or off (black).
- **Repeat toggle** This "toggle" actually has three positions: Repeat forever, repeat once, and off. It affects whatever songs you currently have queued for playback.
- **Previous track/rewind** The button with the two left-pointing arrows serves three functions. A single tap returns to the start of the currently playing track. A double-tap returns to the previous track. And if you tap and hold the button, it rewinds the song—slowly at first, but faster and faster the longer you hold it.
- **Next track/fast-forward** The button with the two right-pointing arrows serves two functions. A single tap takes you to the next track in the list. And if you tap and hold the button, it fast-forwards the song—slowly at first, but faster and faster the longer you hold it.

 If you switch to another app while music is playing, you'll notice a small musical note icon in the notification area at the bottom of the screen. Tap it to bring up player controls you can use without switching back to the Music app! This also works with the Pandora app, as discussed in the upcoming section, "Listen to Streaming Music."

Menu Options

The Music app hides a few intriguing options in its pull-down menu, which is accessible by tapping the Music menu in the top-left corner of the app:

Actually, when you're looking at the Music app's "home" screen (the one that shows Artists, Albums, Songs, and other options), that menu doesn't show much. But when a song is playing, a tap of the Music menu reveals two nifty options (plus Edit and Help):

- **Amazon MP3**   So you're listening to a Brendan Benson track and thinking, "Wow, that sounds great. I wonder what else is in the guy's catalog." A tap of the Amazon MP3 option switches you to the eponymous app and runs a search for the currently playing artist.

- **YouTube**   Same deal here, except that you can quick-search YouTube for either the artist or the track title.

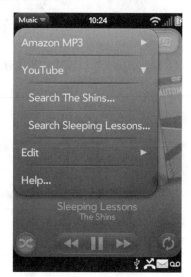

Now that you've mastered the Music app, let's look at another way to listen to tunes on your Pre: streaming Internet radio.

Listen to Streaming Music

Given that the Pre has only a handful of gigabytes for storing music (yes, now is a good time to again bemoan the lack of a memory-card slot), you may get tired of hearing the same small batch of tunes over and over. Granted, you can always swap one batch for another (playlists!), but even that can feel confining.

Fortunately, there's a cool way to listen to a lot more music on your Pre: Internet radio, also known as streaming audio. See, just like regular radio, the Internet can carry music over the airwaves, meaning you're not limited to whatever songs can fit in the Pre's memory. And thankfully, a Pre app makes Internet radio an awesome reality: Pandora.

Using the Pandora App

Universally adored by music fans, streaming-music service Pandora (www.pandora.com) is sure to be equally adored by Pre users, who can get in on the action with the nifty Pandora app (see Figure 8-5). Like its Web-based counterpart, Pre's Pandora app creates custom "radio" stations based on a selected artist, song, or even classical composer. In other words, it lets you create a custom station based on what you like, and it serves up more music it thinks you'll like just as well.

FIGURE 8-5 Without a doubt one of the best apps in the App Catalog, Pandora streams custom radio stations to your Pre.

After downloading Pandora from the App Catalog (see Chapter 10 if you're not already familiar with installing new apps), find the icon in the Launcher and give it a tap. You'll see this screen:

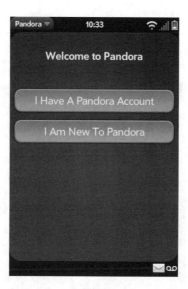

If you've already signed up for the Web version of Pandora (something we highly recommend—you'll love it!), tap the top button and enter your registered email address and password. If not, tap the bottom button to create an account right on your Pre. Don't worry: It's free! Just enter a few bits of information, and then you'll see this:

Now for the fun part. Start typing in the name of an artist, song, or composer. You'll notice that the Pandora app starts showing search results immediately as you type. For example, here's what happened when we tapped out "Brendan" (as in Benson, one of Rick's favorites):

When you see the artist/song/composer you want, tap it, and then break out the headphones! Like some magical genie, Pandora immediately starts playing the music you want:

As you can see, Pandora looks a lot like the Music app, but with a few differences in the controls:

- **Station list**   Tap this button to return to the station list screen, where you can select a different station or create a new one.
- **Information**   Displays biographical information about the current artist or song. Drag your finger up the screen to scroll the text.

- **Thumbs up/down**   Like the song Pandora selected for you? Tap the thumbs-up icon. Don't like it, and don't want to hear it again on this station? Tap thumbs-down. This is how Pandora "learns" your musical preferences and customizes your stations accordingly. Note that if you tap thumbs-down, the app immediately skips to the next song.
- **Options**   The little triangle sandwiched between the thumbs-up/down buttons reveals a list of options, most of which are self-explanatory. The bookmark options save songs and artists in your Pandora profile, which, for the moment, is accessible only via the Web version of the service. If you tap one of the Buy options, you'll get bounced over to the Amazon MP3 app.

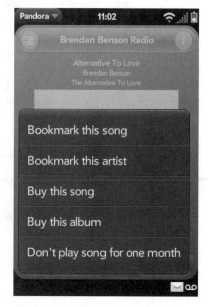

- **Skip** Not in the mood for the current song? No problem: Just tap the Skip button. However, Pandora limits you to six skips per hour, per station. You're also limited to 12 total skips per day.

 Because Pandora relies on "full-time" Internet access (be it Wi-Fi or your carrier's network), it'll drain your Pre's battery quite a bit faster than the Music app. That's really the only downside to this stellar app. Need more power? See Chapter 11 for information on spare batteries and other solutions.

Other Streaming Audio Options

Pandora is awesome, but it doesn't deliver the Holy Grail of streaming audio: your own music library. For example, an app called Simplify Music lets you listen to every song stored on your PC, effectively eliminating the problem of limited storage space. As of this writing, however, it's available only for the iPhone. We have our fingers crossed that the developers will release a Pre version, or that another developer will design a similar app.

In the meantime, check out Net2Streams, a homebrew app (see Chapter 10) that connects with hundreds of "traditional" Internet radio stations. It was a little rough around the edges when we tested it, but with just a few taps we were streaming everything from blues to Top 40 to public radio.

Fans of the famous SHOUTcast, which catalogs thousands of Internet radio stations, will be glad to know that the Pre can stream *some* SHOUTcast stations. Just fire up the Pre's Web browser, head to http://classic.shoutcast.com, and then tap the little yellow Tune In button next to any station. This site looks pretty cluttered on the Pre's small screen, but with a little careful swiping you should be able to navigate well enough.

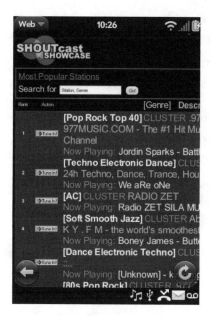

  Some SHOUTcast stations just won't play on the Pre. The only way to tell which ones will play is through trial and error.

Headphones, Earphones, and Other Audio Accessories

The Pre comes with a fairly decent headset that's fine for listening to music (and taking phone calls when they come in). However, if you're serious about music, you may want to treat your ears to something a little better. Because the Pre employs a standard 3.5 mm headphone jack and offers stereo Bluetooth, it's compatible with a huge assortment of headphones, headsets, earphones, and other audio accessories (including speaker docks).

To learn about those goodies and other Pre accessories, skip ahead to Chapter 11.

Rick vs. Dave: Our Favorite Songs

Rick: Trying to choose my five favorite songs is like trying to choose my five favorite TV shows: can't be done. So this is merely a list of five songs I absolutely love. It's by no means complete.

1. "Feel Like Myself," Brendan Benson
2. "Mad World," Gary Jules
3. "Viva La Vida," Coldplay
4. "Step Into My Office, Baby," Belle and Sebastian
5. "Ain't No Sunshine," Bill Withers

Dave: Five favorite songs? What moron thought up this category? You might as well ask me what my favorite kid or my favorite cat is. Actually, my favorite cat is Hobbes, so okay, I'll give this a shot:

1. "I am the Walrus," The Beatles
2. "Pearl," Throwing Muses
3. "I'll Be Your Mirror," Velvet Underground
4. "Overground," Downpilot
5. "Ball and Biscuit," The White Stripes

9

Lights, Camera, Action

HOW TO...

- Use the Camera
- Browse photos
- Get photos onto your Pre
- Share photos from your Pre
- Take screenshots
- Watch video on your Pre
- Get video onto the Pre
- Delete videos

Rick spends most of his time lying on the couch, eating Funyuns, and watching his "picture stories" on the television, while Dave is more interested in creative pursuits; for example, film and TV producer J.J. Abrams is rumored to have relied heavily on Dave's insights to create the hit television show *Lost*, and at least one person claims that Dave ghost-wrote several of the songs on Brendan Benson's latest album.

But you know what? There's something in the Pre for both of us. No matter whether you want to create content or consume it, you'll want to read this chapter. Here, you'll get the skinny on how to use the Pre's camera, browse and share photos, and even how to watch video on your phone.

Using the Pre's Camera

Let's start with one of the Pre's brightest stars: Its 3-megapixel digital camera. It's located on the back of the Pre—turn it over and you can see the lens and the small LED flash.

Flash ——————
Lens ——————

Using the camera is pretty straightforward. Start the Camera app (tap the Launcher and then Tap Camera on the first page).

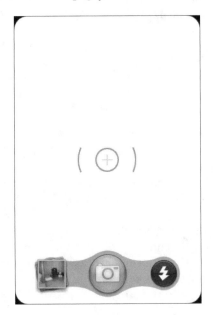

You can take a picture in two different ways—do whichever is more convenient:

- Point the Pre at the shot and tap the green camera icon.
- Point the Pre at the shot and press the SPACEBAR on the keyboard.

Congratulations! You've taken a picture.

You can take a photo with the camera in any orientation. With the phone in a vertical position, you'll take "portrait" photos. With the phone in a horizontal position, your photos will be "landscapes." Notice that as you turn the phone, the three buttons on the Phone app's screen turn accordingly.

 The Pre's camera uses a fixed-focus lens rather than one that can auto-focus. That means it will take reasonably sharp photos over a broad range of distances, but it can't take close-up (macro) photos. You'll need to be at least 12 inches away from your subject to take a photo, and if you're too close, the Pre will not warn you if the subject is out of focus.

Using the Flash

Unlike many phones, the Pre has a small built-in flash. The flash is useful for illuminating dark scenes at close range, and it can help you take pictures otherwise impossible to achieve with a camera phone.

The flash has three controllable modes, all adjusted using the Flash button to the right of the green Camera button. Just tap the button to change the mode, and keep tapping until it lands on the setting you want:

AUTO	Auto	The default flash mode, good for most purposes. In this mode, the Pre will fire the flash when it determines that you need more light to expose the photo properly.
⚡	On	Photographers sometimes call this "force flash." The flash will fire whether you need it or not. This is handy if you're taking a picture of someone outdoors; the flash can help illuminate the subject's face, which would otherwise be cast in shadow from sunlight.
⚡	Off	You don't need no stinkin' flash. Turning it off prevents the flash from firing. This can help save your battery and is handy if you're shooting in a dark room on purpose (such as to photograph a ghost, we suppose) and don't want a flash brightening the scene.

The flash can help you get sharper and better color-balanced photos, though, even in scenes where you think there's enough light already. Compare the two images in Figure 9-1. The one on the right, taken with a flash, is noticeably sharper than the no-flash photo.

We suggest that you just leave the flash turned on—that'll give you the best all-around results. But remember that the flash is quite small and will have little to no effect on subjects that are more than about 4 feet away.

FIGURE 9-1 The same scene taken without the Pre's flash (left) and with the flash (right)

Taking a Self Portrait

So far, the 21st century is pretty much defined by coffee stands on every street corner, Facebook, and people using their cell phones to take self-portraits. (Soon, it will also be defined by the horrific Robot Apocalypse, but let's not get ahead of ourselves. Enjoy Facebook. While you can.)

The Pre can definitely help you with the self-portrait thing, which, in turn, you can use on Facebook. See how it all comes together?

You'll see a handy little mirror on the back of the Pre when you slide open the phone. Hold the Pre at arm's length in front of you, making sure you can see yourself in the mirror, and snap away—you'll be framed in the photo.

Dave vs. Rick: Top Ten Uses for the Pre Mirror

Dave:

10. Drive safely even if your car's rear view mirror falls off.
9. Discreetly make sure Rick isn't following you. (Again.)
8. Cast reflections on the wall to entertain your cats.
7. It's like having a funhouse mirror—in your pocket!
6. Handheld vampire detector.

Rick:

5. Check your teeth for spinach.
4. Watch for sneak attacks from behind.
3. Signal rescue planes from the beach where you crash-landed.
2. Start a fire.
1. Check again: The spinach is still there.

Keep in mind that when you're holding the Pre in front of you with the touch screen facing away, it can be tricky to press the Camera button to trigger the shutter release. Instead, press the SPACEBAR on the keyboard. It's much easier.

Taking Time-Lapse Photos

The Pre doesn't (currently) let you shoot video, only still photos. That's a big bummer. It doesn't necessarily mean, however, that Palm won't upgrade the camera after this book is published to allow video recording. For all we know, if you're reading this book by dim candlelight to hide from the robots, your Pre might already be video capable.

Assuming that you're stuck with only still photos from your Pre, we thought you might like to know that you can assemble a series of still photos into a time-lapse animation, and that's kinda fun, too. You can create a time-lapse video that strings together photos taken on your Pre over a large span of time or photos taken one after the other, in a very short period of time.

Here's what you can do:

1. Take some photos. If you want to take a series of photos as quickly as possible, press and hold the SPACEBAR as you shoot. As long as you hold down the key, the Pre will continue taking photos.

 For even faster shutter action, turn off the flash.

2. Copy the photos to your PC. For details on how to do that, see "Copying Photos from Your Pre to Your PC" later in this chapter.
3. Add the photos to a video editing program. We recommend using Windows Live Movie Maker, which is free (you can find it at http://download.live.com) and easy to use.

4. If you take our advice and give Movie Maker a shot, select all the photos and click the Edit tab.

5. Set the Duration field to a fairly small number. It can be as small as 0.03 second per photo. We've gotten good results with numbers between 0.03 and 0.1 second.

6. Finally, save your movie or upload it to YouTube and wait for the Sundance Film Festival awards to come rolling in.

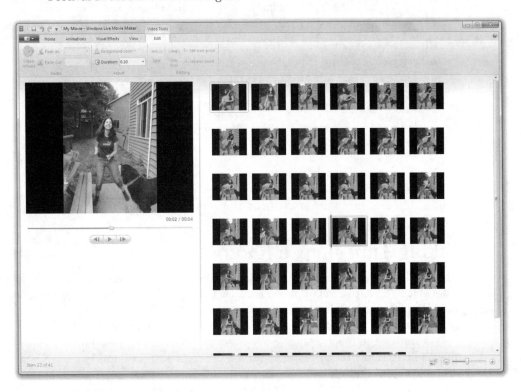

Browsing Your Photos on the Pre

As you take pictures with your Pre's camera, they're automatically added to the Photo roll folder in the Photos app. That means you can browse your photos on the Pre at any time. You can then reach your photos in two ways:

- If you're already in the Camera app, tap the Photos button to the left of the green Camera button. Wait a moment, and the Photo roll folder opens automatically, so you'll be looking at your photo collection.
- Tap the Launcher, and then, on the first page of apps, tap Photos. Then tap Photo Roll. You'll see thumbnail images of all your photos. Tap the first photo—or, in fact, any photo—to see the image appear full-screen.

You'll see something like this:

The menu bar with these three icons disappears after a few seconds, so it does not obscure the photo itself. To see the menu at any time, just tap anywhere in the photo.

Getting Around in Your Photo Collection

You can navigate around your photo collection using the gestures you have come to know and love. (See "Using Gestures" in Chapter 1 if you need a refresher.)

- **Change photos**   Swipe your finger to the left or to the right across the photo to move to the previous and next entries, respectively, in your Photo roll.
- **Zoom in for a closer look**   Use two fingers to pinch in and pinch out to zoom in or out, respectively, for a view of photo details. Alternately, you can double-tap the photo to zoom in immediately to the maximum level of magnification, and double-tap again to zoom back out to the full view.
- **Go back to see the entire photo roll**   Use the back gesture in the gesture area below the touch screen to go back to the thumbnail view. This is handy to quickly find a specific photo in a large photo collection.

Don't forget that the Pre will orient the photo correctly no matter how you hold the phone. So if you're looking at a landscape photo, for example, it will appear relatively small, compressed into the narrow width of the display. You can rotate the

Pre to switch between portrait and landscape views, so when you turn the phone, the picture will automatically rotate so it is in the correct orientation:

Deleting Photos You Don't Want

You needn't keep photos on your Pre forever. To delete a photo, just tap the Delete Photo button at the top-right of the screen. You'll get a warning that the photo is being permanently deleted. Tap Delete, and then, well, true to its word, the Pre permanently deletes your photo.

Keep in mind that even if a photo has been deleted, if you had earlier chosen to use the photo as your Pre's wallpaper or if you selected it as a picture for a contact, the photo will continue to appear in those places even after you delete the photo from the Photos app.

Sharing Photos from Your Pre

Your Pre gives you a lot of ways to use and share your photos. Just tap that Sharing menu in the upper-left corner, and you'll see this:

Each items works pretty much the way you'd expect it to:

- **Assign To Contact**   Tap this menu item to see your contacts list. Choose a contact and you'll have the opportunity to zoom and frame the photo to taste. Tap Set To Contact to save this photo as the picture for that contact.
- **Set Wallpaper**   Tap Set Wallpaper to open the wallpaper selection screen. Zoom and frame the photo, and then tap Set Wallpaper to save this photo as your new Pre background image.
- **Share Via Email**   Tap this entry to open a new email message with the photo already automatically attached. Then just address the email, type in a message, and tap Send. You can also specify the account from which the email will be sent.
- **Share Via MMS**   Similar to Share Via Email, this automatically attaches the photo to an MMS (for Multimedia Messaging Service) message—just assign it to a messaging contact, type your message, and send it.
- **Upload**   This provides one-tap uploads to online services such as Facebook or Photobucket. If you've already configured the Pre with your account information, just tap Upload and then tap the desired account.

If your Facebook or Photobucket account isn't yet configured, you can set it up from within the Photo app. Make sure that you are in the thumbnail view (use the back gesture in the gesture area if you need to get there) and then open the app menu.

Tap Preferences & Accounts, and then tap Add An Account. Then enter your username and password.

 All of these sharing options are two-step processes—that is, you'll need to confirm each one with at least one additional tap—except Upload. As soon as you tap your account name, the photo is immediately uploaded to the Internet.

Copying Photos from Your Pre to Your PC

As you just saw, you can do a lot with your photos while they remain on your phone. But the nice thing about your Pre is that it's easy to move those photos from the phone to your PC as well. Once your photos are on your computer, you can use them as wallpaper for Windows, send them in email messages, and do all the other things you'd do with photos from your ordinary digital camera.

Here's what you need to do:

1. Connect your Pre to your PC using the Pre's USB charging cable. We've said it before, and we'll say it again: Be careful to insert the USB cable into the Pre

properly, with the divot on top. It's possible to insert the cable upside down, and you really don't want to do that. You'll see this screen on the Pre:

2. Tap USB Drive. The Pre's screen will change to a static image. Set it aside—you don't need to use the Pre anymore for a while.
3. You should see the AutoPlay dialog on your PC. Click Open Folder To View Files.

If the AutoPlay dialog doesn't appear, you can do this manually: Choose Start | My Computer. Under Devices With Removable Storage, double-click Palm Pre.

4. In the Palm Pre's open folder, double-click DCIM. Then double-click 100PALM.

You should now see all of your photos. You can selectively copy just the photos you want from this folder to a location on your computer, or, if you prefer, you can drag the entire folder to your computer.

 When you connect the Pre to your computer, you'll find that your photos aren't organized the same way they are in the Photos app—there's no folder called Photo roll, for example.

When you're done, don't disconnect the USB cable right away. In Windows' Notification Area (also known as the system tray), right-click Safely Remove Hardware And Eject Media.

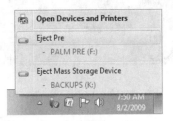

Wait for the balloon message that tells you it's safe to remove the Pre before you disconnect it.

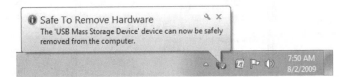

Deleting, Adding, and Organizing Photos Using Your PC

Instead of de-cluttering your photo collection using the controls built into your Pre, you might find it easier to do this with a mouse and keyboard. In other words, you can manage your Pre's photos using your PC while the Pre is tethered to it via the USB cable.

With the 100PALM folder open (using the steps discussed in the preceding section), you can delete photos using your computer keyboard's DELETE key.

Delete a photo (or even the entire 100PALM folder) and they're permanently removed from your Pre.

If you really want to get rid of all your photos, don't worry about just eliminating the whole folder. The next time you take a picture with your Pre's camera, the Pre will automatically create a new 100PALM folder for you, like magic.

You can also rename the 100PALM folder, create new folders on your Pre and add photos there, or generally do anything you'd ever want to do on your own computer to organize your photos. If you create a folder (named, say, Kids, and fill it with photos of your pet goats), then when you next open the Photos app on your Pre, you'll see an entry for that folder. This is a great way to organize your photos and make it easy to find and show off special photos using your phone.

Take Screenshots of Your Pre's Display

Every once in a while you might want to take a screenshot of your Pre's display. You might want to show off a screen for all sorts of reasons. Perhaps you're writing a book on the Pre and need to illustrate how to perform tasks to millions of readers who hang on your every word. (Dave and Rick are unfamiliar with this phenomenon, but we suppose it's possible.)

More likely, you just want to send a screenshot in email or incorporate it in a Word or PowerPoint document. No matter what your end goal, you can easily take a screenshot on the Pre.

Notice, though, that there's no PrintScreen (Prt Sc) button on the Pre as on most keyboards. Instead, you need to press and hold SHIFT-ORANGE and then press P. It might seem like a bit of a feat of gymnastics to get all three of those tiny keys, but we can assure you we've done it a few hundred times now, and it isn't terribly difficult.

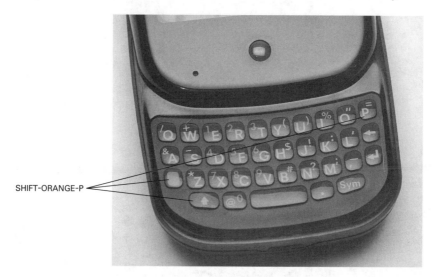

SHIFT-ORANGE-P

Once you take a screenshot, it ends up in a folder on the Pre called, not surprisingly, Screen captures. You can see them by opening the Photos app (tap Launcher, and then tap Photos) and then tapping Screen Captures.

From there, you can share the image via email or MMS by tapping the Share button in the upper-right corner. Alternatively, you can attach a screenshot to an email message.

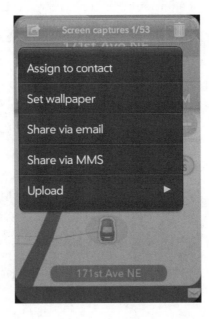

Or you can connect your Pre to your PC and choose USB Drive. Then open the Screen captures folder on the desktop and drag your files wherever you want to place them.

You might notice that the Pre makes two copies of every screen capture you make. What's the deal with that?

JPG   PNG

The screenshots are saved in both JPG and PNG formats. Here's what you need to know:

- **JPG** A common file format that *compresses* the image. That means pretty much anyone on planet Earth can read the JPG image—and it'll work in any program or on any computer—but the image quality is not perfect due to the compression. It's fine for everyday jobs, but not for professional publishing.
- **PNG** A "lossless" file format: there's no compression that results in lowered image quality. If you're publishing the images on the Web or in print, you might want to use PNG. On the other hand, some people can't read PNG files, so it's not quite as convenient to share day-to-day.

If you're copying these files to the desktop, we recommend that you decide which kind of file you plan to use and just delete all the entries of the other file type to keep from getting confused. On Windows Vista or Windows 7, for example, you can type ***.png** in the folder's search box and then delete all the files that appear. When you clear the search box, only the JPG files will remain.

Watching Video on Your Pre

As early as the 1960s, scientists and engineers experimented with pocket-sized devices that could play movies for people on the go. Of course, back then, they were called portable drive-in theaters, and while they were indeed pocket-sized, they required custom pockets that were 200 yards long and wide.

These days, your little Palm Pre can store and play high-quality video, or you can watch video that streams to your phone via the Internet.

No matter what kind of video you watch, it will, almost without exception, play in your Pre's landscape mode to take better advantage of the screen size, so rotating the Pre won't get it to play video in portrait orientation.

Getting Around YouTube

First stop: YouTube. Everyone knows and loves YouTube, a Web site that gets about 20 percent of all the Internet's daily traffic (and almost 60 percent of all the kittens-riding-around-on-Roombas–related traffic). YouTube is a site that lets people share home videos, goofy flicks of their cats (see Figure 9-2), and other personal video, but it's also where you can watch TV show clips, some full-length movies, and all sorts of

FIGURE 9-2 We simply can't get enough of those kittens.

other stuff. Bottom line: If it has moving images and sound, you'll probably be able to find it on YouTube.

Thankfully, a YouTube app is built right into your Pre. To start it, just tap the Launcher and then tap YouTube on the second page of apps. You'll see something like this:

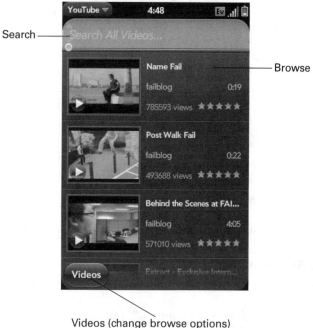

Videos (change browse options)

When you first open YouTube, you'll see videos ready and waiting to be watched. These are the most popular videos, as ranked by YouTube. You can scroll through dozens of these videos, looking for something to watch.

If you prefer, you can tap the Videos button—which you can think of as the Change Browse Options button—and change it to Most Viewed (which will, as the name suggests, show you the most viewed videos as ranked by YouTube) or History, which will show you only the videos you have watched most recently.

 Tip After a while, your history can get long. You can erase your history at any time that you are viewing it by tapping the Clear button on the bottom-right corner of the screen.

You can also search directly for the video you want to watch—just type, tap the search button at the top-right, and the results appear on the screen. This is just like searching on the YouTube Web site, so be sure to type "kitten roomba" to see the best videos. The number of results appear in the upper-right corner.

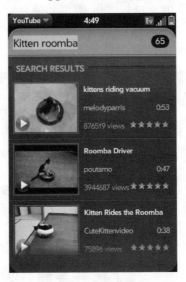

Are 65 kittens riding Roombas enough, we ask? Nay, it is not!

Selecting a Video

When you see a video you want to watch, you have two options:

- Tap the right side of the screen for additional details about the video.
- Tap the left side of the screen to play the video immediately.

Tap the left side to play the video

Tap the right side for details

The details page is chockful of information about the video. You can see the total runtime of the video, the user rating, and a text description.

Want to see more? Tap the More button. You can choose from the following:

- **More From This Author**   Shows other videos that have been uploaded to YouTube by the same person.
- **Related Videos**   Shows similar videos based on theme and keywords—these are not necessarily by the same person.

One more option: Tap Share to send this video link to someone via email or a text message.

Watching a Video

Now that we've gotten all the preliminaries out of the way, it's time to watch a YouTube video. (Yeah, we know—you're way ahead of us. You've already seen the Roomba kitten video on your Pre. But hang with us, because we've got all the details you might have missed.)

You can start playing a YouTube video in two ways:

- From the list of videos, tap a video on the left side.
- From the details page of a video, tap the video preview at the top of the screen.

After that, the video will start playing in landscape mode.

Play/Pause —   — Full screen/original size

Drag to a particular point in the video

The video player controls start out at the bottom of the screen, but they fade after a few seconds. You can tap the screen at any time to get them back.

A couple of handy tricks:

- To skip forward 30 seconds, flick from the left side of the screen to the right side.
- To rewind 10 seconds, flick from the right to the left.

And don't forget that you can get back to the browse screen at any time by making the back gesture in the gesture area under the touch screen.

Did You Know?

Watching Sprint TV

Sure, YouTube is cool, but it's not the only video app on your Pre. Sprint also includes Sprint TV, for example, which you can find on the second page of the Launcher. The main screen is shown at right.

The shows are organized by category—Live, On Demand, Spring Movies, and so on—and while much of the content is free, some channels (identified as Premium Channels) have a cost associated with viewing. If you attempt to watch a premium show, you'll see the charge, and you'll need to tap Subscribe to gain access.

Want more information before you start watching or before you pay for a show? Tap the small info button (the "i") on the right side of the screen.

Watch a Video Saved on Your Pre

It's pretty cool to be able to tune in to videos that stream to your Pre over the Internet, but you can also play videos that are stored on the Pre itself. That's also cool, but we hear what you're thinking. (That's right, we have a machine that lets us hear your thoughts, as we write this, which is months before you'll even read our words, prompting your question. It's a time travel-telepathy thingy machine. Fear us.)

What were we saying? Oh, right. We hear what you're thinking: How do you actually get the video onto the Pre to begin with? You can do it a couple of ways:

- Copy video to your Pre from your computer.
- Send video to your Pre as an email attachment.

Copy Videos to Your Pre Manually

Copying video to your Pre is pretty straightforward—if you can copy music or photos to your Pre, you already know the skinny. Remember how you copied files to the Pre as if it were a USB drive back in Chapter 6? It's basically the same deal to copy video:

1. Connect your Pre to your PC using the Pre's USB charging cable. One more time for emphasis: Be careful to insert the USB cable into the Pre properly, with the divot on top. It's possible to insert the cable upside down, which isn't good for the cable or the Pre. You'll see the screen shown at the right.
2. Tap USB Drive. The Pre's screen will change to a static image. Set it aside, since you won't need to use the Pre for now.
3. You should see the AutoPlay dialog on your PC. Click Open Folder to view files.

Tip   *If AutoPlay doesn't appear, you can do this manually: Choose Start | My Computer. In Devices with Removable Storage, double-click Palm Pre.*

4. Find the video files you want to copy to your Pre on your computer, and then drag them to the Pre's open folder. You can copy the videos to an existing folder or make a new one—you can store videos anywhere you like. We like to create a folder named Video and store all our video files there.

Note   *The Pre is capable of playing video in any of these formats: MPEG4, H.263, H.264, MP4, M4V, 3GP, 3GPP, 3G2, and 3GP2. There are some notable exceptions that won't play: the common WMV format from Microsoft, as well as Apple's QuickTime (MOV).*

Copy Videos to Your Pre Using iTunes

If you use iTunes, you might find that you can sync video from your iTunes library with your Pre—but almost without exception these videos will not play. You'll see an error like this one:

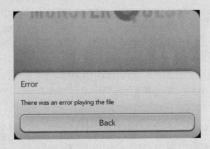

iTunes videos are rights-protected, and the Pre is not capable of playing anything with iTunes rights-protection. In theory, if you have any truly unprotected video files in your iTunes library, the Pre will be able to play them—but that would be pretty unusual.

When you're done, don't disconnect the USB cable right away. In Windows' Notification Area (also known as the system tray), right-click Safely Remove Hardware and Eject Media.

Click Palm Pre and wait for the balloon message that tells you it's safe to remove the Pre. Now you can disconnect the Pre from your computer.

 Videos can be pretty big—even a relatively short video can be several megabytes in size. Since your Pre has a total of only 8MB of available storage, you'll need to be careful and keep an eye on your available space if you play a lot of videos on the Pre.

Play Videos on Your Pre

Once you copy a video to your Pre, you can head over to the Videos app to watch them. Tap the Launcher and then tap Videos on the first page. You'll see something like the list of all the videos on your Pre shown at the right.

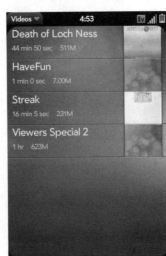

Note that if you've copied videos to your Pre that the Pre can't play—such as MOV or WMV files—they won't appear here. But if you copied right-protected versions of files the Pre does recognize, such as MP4 videos from iTunes, they'll appear in the list but won't play (you'll see an error when you try).

To play a video, just tap it. When the video starts, it'll be oriented in the Pre's landscape mode, and you'll see something like this:

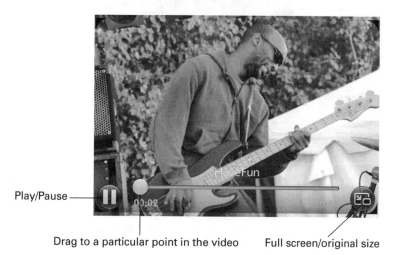

Play/Pause

Drag to a particular point in the video   Full screen/original size

Like the player in YouTube, the video player controls start out at the bottom of the screen but will fade after a few seconds. You can tap the screen at any time to get them back.

You can also use these handy tips to move around in the video:

- To skip forward 30 seconds, flick from the left side of the screen to the right side.
- To rewind 10 seconds, flick from the right to the left.

To get back to the main Videos screen, use the back gesture in the gesture area under the touch screen.

Send Video to Your Pre Using Email or MMS

Here's another way to get video onto your phone: You can email a video to yourself (by adding the video as an attachment)—or, of course, someone can send you an email with video.

If you received a video in email, it'll appear as an attachment, like the screen shown at right.

Before you can watch the video, you must download it to your Pre. To do that, tap the attachment—and wait. Most videos are pretty big, so you'll probably need to wait a few minutes while the multi-megabyte file gets downloaded to your Pre.

When it's done, the attachment's appearance changes to look like this:

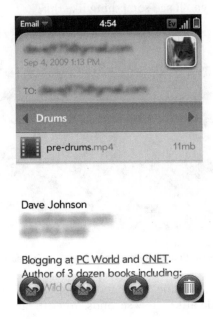

These downloaded videos won't appear in the Videos app—they'll be accessible only from the email in which they arrived. To play the video, tap it, and then the video will start playing using the controls you already know and love from YouTube and other videos.

Did You Know?

Converting Video to Play on the Pre

As we mentioned—and you might have discovered for yourself, the hard way—some common video formats such as WMV and MOV aren't compatible with the Pre. Fortunately, while Dave habitually throws his Pre to the ground and jumps up and down on it when faced with a situation like this, Rick knows there are easy workarounds.

What you need is a *video converter*, a program that can convert incompatible video formats to a compatible one. Start with HandBrake (http://handbrake.fr), a free utility that supports just about every video format. Open the video you want to convert, choose a Preset (we've had good luck with iPhone Legacy), and then specify a destination for the converted file. When the process is done, you'll need to copy the video to your Pre.

With a gazillion other video converters out there, if HandBrake doesn't get the job done, a little Google searching should help you find a program that will. (We've also had good luck with some of Wondershare's products.)

Delete a Video from Your Pre

So what happens when you are done with a video and want to remove it from your Pre? Are you stuck with it forever?

Of course not. You can delete video from your Pre—but you can't delete the video files using the Pre itself. Instead, you have to use your PC. Here's what to do:

1. Connect your Pre to your PC using the Pre's USB charging cable.
2. Tap USB Drive. The Pre's screen will change to a static image. Set the phone aside.
3. You should see the AutoPlay dialog on your PC. Click Open Folder To View Files.

 If AutoPlay doesn't appear, you can do this manually: Choose Start | My Computer. In Devices with Removable Storage, double-click Palm Pre.

4. Find the video files that you want to delete, select them, and press the DELETE key, just as you would to remove any file from your computer.

That's all there is to it. When you're done, don't forget to safely remove the Pre from your PC. Don't just yank out the USB cable.

 You can delete a video you received as an email attachment simply by deleting the email message in which it is embedded.

10

Finding and Using Apps on the Pre

HOW TO...

- Use the App Catalog
- Find and download new apps
- Update your apps
- Delete apps
- Install homebrewed apps
- Use your Pre as a PalmPilot

One of the things that distinguishes modern mobile phones from their less sophisticated ancestors is their ability to run additional programs beyond those that were factory installed. Whether you have a Pre, an iPhone, or some other fancy smartphone, it's hiding a powerful computer under the hood. And computers are really good at running programs. In fact, they live for the excitement of running lots of different apps. Don't have lots of programs on your phone? You're making it sad.

Of course, the Pre doesn't come with a mouse, keyboard, and DVD drive. But that's not going to stop us from running a wide range of apps beyond what came in the box. In this chapter, you'll learn how to add apps to your Pre using the App Catalog, which is an online store you can access right from your phone. You'll also see how to get to "homebrewed" apps that aren't officially in the App Catalog. And you'll read about all the other usual extras and related topics along the way. So get ready to expand your Pre and do a whole lot more than just use it as a phone.

Using the App Catalog

Your Pre comes with its own online store that's filled with apps you can easily download and install. Unlike some phones, such as the iPhone, the Pre requires no extra software or desktop synchronization—it's all right on the Pre.

Many of these apps are free, though some cost money. In almost all cases, though, you can install apps for free on a trial basis. If you don't like the app or don't want to pay for it when the trial period is over, you can easily remove it.

Finding Apps

So let's get started. All the action happens, as we said, in the App Catalog. To get there, tap the Launcher icon and then tap App Catalog, which you'll find in the first position on the second page of the Launcher (assuming you haven't moved it). The App Catalog looks like this:

You can navigate around the App Catalog in several ways:

- **Search** If you know what you're looking for, you can search for it. Start typing and your search term will appear in the Search box at the top of the screen. Press ENTER and you'll see a list of results. You can search for the exact term you're looking for—say, *Pandora* to find Pandora Radio—or you can search for keywords that represent what you are trying to find. Searching for *movies* will turn up Fandango and Flixster, for example. You might have to try several keywords to get good results, though. *Dining* turns up only OpenTable, but *restaurant* returns OpenTable along with at least three other entries, including GoodFood, Where, and LikeMe Mobile.

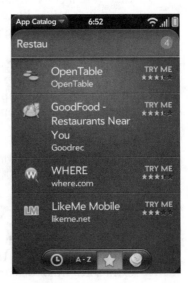

- **Featured**   If you're not sure what you want, but you're in the mood to browse, the Featured and Popular sections are handy for seeing what's hot in the world of apps. In the Featured section, you'll find the apps that Palm wants you to see. That doesn't make these apps popular, or even necessarily good—it's possible (but we don't know for sure) that the app developers might pay a fee for placement in this slot. Presumably, though, Palm has a vested interest in showing off the best stuff here to encourage people to try out the App Catalog and download more apps. Indeed, as we wrote the book, we routinely found apps such as OpenTable, AP News, and AccuWeather here—not too shabby. (Of course, only a small collection of apps was available when we wrote the book to begin with. Hopefully, by the time you read this book, there will be hundreds.) More apps are included in Featured than you can
see on the screen—they continue off the right side of the screen. Use the next and previous gestures to slide the icons left and right across the screen to see them all.

- **Popular**   The Popular category is another good place to browse, but it's kind of the opposite of Featured—you'll find apps that people download a lot. Again, that doesn't necessarily make the apps in this category any good, but you can defer to the wisdom of the masses and try out some app that is extremely popular. Just as in the Featured category, there are more apps than you can see on one screen. Use the next and previous gestures to slide the icons left and right across the screen to see them all.

- **Top Tags**   Under the Featured and Popular sections, you'll find lists of common tags for browsing apps. If you're the sort of person who frequents the App Catalog on a regular basis, the most important one is Most Recent. Visit that list to see the latest additions to the App Catalog, so you don't miss out on new apps of interest. If you don't use the App Catalog a lot, you might be more interested in Top Rated, which lets you browse apps that other Pre users have voted as the best. Otherwise, you'll find a slew of tags that divide the apps into categories such as Lifestyle, Entertainment, and Productivity. Pick the one that represents the kind of app you're on the hunt for.

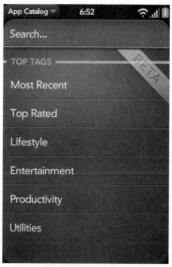

- **All Tags** At the bottom of the list, you'll see All Tags. This displays a "tag cloud" of all the tags associated with apps in the catalog. The size of the tag represents the relative number of apps bearing that tag—so there are a lot more productivity apps than health or navigation apps, for example. (At least this was true when we wrote this; by the time you try it out for yourself, health could be the biggest tag category. Though, if Rick's pizza-beer-and-pretzel diet is any indication, that's pretty unlikely.)

 You can get back to the main App Catalog screen from any tag or category page by using the back gesture in the gesture area.

Browsing a List of Apps

So now you've searched or browsed your way to a list of apps. You probably see something like this:

If only a couple of results appear here, you can probably see everything on one screen and tap the one you want. If a lot of results appear, though, they might scroll way off the bottom, making it harder to choose the one you want. That's where the buttons at the bottom of the screen come in handy. You can sort the results to see apps listed in any order you prefer.

When you see an app you want to investigate further, tap it.

Also, remember that you can type a new search term to look for a specific app, or use the back gesture in the gesture area to go back to the tag or category screen.

Newest to oldest — Alphabetical — By star rating — By price

Inspecting an App Before You Download

You've reached the app's page. Here, you can skip all the preliminaries and just download it right away—see "Downloading an App" for more on that—or you can loiter a bit and see all sorts of information about the app you're thinking of adopting. There's a lot of information on this page, and it can go on for quite a bit, so let's look at it in sections.

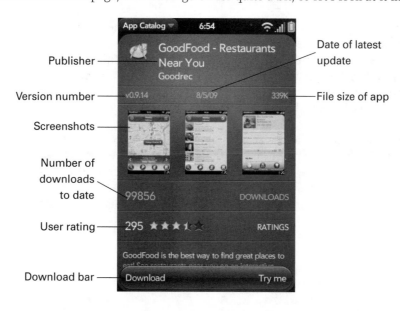

Publisher — Date of latest update

Version number — File size of app

Screenshots

Number of downloads to date

User rating

Download bar

If you want to see a better view of the screenshots, tap one to make it appear full screen. You can then flip through them all using next and previous gestures.

You can also tap the user rating to read all the reviews that have been written for the app. This can give you a lot of insight into the pros and cons of the app, and whether it's worth downloading or—more importantly—paying for.

Scroll down a bit, and you'll see even more information about the app:

The app description comes courtesy of the publisher and usually contains a handy summary of the app's best features.

Some apps might include additional information, such as this GPS disclaimer. It tells you that the app will tap into your GPS receiver to determine your location. You can control whether this happens automatically or at all—see Chapter 6 for the skinny on that—but this warning helps you avoid apps that might use GPS in case you want to avoid installing those kinds of apps in the first place.

You can read all the reviews by tapping See Reviews. This is the same as if you tapped the star rating higher up on the app's page.

You can also write a review, but the Add Review link will work only if you have already installed the app. Not surprisingly, publishers want to avoid letting people write reviews about apps they have not actually installed and tried firsthand.

Finally, each app page also shows these links below the review section:

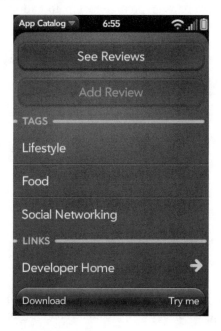

You'll find all the apps' tags here—it's handy if you say to yourself, "I'm not sure I like this app, but I'd like to see other apps that have the same tagging instead."

You can also go directly to the developer's Web page and support page. So if you're having trouble with an app you've installed, return to the App Catalog and navigate to the publisher's support center through the app page.

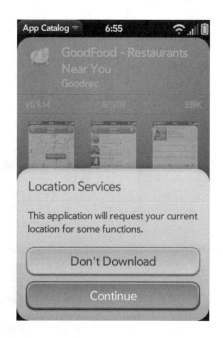

Downloading an App

Ready for some download magic? To download an app, tap the Download/Try Me bar.

At this point, the app might ask if you really want to install it. GPS-enabled apps, for example, warn that they use location services. If you tap Continue, the installation will proceed.

You should see the progress of your download, as shown next, and after a few moments, the Download bar will change to Tap To Launch.

 You can launch an app in two ways. You can find and tap the app's icon in the Launcher, or you can open the App Catalog and tap "Tap to launch" on the app's page.

Review an App

If you found the star ratings and product reviews helpful as you considered selecting an app from the catalog, you might want to return the favor by adding your own reviews. It's quite easy to do.

To review an app you've already installed, find its entry in the App Catalog and scroll down to the review links.

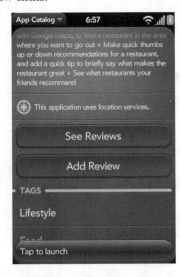

Then, just do this:

1. Tap Add Review. The review form will appear.

2. Tap a star to assign a star rating. You can apply from one to five stars—sorry, no half-stars allowed.
3. Type your review.
4. If you don't want your name to appear online, tap the Post Anonymously button to On.
5. When you're done, tap Submit.

After you submit the review, it shows up online immediately:

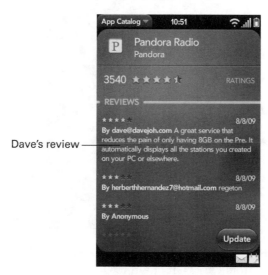

Dave's review

Updating Your Review

You can update an existing review at any time. Just return to the App Catalog, find the app's page, and scroll once again to the review links. Notice that now, instead of Add Review, the button shows Update Review. Make your changes and tap Update—the changes occur almost immediately.

Here's another way to update the review: Go to the reviews page (for example, by tapping See Reviews). Notice the Update button at the bottom of the page, which you can tap to update your review.

Dave's updated review ⎯

Tap to update again

You can change the star rating or the text of your review, or even switch your anonymous status from On to Off or Off to On.

Flag an App as Inappropriate

Have you downloaded an app only to find it is somehow inappropriate? Perhaps it includes offensive language or explicit images. That's not too likely, but if you do find something like that, you can pass on that information to Palm, so they can investigate and determine whether they want to remove the app from the catalog.

To flag an app, open the app's page in the App Catalog. Then tap the app menu in the upper-left corner and tap Flag As Inappropriate.

Update Your Apps

Just as with all the programs on your computer, Pre apps are often updated and released with improved versions. Having the most up-to-date version of your apps is important—they often include new features, fix bugs, and improve security and stability. And updates are usually free.

So how do you get your hands on updates? Your Pre actually makes it pretty easy. You can update each app individually, or you can check for updates for all your apps at once and install them with a single tap. It doesn't really matter which method you choose, but clearly updating all your apps at once is faster and easier.

Updating a Single App

You might want to update a single app if you want to get your hands on an updated app quickly, but you don't want to make the time to update all your other apps at the same time. Or perhaps a WebOS update will upgrade your entire phone—and that will take a while and require your phone to restart at least once. You can leave that for another time and just update the app you need right now.

Here's what to do:

1. Tap the Launcher icon to open the Launcher.
2. Tap App Catalog.
3. Navigate to the app's page.
4. Tap Update Available.

The Download bar turns into Update Available when the app has been installed and an update is, in fact, available. After installing the update, the bar changes to Tap To Launch.

Updating All Your Apps at Once

Aside from the special situations we just described, you'll probably want to update all your apps in one fell swoop most of the time. Obviously, updating one app at a time is too much work. Instead, do this:

1. Tap the Launcher icon to open the Launcher.
2. Tap Updates (you'll find it on the third page if you haven't moved it). Wait a few moments while it searches the Internet looking for available updates.
3. Tap Install Free.

All of your updates will be installed, one after the other, and you can track the process via the progress bars for each app. As each update is completed, you'll see a checkmark on the right.

Deleting Unwanted Apps

If you're anything like us, you probably downloaded everything in sight when you first found the App Catalog. No program was too silly, pointless, or impractical. You had to have every news reader, every restaurant guide, and every flashlight. But at a certain point, perhaps, you realized that you rarely used that quiz game or video player you downloaded. Yet it still clutters up your Launcher and takes up precious memory. Is there some way to get rid of it? Absolutely.

You can easily remove unwanted apps from your Pre or just get some information about your Pre and its software, if that's all you need. Do this:

1. Tap the Launcher icon to open the Launcher.
2. In the app menu, tap List Apps...

The Apps List is divided into three sections:

Scroll down to see Built-In Applications

3. Tap any entry in the Downloaded Applications section, and you are offered the ability to delete the app or tap Done:

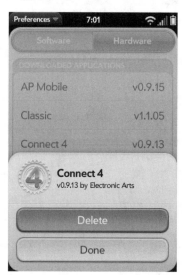

4. If you tap an entry in the Built-In Applications section, you see only the app name and version information—you can't delete built-in apps.

Finally, the Hardware view rolls up all sorts of ultra-geeky information about your phone's hardware and version numbers in case you ever should need to provide it to a tech support rep.

Did You Know?

Viruses: Should You Be Worried?

Unless you have been living under a rock for the last ten years, you know that software viruses and other malicious software can wreak havoc on a desktop computer, and anti-virus software is marketed heavily to PC users. A dozen popular anti-virus programs are out there, along with another dozen less popular ones.

So, the thousand dollar question: Should you run some sort of anti-virus software on your Pre?

Eh, probably not. We predict that by the time you read this book, a handful of companies will be offering anti-virus software for the Pre, but the reality is that the risk of infection is low. Really low. In the many years that Palm sold PDAs such as the Palm III and the Tungsten, for example, not even a single instance of a virus ever harmed a Palm device or the data on it. So if you see ads for anti-virus software for your Pre, ignore them and save your money.

Using "Homebrewed" Apps on the Pre

Have you ever thought it would be cool to do a little computer hacking? Perhaps you wanted to be Tom Cruise in *Mission: Impossible*, hanging upside-down in front of a computer console, or Sandra Bullock, doing...whatever it was that she did in *The Net*.

Well, homebrewed apps let you capture a teeny bit of the hacker mystique. (Not to be confused with Mystique, the blue changeling from X-Men, who, we'd like to point out, was not played by Sandra Bullock).

Homebrewed apps are just like any other Palm app, except that you won't find them in the App Catalog. They're usually labors of love, written by small or one-person development teams, and provided to the community for free. Some of these apps might eventually find their way to the App Catalog, but for now, they live on the outside, like a cybernetic rebel without a cause.

The Origins of Homebrew

Homebrewed apps came about shortly after the Pre was released, because Palm hadn't made it easy for developers to create official Pre apps and get them in the app store. It took Palm a relatively long time to release the official Software Development Kit (SDK) and set the App Catalog submission process in place, meaning that for many months after the Pre's release, only about 30 apps existed for users hungry for more things to do with their Pre.

So while only a handful of apps were in the App Catalog for many months after the Pre first hit the stores, it didn't take long for folks to fill in the gap by writing Pre apps and making them available outside of the App Catalog.

This is actually kind of a big deal and really cool. While some phones—you know, like those from companies with fruits in their names—actively discourage homebrew applications, Palm embraced it.

That means you can install the stuff already in the App Catalog and leave it at that if you want to, but you can also explore homebrewed apps as well. If you get this book before zillions of apps appear in the App Catalog, homebrewed apps will give you a lot of other options. And even if the catalog has lots of apps, the homebrewed alternative can give you some other places to explore.

Getting Ready for Homebrewed Apps

To install homebrewed apps, you need to prep your Pre (and your PC) by installing some software first. This is admittedly the most daunting part of the process. And though you might think that this "homebrew" thing sounds a bit like hacking, let us assure you of a couple of things:

- *It's not really that hard.* Even Rick can do it, and he is required by his state-mandated counselor to use safety scissors and juice boxes with rounded corners.
- *It's perfectly safe.* You're not in danger of damaging your Pre or your PC by configuring them to receive homebrewed apps.
- *It's legal.* Installing homebrews does not void your warranty, break any laws, or compromise your support plan with Sprint or Palm. It's totally kosher.

Now that we have the preliminaries out of the way, let's get started. You can get your Pre ready for homebrews in several ways, but we think the following process is the easiest. If you have a friend or see a Web site that recommends a different approach, that's cool. Do whatever works best for you—you won't hurt our feelings. Do this:

1. Start by putting your Pre into Developer Mode. Turn on the Pre and close any apps, so you are looking at the Pre in Card view with no cards.

2. Type this, exactly as it appears: **upupdowndownleftrightleftrightbastart**.

 Tip To make it easier to enter, it's just "up up down down left right left right ba start" without any spaces. If you're not a computer game geek, here's some trivia for you: that's a classic cheat code for Nintendo games.

3. Tap the Developer Mode icon and then switch Developer Mode from Off to On. Allow the Pre to restart, as directed. Set the Pre aside for the next few steps.

4. On your PC (specifically, on a Windows PC), download and install the PreBrew installer. You can get a copy from http://tinyurl.com/mklqw4. This Web page is needlessly confusing, so be sure to click the latest version of the Installer icon at the upper-right, and then click the Download link at the upper-left.

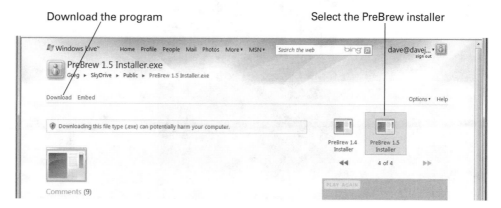

Download the program

Select the PreBrew installer

5. After the installation is complete on your PC, double-click Setup.vbs and, when it's done (it might take a while), restart your PC.

Whew, still with us? That's the bare essentials. In a minute, we'll add one more flourish to the process that isn't essential, but that will make installing homebrewed apps much more convenient.

 Homebrew setup will no doubt continue to involve and improve. You might want to check http://tinyurl.com/kk44k9 for the latest details on how to do this.

Installing Your First Homebrew

Now it's time to install something.

1. First, find an app you want to install. You'll find a comprehensive collection at PreCentral.net (http://forums.precentral.net/homebrew-apps/). In order to download apps from there, you will need to register at the site with a username and password, so do that first. Go ahead, we'll wait.
2. Okay, done? When you find an app you want to install, download it to your PC. You'll get a file that has an .IPK filename extension. Save it somewhere convenient, such as on the desktop or in your Downloads folder.
3. Next, connect your Pre to your PC using the USB cable. Tap Just Charge, not USB Drive or Media Sync. (Actually, you could do this step at any point; you don't have to wait. Just make sure the Pre is fully restarted after entering Developer Mode.)

Notice that when you ran the setup.vbs script earlier, an icon named Drop File Here To Install Pre App appeared on your desktop.

4. Here's the magic part: Drag the .IPK file onto the desktop icon, and let go. You'll see a DOS-style window reminding you that the Pre is connected and in Developer Mode. Press ENTER.

```
C:\Windows\system32\cmd.exe

Install Application 1.5 by Greg Roll 2009
Installs an application on the Palm Pre
Ensure your Palm Pre is connected and running in developer mode.

Press any key to continue . . .
```

5. It'll only take a moment, and the window will go away. Now you can check your Pre—the app is installed and will appear at the bottom of the first page of the Launcher.

From now on, you can install additional apps via your Windows desktop by dragging files onto the icon, which you'll probably want to keep tucked away in the corner of the desktop.

 Tip   Even if you restart your Pre, it'll remain in Developer Mode. You don't have to re-enter the code each time.

Easier Installing with fileCoaster

So far, we've shown you how to install homebrewed apps using your Windows PC. But that's kind of clumsy, don't you think? There's an easier way: fileCoaster.

This program lets you install apps directly from your Pre, wirelessly, just like the App Catalog. In fact, fileCoaster is sort of its own App Catalog. Find it at

PreCentral.net (http://forums.precentral.net/homebrew-apps/) and install it on your Pre. Once it's running, you'll see a screen like this:

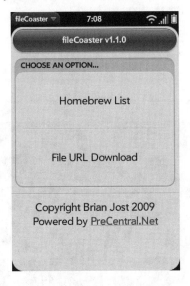

Tap Homebrew List and you'll see the entire library of apps at PreCentral.net, and you can tap apps to see screenshots, see app summaries, and install apps. It's quite elegant, actually, and a handy way to install homebrewed apps.

 The Pre's Developer Mode interferes with your ability to "eject" the Pre from Windows when you're done connecting it with the USB cable. After you start using fileCoaster, you don't need to use Developer Mode anymore, so we recommend that you re-enter the code, disable Developer Mode, and restart your Pre.

Using Your Pre as a PalmPilot

If your Pre is the first thing you've ever bought with Palm's name embossed on the back, you might not care very much about compatibility with the old Palm operating system. But if you carried a PalmOS device like the Palm Pilot, Palm III, Tungsten, Treo, Visor, Clie, or any of a dozen similar devices—or if you even still use one of those gadgets—then having "backward compatibility" might be really important to you.

So, for you, we happily report that, yes, you can run many of your old Palm OS apps on the Pre. (But it's going to cost you another $30.)

Installing Classic

What you'll need is an app called Classic, and it's available in the App Catalog.

You can try Classic for free for seven days, but after that the program will stop working and you'll have to purchase it.

To get to Classic, just start the App Catalog and then look in the Productivity category, or type **Classic** in the search box at the top of the screen.

Getting Around Classic

Classic is a fairly complete Palm OS emulator—the app makes your Pre look and work very much like a typical Palm OS device. When you first start the program, it looks like this:

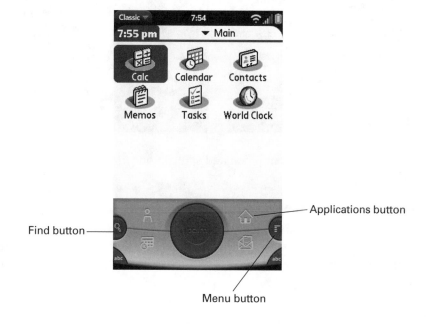

Classic is pretty easy to figure out. After all, it's just a Palm OS device living inside your Pre, so if you already know how to use the Palm, you're set. That said, you should be aware of a few differences. We'll highlight things about Classic that you'll want to know right away to get the most out of this app.

The Keyboard Replaces the Graffiti Area

Just like the headline says—it's worth noting that there's no Graffiti gesture area. You input information using the Pre's keyboard.

Zoom into the Pre Screen

One nifty trick you will like is the fact that you can zoom in on details in the Palm's screen using the familiar pinch in/pinch out gesture to zoom in anywhere on the screen. Here is the World Clock app, at normal size and also zoomed in:

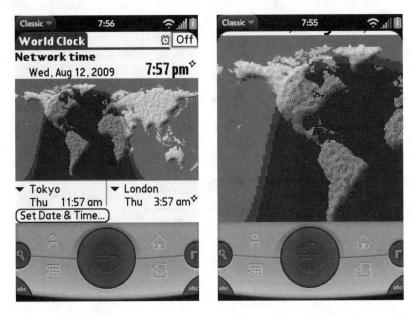

To zoom back out, you can pinch and spread your fingers, or you can double-tap the screen.

Beware of the Dual Menus

Even though they totally make sense, that hasn't stopped the two different menus from occasionally confusing us anyway. Remember that the Pre and the Palm menus are stacked right on top of each other. You can use your finger to tap both of them, but it's probably a little easier to open the Palm's menu by tapping the menu button on the right side of the screen.

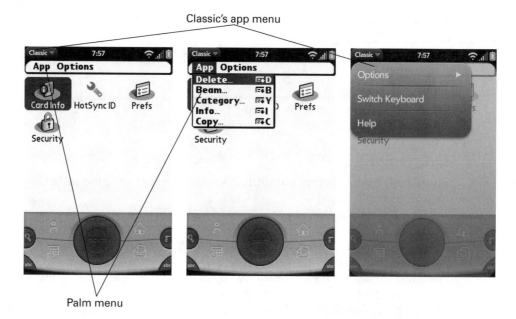

Classic's app menu

Palm menu

The Palm's menu does all the things the Palm menu always does. The other menu is the Classic app menu, which contains all the preferences for configuring the app, along with controls for resetting the Palm.

Resetting the Palm

Remember the button you'd have to depress with a paperclip or the point of your stylus to reset your Palm? Well, the Pre has no reset button. But you can reset the Pre like this:

- To do a soft reset (the equivalent of inserting a paperclip in the reset button), close the Classic app and then restart the app.
- To do a hard reset (the equivalent of depressing the reset button while holding the power button), tap the app menu and then tap Hard Reset.

Installing Palm Apps

So playing with a plain vanilla Palm Pilot is fun in a nostalgic sort of way, but can you actually do something useful with it? For starters, you'll probably want to install some of your old Palm apps.

There are two primary ways to install apps: using HotSync, or dragging files.

Using HotSync

As a Palm veteran, you already know how to install apps via Palm Desktop. No surprises here.

Dragging Files

If you don't want to bother with Palm Desktop, you can drag the install files directly to the Pre.

Here's what you need to do:

1. Connect your Pre to your PC using the USB cable.
2. Tap USB Drive.
3. You should see the AutoPlay dialog on your PC. Click Open Folder To View Files.
4. Open the ClassicApps folder. Then open Install.
5. Copy any installation files—usually, these files have .PRC and .PBD filename extensions—from your PC to the Install folder.

Safely disconnect your Pre from the PC and then start Classic. You should find that the app has been installed in your simulated Palm.

What Won't Classic Do?

Classic is an impressive app that can really extend the value of your Pre if you've been using a Palm device in the past. But it has some limitations. Here are some important things that Classic can't do:

- Classic can't give the Palm access to the Pre's camera.
- Classic can't let the Palm use the Pre's Bluetooth, Wi-Fi, or GPS.
- You can't run apps designed for later model Palm OS devices that had a 480-pixel display. Classic models a traditional 320×320 pixel color screen Palm, like the Palm IIIc.

Dave vs. Rick: Note-taking on the Pre

Dave: Back in the day, the Palm's Memo Pad was just about my favorite application. I'd whip out my Palm a dozen times a day to jot down notes and reminders. But my, times have changed. I once had a memo called "movies," for example, where I'd keep notes of what movies I wanted to see and what the various show times were, so I was all set on Friday evening. These days? I just open Fandango on my Pre while we're out to dinner on Friday, and I can instantly find movies, show times, and theaters. In many ways, the Pre's apps have replaced the note-taking I used to use my Palm for. On the other hand, I'll always have a need to capture brilliant and hilarious thoughts that pop into my head, like this list of "Top 10 Restaurants No One Would Want to Eat At":

10. Kafka's Costumed Eatery
9. The Pikachu Grill
8. Mama Cud's Prechewed Food Emporium
7. The Lil' Elian Inn
6. Newfoundland's Finest Burrito
5. The Moldy Melon
4. The Mad Cow Cafe
3. Worms! Worms! Worms!
2. Blowfishwiches
1. TGI Mondays

Rick: Much as it pains me to say this, those were actually pretty funny. On the other hand, what's with the totally random non–Pre-related topic? In that spirit, here are my picks for "Nature's Cruelest Acts":

5. Mosquitoes
4. Pugs
3. Wasps, hornets, and horseflies
2. Hurricanes
1. Dave

11

Accessorizing Your Pre

HOW TO...

- Use the Touchstone charger
- Recharge on the road
- Install a higher capacity battery
- Protect your screen
- Choose a case
- "Skin" your Pre
- Mount your Pre in your car
- Dock your Pre on your desk
- Choose headphones and headsets
- Connect a speaker dock
- Find Pre accessories online

The Pre may be the new kid on the smartphone block, but that hasn't stopped accessory makers from cranking out tons of terrific add-ons and extras. You'll find Pre cases, Pre docks, Pre headsets, Pre battery chargers, and a whole lot more. In this chapter, we'll spotlight some of the best accessories we've found for the Pre and tell you where to find them and how to score better deals.

 Note Let's get this out of the way right up front. There are a gazillion more accessories for the iPhone than there are for the Pre, in part because the former has been around a lot longer. The good news is that many iPhone accessories work like a charm with the Pre, meaning you have a much larger selection than you otherwise might think. So please don't be offended if we invoke that "other" device along the way. It's actually a good thing!

The Touchstone Charging Dock

Wires? The Pre don't need no stinkin' *wires*. Unlike every other phone, camera, MP3 player, and gadget on the planet, the Pre can charge and recharge just by resting atop the magical Touchstone (see Figure 11-1). If you buy just one accessory for your phone, make it this one.

What you'll need, actually, is the Touchstone Charging Kit, which includes the dock itself and a replacement battery door for the Pre. See, the Touchstone relies on magnets to "lock" the Pre in place, and the standard battery door has no metal. That's why you need the replacement, which is identical to the standard door save for a matte finish (the glossy one just shows fingerprints anyway) and a special "magnetic induction" panel.

 The good news is the replacement battery door doesn't change the weight or dimensions of your Pre. That bad news is that it won't work with oversize replacement batteries, which you'll learn more about in the upcoming section, "Bigger, Better Batteries." Of course, you can always change your battery/door configuration depending on the circumstances, like if you're going on a long trip and won't be using the Touchstone anyway.

FIGURE 11-1   The Touchstone charging dock relies on a technology called *induction* to charge your Pre without wires.

The Touchstone is not only cool, it's also smart. For example, if you're on a call and you place your Pre on the dock, it automatically switches to speakerphone mode. And if your Pre rings while docked, the simple act of lifting it up answers the call.

Palm sells the Touchstone Charging Kit for a fairly steep $69.95, but as of this writing it's available from the PreCentral Store for $49.95 (http://tinyurl.com/mc374j). If that deal's no longer around by the time you read this, a little Google searching should help you find a price at least $10 below Palm's.

Tip A few clever Pre users have figured out a way to mount the Touchstone in their cars, making for a great mobile charger and dock. To see an example, check out this photo-illustrated success story in the PreCentral user forums: http://tinyurl.com/p6qddg. Also, if you already own the Touchstone kit and just need an extra dock, they're available separately.

Recharge on the Road

In Chapter 6, you learned loads of strategies for keeping your Pre charged while traveling, including battery-saving measures like lowering the screen brightness and turning off Bluetooth. Of course, what's the point of having a Pre if you can't use every bell and whistle? We want a blindingly bright screen, every wireless feature cranked to maximum, and non-stop Sprint TV. And we want them everywhere, all the time. *Life in the fast lane, surely make you lose your mind, life in the fast lane....* (Whoa, sorry to go all Don Henley on you there. Where were we?)

By packing the right power-providing accessories, you won't have to worry about the Pre's battery life (which, let's face it, isn't terrific). Let's take a look at the chargers, external batteries, and other goodies you'll want to pack on your next trip—or long commute.

Car Chargers

Want to top off your Pre between home and the office? The office and your lunch meeting? Your lunch meeting and the airport? Or maybe you're taking a road trip and letting the Pre's battery-hungry navigation app show you the way. Whatever the case, a car charger is absolutely essential.

As you may know, Palm sells one: the aptly named Vehicle Power Charger. What's nice about this little kit is that it doubles as a spare USB sync cable, as the larger plug can disconnect from the cigarette-lighter adapter. So if you are indeed headed to, say, the airport, you can charge your Pre on the way, then bring along just the USB cable for PC charging/syncing.

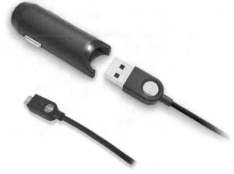

Palm sells the Vehicle Power Charger for $29.99, but you can get it from the aforementioned PreCentral Store (store.precentral.net) for $19.95.

That same store also sells the Motorola Micro USB High Performance Car Charger for $14.95 (http://tinyurl.com/msz4rw). The only difference between the two? The Motorola doesn't pull double duty as a standard USB cable. If you don't need that capability, you might as well pocket the five bucks you'll save.

The Pre's Micro USB Port: Your Ticket to Cheap Chargers

Palm may have designed the Pre without a microSD slot (rats!), but at least the phone employs a standard charge/sync connector. It's called micro USB, and it's a universal port, meaning it will work with just about any micro USB cable or charger on the planet. In other words, you're not limited to buying Palm- or carrier-branded accessories, or to a smattering of third-party accessories designed especially for the Pre. Any item that has a micro USB connector should work.

Specifically, if you're looking for a basic sync cable to connect your Pre to your PC, look for any generic one that has a standard USB connector at one end and micro USB at the other. Palm charges $14.99 for the Travel Micro USB Cable, but a quick search of eBay ("micro USB cable") reveals similar products selling for as little as $1.

You need to be a little more careful when dealing with chargers, as it's critical that you use one that supplies no more than five volts (5V) of power. For example, you might have a micro USB cigarette-lighter adapter for your GPS—but before you try plugging it into your Pre, double-check its power output. Same goes for any kind of power supply, whether it's a car charger, external battery, or whatever. An incompatible power supply could fry your Pre in a matter of seconds. Yikes!

The other caveat here is that cheapo cables and chargers aren't always the best quality. Using them could put your Pre at risk, so you'll have to decide if that's worth saving a few bucks. Dave would probably say no, but Rick—a self-proclaimed cheapskate—has no problem rolling those particular dice.

Of course, don't base your decision on our opinions alone. We highly recommend perusing the user forums at sites such as PreCentral.net and EverythingPre (www.everythingpre.com), where you'll find lots of discussion about Pre chargers, including many third-party and generic products that have been tested by your fellow users. In other words, if you're eyeballing a charger and want to know if it'll work safely with the Pre, chances are good someone has already tried it.

Travel Chargers

By far the best way to charge your Pre on the road is with the wall adapter that came in the box and an AC outlet. Of course, the latter are hard to come by in airplanes, taxis, trains, and the like. If you need power that's available anywhere, any time, you need a travel charger—specifically, an external power supply that packs its own battery.

These accessories, also known as emergency chargers, come in all shapes and sizes. As we noted earlier, any external charger that relies on a micro USB connector should work with the Pre. And there are tons of them, as some BlackBerry phones employ micro USB. So you needn't limit your charger search to Pre-specific products; the door's open to just about any charger that's BlackBerry-compatible.

Let's take a look at some of the more intriguing chargers you can toss in your bag, briefcase, purse, or even pocket.

The Ecosol Powerstick

About the size of a pack of gum, the Ecosol Powerstick (http://tinyurl.com/ltfgnb) charges by plugging into a computer's USB port. That means you can leave it plugged in, and then grab it when you head out the door. When your Pre is low on power, simply connect the Ecosol to the Pre's micro USB port and let it recharge the smartphone. The Powerstick features a cool LCD gauge that shows how much of its battery power is remaining—a major plus compared with other chargers.

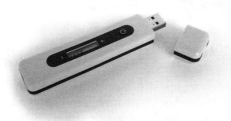

Another perk: The Powerstick is compatible with other devices besides the Pre, and it in fact comes with nine different connectors for plugging into other gizmos. Palm sells the charger for $79.99, but if you shop around online you should be able to find it for as little as $50.

AA Portable Emergency Charger

The AA Portable Emergency Charger relies on a single double-A battery, which is handy because they're sold just about everywhere on the planet. (Gas stations? Check.

Airports? Check. The mental institution where Dave gets his weekly treatments? Believe it or not, check!)

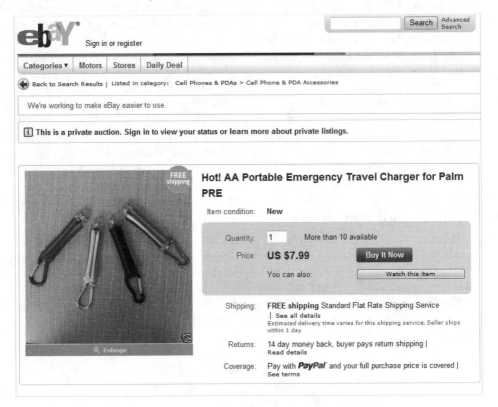

Equally handy, the charger sports a carabiner-style clip so you can easily wear it on a keychain, belt loop, or just about anyplace else. And they're inexpensive. We found one on eBay selling for the bargain price of just $7.99, shipping included. You'll almost certainly be able to find something similar.

iGo powerXtender

Like a slightly more robust version of the previous charger, the iGo powerXtender (http://www.igo.com) relies on two AA batteries to power your Pre. However, you'll need a Pre-specific connector tip to go with it (iGo Power Tip A138). So plan on spending $15.99 for the charger and $9.99 for the tip.

Another Power Option: Spare Batteries

The Pre's battery is removable, so if yours is out of juice, why not just swap in a fresh one? That's certainly an option, but it presents a couple of challenges. First, you need a way to charge your spare battery while it's outside your Pre. Second, the actual act of swapping batteries involves powering down the Pre, removing the battery door, making the switch, and waiting on a lengthy power-up process. Granted, that's really more of a hassle than a challenge, but it's something to keep in mind.

If you still like the idea of keeping an extra battery (or two) on hand, head to the PreCentral Store and check out the Palm Spare Battery Charger for Pre (http://tinyurl .com/lqdmdk). This $29.95 item not only charges your extra battery (via wall adapter, USB cable, or vehicle charger), but it also doubles as a battery carrying case.

As for the spare battery itself, the aforementioned PreCentral Store sells them for $39.95, but we found Palm-branded OEM replacement batteries selling on eBay for as little as $12. Our advice: Buy the $12 one. There's absolutely no reason to spend more.

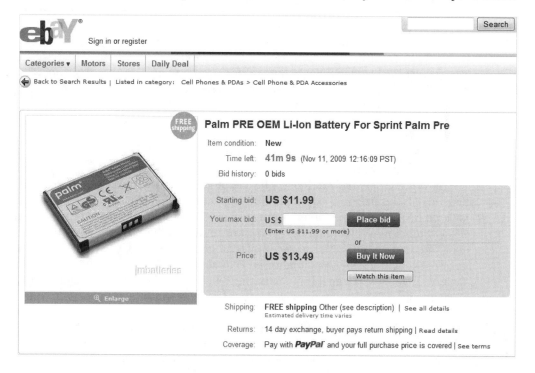

Bigger, Better Batteries

There's another way to solve the problem of never-enough-battery-life: Install a bigger battery. See, the stock Pre battery has a capacity of 1150 milliampere-hours (mAh), and as you've probably discovered by now, that's barely enough to get you through a day's worth of walking around.

Ah, but what if you could shoehorn a 1400-mAh battery into your Pre? In theory, that would net you about 20 percent more runtime. Okay, then, how about a 2600-mAh battery or even a whopping 3800-mAh battery? The latter would run more than three times longer on a single charge. Hey, wipe that drool off your chin!

TABLE 11-1 Extended Batteries for the Pre

Product	Capacity	Price	Where to Get It
Amzer SmartCell 1400	1400 mAh	$49.95	http://tinyurl.com/ku8d4o
Amzer SmartCell 2800	2800 mAh	$89.95	http://tinyurl.com/lav7lp
Amzer SmartCell 3800	3800 mAh	$129.95	http://tinyurl.com/kkxjox
Seidio Innocell 2600mAh Extended Life Battery	2600 mAh	$64.95	http://tinyurl.com/mbsj4h

All this can be yours—for a price. Not just the price of the battery, but also of your Pre's svelte figure. You know how Robert DeNiro famously bulks up for certain movie roles? If you want your Pre to deliver more power, you'll have to accept added bulk. That's because these larger batteries are physically larger, protruding extra millimeters from the battery slot. Take a look, for instance, at a Pre with the Seidio Innocell 2600mAh Extended Life Battery installed, shown here.

As you can see, the Pre looks a little stouter about the tum. Just how much stouter depends on the size (and corresponding capacity) of the battery. The Seidio product isn't too bad: It adds only about 4mm of overall thickness to the Pre. However, and this is true of most extended batteries, it necessitates the use of a replacement rear door, one that's a bit deeper to accommodate the deeper battery.

Consequently, when you opt for an extended battery, such as one of those shown in Table 11-1, you lose compatibility with the Touchstone charger. That's a disappointment, to say the least, but it's the price you pay for extra power on the inside.

 The one exception to this is the Amzer SmartCell 1400, a 1400-mAh battery that's the same size as the standard battery. Consequently, it doesn't require a replacement door, and it should work with the Touchstone.

Protect Your Screen

A scratched Pre screen can ruin your day faster than sitting through one of Dave's "jokes." Fortunately, it's pretty easy to avoid both. For starters, never get on the phone with Dave. Then, apply a screen protector to your Pre. Problems solved!

A screen protector is basically a clear, self-adhesive sheet of plastic cut to fit the front of your Pre. In addition to preventing scratches that can occur when, say, your Pre meets your keys inside your pocket, these sheets can reduce both glare and fingerprints. Definitely a worthwhile investment, especially considering that most screen protectors sell for $10 to $15. Table 11-2 lists some options.

TABLE 11-2   Screen Protectors for the Pre

Product	Price	Where to Get It
BoxWave ClearTouch Crystal	$12.95	http://tinyurl.com/nbcser
Palm Pre Clear Screen Protector with Cleaning Cloth	$8.95	http://tinyurl.com/mx449c
ScreenGuardz	$9.99	http://tinyurl.com/lh392v
Smartphone Experts Screen Protectors (3-Pack)	$14.95	http://tinyurl.com/npsljv

Choose a Case

The Pre is slim and compact enough to ride easily in a pocket or purse. But, let's face it, you've got all kinds of dangerous flotsam in there. (Dave's purse in particular is a gadget deathtrap, what with all the bobby pins and such.) What's more, when your Pre is tucked away somewhere, you're less likely to hear it ring when a call comes in.

All the more reason to consider a case. They're good for showing off your style, keeping your Pre safe from scratches (to say nothing of accidental drops to the pavement), and even securing your Pre to your belt for easier access (and more audible rings).

Here are some things to keep in mind as you shop for a case:

- **Style**   If you're a briefcase-carrying, suit-wearing executive type, you may want a case to match. That means leather. Here's the Smartphone Experts Side Pouch, a fine example of corporate style:

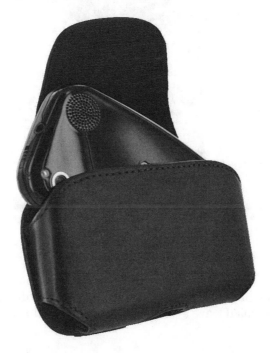

- **Portability**   In the summer, when the tight clothes come out and the jackets get stowed, pockets are hard to come by. That's when something like a belt-clip case can come in mighty handy. Check out the Seidio Holster, seen here at right.

- **Screen protection**   When your Pre is bouncing around in a pocket, purse, or briefcase, the last thing you want is for some piece of flotsam to gouge or scratch the screen. That's one of the main reasons behind getting a case in the first place.

- **Drop protection**   Gravity—it strikes without warning (especially if you're a klutz like Dave), and it can fatally wound a Pre in a matter of milliseconds. A case made of neoprene or even metal can save the day if your Pre gets knocked or dropped to the floor. Check out the Body Glove Faux Nylon Snap-on:

- **Moron protection**   We used to hear stories of people driving over their PalmPilots. Why anyone would leave a PDA in the driveway in the first place is beyond us, but there are aluminum and metal cases that can handle such punishment. Or maybe you just need to survive a day at the beach, in which case something like the Aquapac Handheld Case might be a good choice:

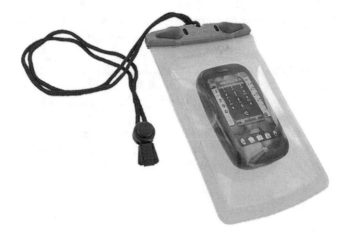

Dozens of different cases are available for the Pre. In Table 11-3 you'll find a smattering of them—a little something for everyone. But with so many options available, you should definitely shop around until you find just the right case for your lifestyle.

Tip Why stop with just one case? We have a leather belt-clip holster for our days at the office, a ruggedized hard/soft shell for weekend combat maneuvers, and a colorful plastic shell for nights on the town.

TABLE 11-3 Pre Cases

Product	Description	Price	Where to Get It
Aquapac Handheld Case	Waterproof, sandproof, and sunlight-resistant; also floats in water	$24.95	http://tinyurl.com/nqkoxm
BodyGlove Faux Nylon Snap-on	Drop-proof hard shell with textured corners for easier gripping	$29.95	http://tinyurl.com/n8nsxy
PDA Skins PDA Plus	Zippered case with slots for cash and credit cards and an outside pocket for your headset	$39.95	http://tinyurl.com/mxvfuh
Seidio Holster	Belt-clip holster protects the screen, leaving the speaker unobscured	$24.95	http://tinyurl.com/kpjv8c
Smartphone Experts Click Case	Shiny, colorful plastic shells clip onto the Pre backside	$17.95	http://tinyurl.com/m9ur5m
Smartphone Experts Top Pouch	Top-loading leather belt-clip case, available in several colors	$24.95	http://tinyurl.com/nwyelo

"Skin" Your Pre

To paraphrase Henry Ford, you can get a Pre in any color you want, as long as it's black. While that's fine for Dave, whose entire wardrobe consists of black t-shirts and jeans, Rick prefers to spruce things up a little. As you learned in the preceding section, certain cases can add a dash of color to your Pre. But for serious flair, nothing beats a skin.

Skins are really just special decals that add some personal style to your Pre. Options range from colorful patterns to sports team logos to a photo of some cute kittens. Or you could even design your own skin with text, graphics, or even a snapshot of your kids. That's one reason we're partial to Unique Skins (www.uniqueskins.com), which lets you build your own skin from scratch. And the design process happens right in your Web browser using a simple (and, dare we say, fun?) set of tools. Check it out in Figure 11-2.

The company promises that its skins will never fade or smudge, and that the adhesive won't leave behind any residue when you peel one off. What's really amazing is that these custom-designed skins cost just $6.99 apiece.

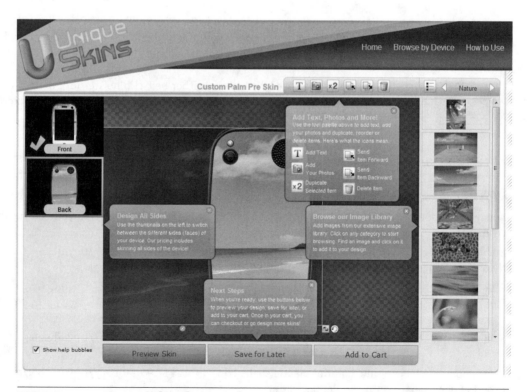

FIGURE 11-2 Unique Skins lets you design your own Pre skin, complete with text, graphics, and even your own photos.

Rick vs. Dave: The Accessories We Can't Live Without

Rick: While Dave prefers accessories of the pink and sparkly nature, I like manly leather cases and bullet-stopping screen protectors (because I get fired on a lot).

Actually, I spend a lot of time chained at my desk, and much as I love the Touchstone charger, I prefer a more traditional dock. That's why my Pre accessory of choice is the Mobi Products Cradle, which holds the Pre more upright than the Touchstone and provides a slot for keeping a spare battery charged and at the ready. I'm also partial to the Griffin TuneBuds Mobile, which, though designed for iPhones, work very nicely with the Pre (as do most headsets).

Dave: I can't fathom why Rick needs any accessories at all since he never leaves his parents' basement, but I suppose it can be fun to pretend you have friends. In any event, my favorite (and utterly indispensable) Pre accessory is a pair of Bluetooth stereo headphones. They're from Dell, and they came with some PC I bought a year or two ago. Nonetheless, despite their inauspicious origins, I use them absolutely daily to listen to music while on the go. Without them, my Pre would not be nearly as awesome.

Mount Your Pre in Your Car

In Chapter 6 you learned how to use your Pre as a GPS navigation system. What you didn't learn was how to use it safely in your vehicle. That means mounting the phone on your windshield or dashboard so it's at eye level, just as a standalone GPS would be.

While we've yet to see any car mounts designed expressly for the Pre, plenty of universal mounts work just fine. Arkon Resources (www.arkon.com) and iGrip (www.igrip.net) are among the companies that make such products, and you can find several of them in the oft-mentioned PreCentral Store (http://store.precentral.net/palm-pre-car-mounts.htm). For example, here's the Arkon SM315 Universal Windshield/Dashboard/Console Mount, which suction-cups your Pre to your windshield:

If your windshield is too deep to make a suction-cup mount practical (or your state has laws against windshield-mounted devices), you might be better off with a cigarette lighter mount, which plugs into your car's cigarette lighter (but may not charge your Pre, alas).

Other options include "weighted" mounts that rest on your dashboard and vent mounts that clip into your air vents. Bottom line: If you plan to use your Pre as a GPS, or you just want a safer way to interact with it while driving (something we absolutely positively don't recommend), a car mount is a must.

Dock Your Pre on Your Desk

Back when Palm made PalmPilots, desktop docks were standard equipment. These days, not so much—something we don't fully understand. Don't most of us still spend our days chained to a desk? And isn't it more convenient to have our phone/information manager at arm's length rather than stuffed in a pocket or clipped uncomfortably to a belt? (It's the rare belt-clip case that isn't uncomfortable when you're sitting down.)

Palm doesn't make a traditional dock for the Pre, though the Touchstone sort of qualifies: It holds your device at a semi-upright angle and simultaneously charges it. However, if you want an honest-to-goodness dock, check out the glamorously named Mobi Products Cradle w/Spare Battery Slot (http://tinyurl.com/nybodb). Take a look:

As you can see, the dock relies on a coiled USB connector for charging, meaning you can't just drop the Pre into the cradle and trust that its battery will magically recharge. You have to perform the manual step of carefully plugging in the connector.

On the plus side, the cradle includes a slot for a second battery (see "Another Power Option: Spare Batteries" earlier in this chapter), one that stays charged and at the ready. You can see the slot in better detail here:

You may have noticed that the cradle also comes with a plastic stylus and holder, which is amusing given that the Pre doesn't respond to stylus input. (It's not a PalmPilot, silly Mobi Products!) The only way to navigate the touch screen is with a finger.

Anyway, the dock sells for $24.95—a reasonable price if you spend more time at your desk than you do on the move.

Choose Headphones and Headsets

As you learned in Chapter 8, the Pre makes a fine MP3 player. Of course, it's also a phone. Consequently, you might want to treat your ears to something a little better than Palm's bundled headset. Don't get us wrong: It's fine, but there are better and more versatile ways to listen to music—and hold conversations.

Bluetooth Headsets

For example, a Bluetooth headset allows you to place and receive phone calls while your Pre stays tucked away in your pocket, briefcase, or somewhere else on your person—no wires required. You learned all about Bluetooth—how to enable it on your Pre, how to pair a headset, and so on—in Chapter 6, so hop back there if you need a refresher.

In the meantime, let's talk about some actual headsets you might want to buy. They come in all shapes and sizes, with prices ranging from $20 to more than $100.

Choosing one can be a challenge, indeed, as it's hard to know how well a headset will fit your ear(s) without actually trying it on (rarely an option) or how good it will sound without actually listening to it (ditto).

> There's also the matter of style. Rick wouldn't be caught dead wearing the fashion equivalent of a Borg implant, but Dave has no problem walking around with a shiny, flashing woman-repellant sticking out of his ear. And looking like he's talking to himself.

Consequently, your best bet is to search out reviews. We recommend perusing CNET.com for professional coverage of the latest and greatest headsets and Amazon for user reviews (which are often just as valuable).

That said, we can recommend one Bluetooth headset here and now: the Aliph Jawbone 2 (www.jawbone.com). It's widely regarded as the gold standard among headsets (though there is a newer model, the Jawbone Prime, that's reputed to be even better).

The Jawbone offers unsurpassed sound quality and noise-cancellation features. Our only complaint with it is the quirky volume control. Oh, and the list price: $129.99. Fortunately, it's easy to find online for as little as $50.

FIGURE 11-3   Jabra's HALO headset offers music—and conversation—without wires. It has a list price of $129.

Stereo Headsets

If you can wirelessly listen to callers in one ear, why can't you wirelessly listen to music in two ears? That's the idea behind stereo Bluetooth headsets, which resemble traditional earbuds or headphones—but without the cord. A perfect example is the Jabra HALO (see Figure 11-3), which you might mistake for an elegant, folding pair of regular headphones if not for the conspicuous lack of wires descending from the earpieces.

Because the Pre supports a Bluetooth technology called A2DP, it's able to stream music wirelessly in stereo. And trust us: Once you cut the cord, you'll never go back to wired headphones.

As you can see in Figure 11-3, the HALO looks like a pair of headphones. But it still allows you to hold phone conversations thanks to a built-in microphone. When a call comes in, the music fades out until the call is over. The same is true of most other stereo headsets, including these popular models:

- Motorola Motorokr S305
- Motorola S9
- Plantronics Voyager 855
- Pulsar 590E
- Samsung SBH 600

Wired Headsets

If you don't mind being tethered to your Pre, wired headsets offer terrific sound, freedom from yet another battery to keep charged, and affordable prices. Obviously, your Pre came

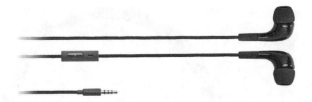

FIGURE 11-4 The Griffin TuneBuds Mobile is much like the bundled Pre headset, but with noise-isolating earbuds and a tangle-free cord.

with one such headset, so we won't spend too much time talking about replacements—except to name Rick's favorite, the Griffin TuneBuds Mobile (see Figure 11-4).

Designed for iPhones but compatible with the Pre, the TuneBuds combine noise-isolating earbuds with a talk-ready microphone and a play-pause control. They're not perfect, but they're definitely worth the $39.99 list price. What's more, if you hit up a price-comparison site such as PriceGrabber (www.pricegrabber.com), you should be able to find them for as little as $20.

The TuneBuds come with three pairs of rubberized earbuds so you can get the best fit for your ears. We particularly like the nylon-coated cord, which helps prevent tangles. To that end, it would be nice if Griffin supplied some kind of plastic cord wrap, but at least you get a zippered carrying case.

As with Palm's headset, the earbuds include an in-line microphone for phone conversations. A small button lets you answer incoming calls or send them to voicemail. When not pulling phone duty, the button can play or pause your tunes or skip to the next song.

How's the sound quality? To Rick's ears, excellent, though he's the first to admit he's not the best judge of audio fidelity. If you can, borrow a pair from a friend and try them for yourself.

Connect a Speaker Dock

You know what Three Dog Night said about one being the loneliest number, right? Why not share that goofy song (and others) with friends and family members instead of sitting there all alone with your headphones? All you need is a speaker dock.

Although no speaker docks are designed expressly for the Pre (not yet, anyway), most such products have compatible line-in jacks. All you need is a 3.5mm patch cable, which you can find at any Radio Shack (sorry, we just can't bring ourselves to call it "The Shack," any more than we can bring ourselves to refer to *Star Wars* as "Episode IV"). Just plug one end into the Pre's headphone jack and the other into the dock. Presto: You've got one killer MP3 jukebox.

You can pick up a small, portable speaker dock for as little as $30 or spend upwards of $200 on a big 'un. However, this is one category that's going to require you to focus on iPod and iPhone products, as that's where all the action is, speaker dock-wise. The good news is that you can find plenty of reviews at sites such as Amazon, CNET, and iLounge (www.ilounge.com). And we've yet to find a company with a wider selection of speaker docks than Altec Lansing (http://www.alteclansing.com), which at press time had no fewer than a dozen Pre-compatible models (meaning they all have 3.5mm input jacks). See Figure 11-5 for some examples.

Wireless Docks

Not one for wires? Then take advantage of Bluetooth. Just as the Pre can wirelessly stream audio to Bluetooth headsets, so can it connect with Bluetooth speakers. We're partial to the Blueant M1 Bluetooth Stereo Speakers (http://tinyurl.com/mdz6ek), a standalone, bookshelf-ready "speaker bar" that features a built-in subwoofer and a rechargeable battery (for easy moving from room to room). The M1 lists for $199.95, but we've seen it selling online for around $155.

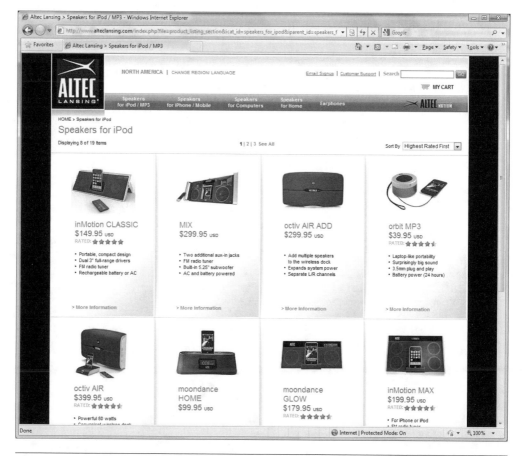

FIGURE 11-5 Altec Lansing's speaker docks may say iPod and iPhone all over them, but those with analog input jacks will work just fine with the Pre.

12

Pre Problems and Solutions

HOW TO...

- Find Pre help in user forums
- Reset your Pre
- Keep your battery properly calibrated
- Use the Pre's built-in help system
- Clean your Pre
- Make room for more apps or data
- Learn what's in each WebOS update
- Find replacement parts and service
- Contact Palm for service and repairs

In an ideal world, people would be able to fly, taxes would be optional, and your Pre would work perfectly 100 percent of the time. In the real world, only we can fly (we *are* superheroes, after all), taxes definitely aren't optional, and your Pre suffers from occasional issues.

We're here to help (with the Pre—taxes are your problem). In this chapter you'll learn about common Pre glitches and how to resolve them. We'll also tell you where to get help with any problems not covered in this book, how to find replacement parts, what you can do to keep your Pre running smoothly (in an effort to prevent problems from occurring in the first place), and much more.

 Many common problems are addressed on Palm's Web site (http://kb.palm.com/support). We're not going to rehash them here, but we are going to suggest you check there first if you've got a problem we haven't addressed. Chances are good you'll find a solution.

Before we get started, we should note that during the several months we spent poking and prodding our Pres, we encountered very few issues. That's pretty impressive given the "1.0" nature of the device and its operating system. However, just because we didn't experience a particular problem doesn't mean you won't. So we're kicking off the chapter with our recommendation for finding help beyond these pages. If it's not covered here, you can rest assured it's probably covered somewhere out there.

The Best Way to Get Help with Your Pre

Much as we wish we could address every possible Pre problem in these pages (and continue this sentence's awesome alliteration for ages), it simply can't be done. Not only does space not allow for it, but it's inescapable that new problems will develop long after we've dotted the final "i" and crossed the final "t."

Fortunately, while we can't predict the future, we can assist with the present. If you've encountered a problem that's not addressed in this chapter (and/or elsewhere in the book), it's time to turn your attention to the Web—and its community of whip-smart users. In other words, if you need help, look no further than *user forums* (see Figure 12-1).

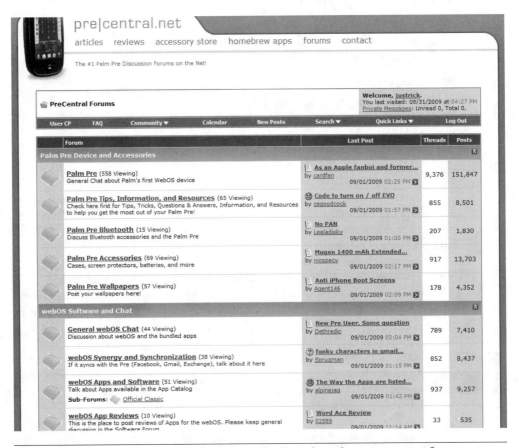

FIGURE 12-1 Looking for help? Look no further than the community forums on sites such as PreCentral, where fellow Pre owners are usually happy to help you troubleshoot.

Various Pre blogs and Web sites maintain active forums (sometimes known as bulletin boards) populated by other members of the Pre community: fellow device owners, software developers, accessory makers, and sometimes even Palm employees. It's like having instant access to a worldwide Palm Pre brain trust!

 Why not take your problem straight to Palm or Sprint? You definitely should, though in our experiences, so-called "professional" tech support is helpful only about one-third of the time. The users are the folks in the trenches, the folks who own and use Pres and encounter the same problems you do. They're not just reading from scripts like most support staffers.

You can get help from one of these forums in two basic ways:

- Browse and/or search the existing posts for information related to your problem. Chances are excellent that whatever's happened to you has also happened to someone else.

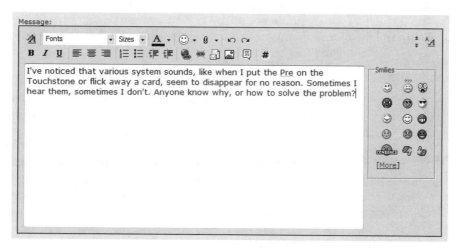

- Create a new post with an explanation of your problem, and then wait for the responses to roll in.

The vast majority of online forums require you to register before you're allowed to create a new post. This is a simple, free, one-time process: Usually, you just pick a username and password, supply an email address, and then tweak a handful of settings pertaining to how you want the forum to communicate with you. (For example, do you want an e-mail notification every time someone replies to one of your posts?) From there, you'll receive a confirmation email with a link you click to verify your identity. Once that's done, you're all clear to start posting.

Increase Your Chances of User Forum Success

It's all well and good to post a cry for help in a user forum, but keep in mind that you're relying on the time and kindness of volunteers, not paid staff. There are no guarantees that someone will post a solution to your problem. You can, however, increase your chances of success by following these tips:

- *Keep it short.* Your problem may be complicated, but your explanation of it shouldn't be. Keep your description as brief as possible, with a simple overview of the issue and a call for help. Anything longer than a couple paragraphs will seriously decrease the chances of anyone reading and responding.
- *Don't whine.* You may be mad as hell at your Pre, Palm, the universe, and Dave, but leave your griping out of the post. Nobody wants to hear it, and you could wind up offending the very people you're asking for help. Sure, it's okay to cap a post with a statement like, "Very frustrating!" But that's as heated as you should get, at least online.
- *Post to multiple forums.* Different Pre users frequent different online forums. By posting your problem to multiple locations (but *not* to multiple areas within the same site—that's considered bad form and could actually get you kicked out), you'll reach a greater number of users. More users equals more possibilities for help. And, hey, even if you get responses in multiple forums, there's nothing wrong with a second (or third, or fourth) opinion, right?

 Don't be surprised, and don't take it personally, if someone posts a nasty, mean-spirited, or otherwise unhelpful response to your post. While most forum dwellers are friendly, helpful folks, you're almost sure to encounter a "troll" from time to time. And there's only *one* way to deal with these meanies: ignore them. Don't reply, don't get dragged into the argument, don't sink to their level. We've seen some bitter "flame wars" erupt in user forums over the silliest things. They're a waste of time and energy, and they always leave you feeling crummy. Ignore the yahoos and move on.

The Best Palm Pre User Forums

Now that you know user forums are the answer to many a problem-solver's prayer, where can you find them? Here are the ones we like best, if only because they're the most heavily trafficked:

Site	Address	Comments
EverythingPre	www.everythingpre.com/forum	Moderately active forums, plus a blog, store, and more.
Palm Pre Forum	www.palmpreforum.org	Not a lot of activity on the home page, but some very active forums—including one specifically devoted to "Help."
Palm Support Community	http://forums.palm.com	Palm's own forums attract lots of users, but it's hard to find Pre-specific stuff amidst all the other Palm-related posts. (Look for forum headings containing "WebOS.")
PreCentral	http://forums.precentral.net	One of the Web's most active Pre communities, plus Pre-related articles, reviews, and accessories.

Reset Your Pre

Just as rebooting a computer will often resolve a glitch or lockup, resetting your Pre is the solution to many a problem. And it's usually the first thing you should do if your device crashes—or just acts a little strange.

There are several ways to reset your Pre:

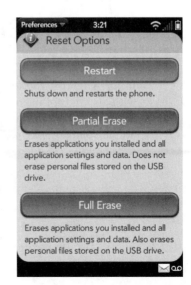

- **Keyboard**   All at the same time, press the ORANGE, SYMBOL, and R keys.
- **Menu**   Tap the Launcher button, swipe your finger to the left until you reach the third page of icons, and then tap Device Info. The Preferences screen appears; scroll down to the bottom and tap Reset Options. Then tap the Restart button.
- **Battery**   When all else fails, you can remove the Pre's rear cover and pull out the battery. Wait about 30 seconds, and then reinsert it, replace the cover, and turn the phone back on.

As we've discussed in previous chapters, the Pre takes a painfully long time to start up after a reset, so perform this step only when it's absolutely necessary.

How to... **Keep Your Pre Battery Calibrated**

Please welcome special guest writer Aaron Vronko, CEO of gadget-repair service Rapid Repair, who generously offered to share some insights on Pre maintenance and preservation (should that be Pre-servation?). First up: battery calibration.

Don't forget to change the oil and check the tire pressure on your Palm Pre! Well, there isn't any oil, but following a few simple maintenance tips will help keep your smartphone running at its best.

Devices with lithium-ion batteries, such as your Palm Pre, use a coordinated system of inputs to estimate the remaining battery life during each use. The device even subtracts for the gradual permanent battery degradation that naturally occurs. However, the sum of these estimations can cause your phone's battery meter to lose accuracy over time.

Help keep the battery meter synced with the battery by calibrating it once per month. To do this, simply charge your phone fully (4 hours or more), and then use it normally until the battery runs completely dead and the phone shuts off. (Then fully charge it again, natch.)

However, don't be tempted to subject your Pre to daily "calibrations"—you should know that frequently running your battery below a 10 percent charge will shorten its total useful life.

Finally, while calibrating your Pre's battery on a monthly basis will help extend its total useful life, lithium batteries still wear out over time and need replacing. If your digital lifeline sees heavy daily use, this can happen in as little as 9 months. Most average users, however, can expect to replace the battery in 12 to 18 months. Just remember that if your time between "fuel-ups" doesn't fit your lifestyle, don't torture yourself! Replace the battery—it's inexpensive and easy.

Use the Pre's Built-In Help System

It may surprise you to learn that the Pre comes with all kinds of useful information built into the device. It's all found in the Help app, which offers an ample selection of tips, how-to videos, and feature overviews. Take a look.

As you can see, Help has three sections:

- **Tips** Tap Tips for an alphabetical list of, well, tips, covering everything from Amazon MP3 to YouTube. (You can also sort the list by category by tapping Sort By Category.) Here's an example:

- **Clips** What's better than a set of instructions? An instructional video, of course! (Hey, if we could, we'd make this book one giant video.) Tap Clips for an alphabetical list of videos covering everything from adding an IM account to zooming in and out.

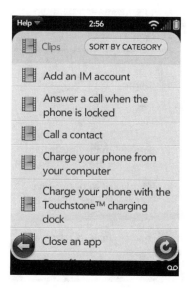

- **Featured** This is a random collection of articles covering a handful of mostly unrelated basic topics, such as running applications from the Launcher and using the back gesture.

You can also search for any topic by typing in the Search field, and then pressing the ENTER key.

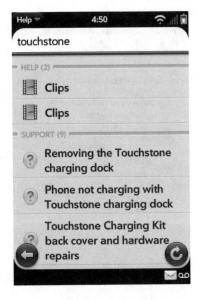

Tip The Search function produces results not just from Tips and Clips, but also from Palm's support library.

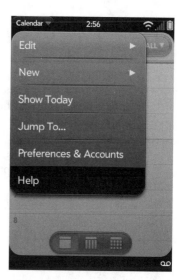

Of course, the Pre's help options don't end with the Help app. As you've probably discovered by now, there's a Help option at the bottom of the pull-down menu for just about every app on your device. The screen at right is an example.

This is context-sensitive help, meaning it'll take you to information related to the particular app or feature you're using. How handy is that!?

How to... **Clean Your Pre**

Let's once again welcome the sage advice of Rapid Repair CEO Aaron Vronko, who's got tips to share on cleaning a dirty Pre.

Are your Pre's camera photos not as clear or its speaker not as loud and crisp as it once was? In this dirty world, it's easy for these components to get covered and clogged with dust and grime, but they are also easy to clean. You'll need the following:

- An optical grade soft cloth (found in an eyeglass or camera lens cleaning kit)
- A can of compressed air
- Strong rubbing alcohol (85 percent or higher, which can be found at drug stores)
- An old toothbrush

1. Remove the back panel by pressing in the button on the bottom of the Pre, and then gently pry up the back starting from the bottom.
2. With the canned air, carefully blow any loose dust from the speaker grille, which is located on the battery door. (Note: For delicate electronics such as the Pre, you should use about only a half-trigger on the canned air, keeping the straw nozzle 2 inches from the target.)
3. Apply alcohol to the toothbrush to wet it, and then shake off the excess so it's not dripping. Gently scrub the fine mesh screen in a circular motion, using the air to expel any loose debris and dry the alcohol. Repeat as necessary.
4. To clean the camera lens, first blow off any loose debris.
5. Apply a small amount of rubbing alcohol to the cloth, and gently wipe the lens in a circular motion. Finish by blowing with canned air. Repeat as necessary.
6. Re-attach the back panel and you are ready to go.

These cleaning procedures should be performed every two or three months, depending on your usage and environment. Letting dirt build up too long may make cleaning difficult and increase the potential for damage.

Make Room for More Apps and Data

As we've noted (okay, complained about) many times already, the Pre comes with only 8GB of storage space—and no way to add more. That may well have changed by the time you read this—we absolutely, positively believe Palm will offer a 16GB model in the near future, if not one with a microSD expansion slot—but the fact remains that there's never enough room for all the stuff you want to carry.

For example, maybe you need to make room for the DVD movie you ripped in Chapter 9. Or you don't have enough space to download a cool new game. Whatever the case, your only option is to clear out the old to make room for the new:

- *Delete unwanted apps.* To delete an app you're no longer using, press and hold the ORANGE key, and then tap the icon for the app you want to delete. Tap the Delete button to confirm the action.

- *Delete unwanted songs.* As you learned in Chapter 8, MP3s and other music files can consume a considerable amount of Pre storage. You can free up hundreds of megabytes just by deleting a few albums. However, you can't do this on the Pre itself; you'll need to use iTunes or your preferred music manager. To remove songs, just delete them from the playlist(s) where they reside, and then re-sync your Pre. (Remember that deleting a song from a playlist is not the same as deleting it from your PC.) Find out more in Chapter 8.
- *Delete unwanted movies.* If you've already watched, say, *Iron Man* on your Pre, there's no need to keep it in memory. So get rid of it! See Chapter 9 if you need a refresher.
- *Delete unwanted photos.* If you've been snapping tons of photos with the Pre's camera, now would be a good time to go through your photo library and remove any snapshots you no longer want. Just view any photo full-screen, and then tap the trashcan icon to delete it. Wash, rinse, repeat with other photos.

Check How Much Memory Is Available

Not sure how much storage space your Pre has left? There's a simple way to find out: Tap the Launcher icon, and then tap the Device Info icon. Here's what you'll see:

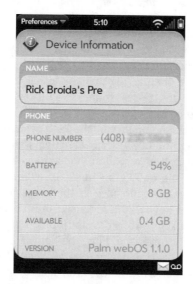

The Memory field shows you the total storage in your Pre, while the Available field tells you how much is unused and, well, available.

Learn What's in Each WebOS Update

If you've owned your Pre for a while, you've probably noticed that WebOS updates appear on your Pre from time to time. That's actually a very cool thing: These updates get "pushed" to your device and installed without any action on your part, other than tapping the Install button.

Okay, but what features did the latest update add? What fixes did it apply? You can find out by visiting the Software Update section on Palm's Support site (http://kb.palm.com/support). Just click Phones, Palm Pre, Sprint (or the name of your carrier), and then click the big Software Update News button on the right side of the page, as shown here.

Software update news

Now you can review the complete list of new apps, new features, feature changes, and bug fixes. Happy reading!

Top 5 Pre Problems—and Their Solutions

Our next special guest is Jason Robitaille, owner of Canuck Software (http:// canuck-software.ca/) and a writer for PreCentral, one of our favorite Pre sites. Take it away, Jason!

5. Lack of Palm OS compatibility The Palm OS may be incredibly outdated, but it had a huge collection of applications available for its users. Fear not: MotionApps (*www.motionapps.com*) has created a shareware Palm OS emulator named Classic (see Chapter 10) that will let users enjoy most of their favorite Palm OS programs and games. There's even a Classic software store (http:// classic.mobihand.com).

4. No Adobe Flash support in the Web browser Unfortunately, for this problem (which prohibits you from watching streaming video), you'll need a bit of patience—but not for very long. Adobe has announced that Flash Mobile 10 will be coming to the WebOS in early 2010. When it's ready and approved by Palm, you'll receive it free in an over-the-air device update.

3. No onscreen keyboard An onscreen keyboard is always handy. While the Pre's slide-out keyboard is nice for typing long texts, sometimes you just want to send a quick message. Plus, the hardware keyboard doesn't work well in landscape mode. To that end, the folks at WebOS Internals have created a handy free virtual keyboard (www.webos-internals.org/wiki/Keyboard).

2. Bad battery life You can do a number of things to get better battery life. One obvious option is to get a larger battery, though these generally cost at least $40 (see Chapter 11). Another option is to use Wi-Fi instead of the phone network, as Wi-Fi uses less power. Oh, and be sure to charge often; the battery has a longer life when it is topped off frequently.

1. Not many applications in the App Catalog This issue was one of the first solved by avid fans, who wanted more than what the App Catalog was offering. PreCentral.net has a large selection of user-developed applications (see Chapter 10), and there's even a full how-to guide ready-made for new users (www.precentral.net/how-to-install-homebrew-apps).

Find Pre Replacement Parts and Service

Let's face it: The Pre doesn't have many "parts." The most common item you'll need to replace is the battery, and you learned all about that in Chapter 11. Perhaps unsurprisingly, then, a Google search for "Palm Pre replacement parts" produces few results. Indeed, as of this writing, we found just a smattering of companies offering Pre parts or repair services.

For example, PDASmart.com (www.pdasmart.com) had exactly one part: a replacement LCD screen. It was priced at $110, or $135 if you send your Pre to the company and let them perform the repair. That probably seems like a lot, but if you've cracked your screen, it's definitely less than the price of a new Pre.

Another source for screen repair: Dr. Cell Phone (www.drcellphone.com), which charges $149.99 for the parts and labor.

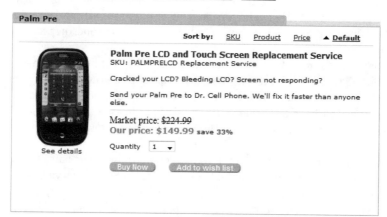

As time goes on, you should be able to find more third-party options for Pre parts and service. In the meantime, keep your baby protected in a good case (see Chapter 11) and try not to break it!

Get Help from Palm or Sprint

Need help solving a problem not addressed in these pages? Online forums are a great alternative, but sometimes you just need to go to the company that sold you the product. In this case, that means Palm and/or Sprint (or whoever your carrier might be). Ah, but which company should you contact for which kind of problem? Here's a simple set of guidelines:

Contact...	For problems with...
Palm	Hardware and software, synchronization, and other device-specific issues
Sprint (or your carrier)	Poor reception, dropped calls, voicemail, and other phone-service issues

To get in touch with either company, you'll need your dialing finger or your Web browser. Here's all the pertinent contact info:

Palm Customer Service	866-750-7256
Palm Online Support	www.palm.com/support
Sprint Customer Service	888-211-4727 or press *2 on your Pre
Sprint Online Support	www.sprint.com/palmpresupport

Rick vs. Dave: The End of the Book

Rick: Well, here we are at the end of yet another book. I'd like to say it's been my pleasure to work with such a talented, tireless co-author—but I can't, because I'm talking about Dave. I will say he's made a lot of progress with his sentence structure, which no longer calls to mind Yoda on a bender. ("Smartphones not make one great! Tap it, you must!")

What's next for me? Well, now that the yoke of another book has been lifted, I'll be returning to the soup kitchen where I volunteer three times a week, though not before I finish the urban-beautification program I spearheaded and the fundraiser for Greenpeace. Just have to decide which charities will be getting my royalty checks this year—always a tough choice. Honestly, there's no better reward for months of hard work than good old philanthropy.

Dave: Oh, posh. We all know that you are going to use your half of the book royalties to finish that gigantic water fountain statue of Aaron Sorkin you've been sculpting in your backyard. Me? I'll be retiring to a private island where my army of trained monkey butlers will cater to me and my wife, Halle Berry. We'll form our own two-person band, sort of like the White Stripes, with Halle playing guitar and me on drums.

Oh! And I'm planning to visit the International Space Station aboard the space shuttle, as well. Later, sucker!

Index

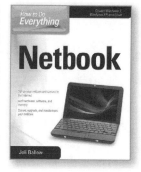

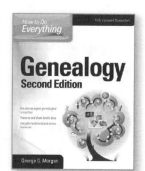